GLOBAL UNIONS, LOCAL POWER

GLOBAL UNIONS, LOCAL POWER

The New Spirit of Transnational Labor Organizing

JAMIE K. MCCALLUM

ILR PRESS
AN IMPRINT OF
CORNELL UNIVERSITY PRESS
ITHACA AND LONDON

First published 2013 by Cornell University Press

First printing, Cornell Paperbacks, 2013
Printed in the United States of America

Library of Congress Cataloging-in-Publication Data

McCallum, Jamie K., 1977– author.
   Global unions, local power : the new spirit of transnational labor organizing / Jamie K. McCallum.
        pages cm
   Includes bibliographical references and index.
   ISBN 978-0-8014-5193-5 (cloth : alk. paper) — ISBN 978-0-8014-7862-8 (pbk. : alk. paper)   1. International labor activities.   2. Labor and globalization.   3. Labor movement—International cooperation. 4. Transnationalism.   I. Title.

   HD6475.A1M33 2013
   331.88—dc23   2013002325

Cornell University Press strives to use environmentally responsible suppliers and materials to the fullest extent possible in the publishing of its books. Such materials include vegetable-based, low-VOC inks and acid-free papers that are recycled, totally chlorine-free, or partly composed of nonwood fibers. For further information, visit our website at www.cornellpress.cornell.edu.

Cloth printing   10 9 8 7 6 5 4 3 2 1
Paperback printing   10 9 8 7 6 5 4 3 2 1

To my family, with gratitude

Events belie forecasts.
—Henri Lefebvre, *The Explosion*

CONTENTS

74-122

ACKNOWLEDGMENTS

This book owes its life to the unionists and workers who shared their time and stories with me throughout the years I conducted research. You are the ardent couriers of an old idea made new again. In particular, I must recognize Mr. Cheeks, whose singular wisdom, courage, and compassion were so important.

It is not a book about why David sometimes wins or a recipe for labor union success. Nor was it written to "give voice" to low-wage workers struggling for a better life. Rather, I undertook the project to make sense of a particular historical conjuncture for labor. Along the way—and it was quite a journey—I accrued many personal debts.

At the City University of New York I owe endless appreciation to Frances Fox Piven, Ruth Milkman, John Torpey, and Stanley Aronowitz for their mentorship and insights over many years. I benefited from the support of a research grant from the Graduate Center and a fellowship at the Center for Place, Culture, and Politics, where I had the insightful criticism of David Harvey, Peter Hitchcock, Ruthie Gilmore, Manny Ness, and others.

Blair Taylor was an astute editor and critic. Patrick Inglis helpfully challenged some of my assumptions, forcing a greater degree of clarity. All in all, the lumpen intelligentsia of New York City was an amazing resource, and I have drawn on many people within important institutions as this work has moved forward—my comrades at Left Forum, Brecht Forum, and Bluestockings deserve special mention.

Peter Evans and Dimitris Stevis lent their considerable talent and expertise to reviewing this manuscript. I am grateful to have had such politically engaged and intellectually rigorous scholars improve my work. The book changed considerably as a result of their insights.

Outside the United States I am grateful for the guidance, feedback, and friendship over the years of Ian Greer in London. At the Freie Universität, Mike Fichter roped me into a four-country study of global framework agreements, funded by the Hans-Böckler-Stiftung, that significantly influenced my views on governance. Eddie Webster offered me space to work and sage advice at the Sociology of Work Unit at the University of the Witswatersrand in Johannesburg, as did Supriya RoyChowdhury at the Institute for Social and Economic Change in Bangalore. In Geneva, my work was aided by Dan Gallin at the Global Labour Institute and Konstantinos Papadakis at the International Labor Organization. Lisa Berntsen in Rotterdam provided important translation assistance.

On the first day of my research abroad I acquired swine flu (H1N1), foisting me into the epicenter of a global pandemic. This presaged a series of research trips fraught with minor calamities that nearly ended my fieldwork numerous times—a bus crash near the Nepal border, a near-drowning in the Bay of Bengal, and a violent attack in Soweto. All of this contributed to the alienation and sensory overload that major cities in the developing world are famous for bestowing on new arrivals. For their care and patience during these times I owe heaps of gratitude to Lotta Staffans, Jason Hopps, Rebecca Harrison, Gretchen Wilson, Sowmya and Sriraj Reddy, Auntie and Uncle Ramalinga Reddy, Harish N., Anushree Sahay, and Sunil Kumar. In South Africa I would have been useless without the expert advice of Crispen Chinguno.

Over the years my research was aided by a network of global trade unionists and political activists who were sympathetic to my project and became important stakeholders in my success. Though most of them remain nameless in the book, their imprint is on every page. I am grateful for the help of several veteran organizers who took time to read versions of the manuscript, bluntly correcting me when I simply did not "get it." In particular, I thank Audra Makuch, Muni Citrin, and Jane McAlevey for their careful insights into the world of labor. Jenna Latour-Nichols and Alan Sutton offered considerable help editing the manuscript as well as vital research assistance.

Some of this was written while I was actively engaged in labor union activity, on the margins of the proverbial trenches. The final stages took place while I contemplated various editing decisions from the comfort of an Adirondack chair overlooking the Green Mountains. I credit a handful of my students with reminding me that one's perspective and vantage point matters and to be mindful of that when considering pronouncements on the fate and future of movements. My colleagues in sociology and anthropology at Middlebury also shared their wisdom and varied expertise as I set about making revisions.

Fran Benson challenged me to write this book the first day we met, and her guidance throughout the process gave me the confidence to make the big decisions necessary to finish the job. I thank her and the wide array of talented folks at Cornell ILR Press.

Finally, my family, to whom this book is dedicated, deserves their own special roped-off area of gratitude. For making Vermont feel like home (where the heart is), I thank Erin. Her support made my life full of laughter and love when it was most needed. Her take on the world—a committed bottom-up perspective—always challenged my well-worn ways of thinking. My brother, Fox, doubles as a best friend, and I am indebted to him for all that accrues from blood and comradeship. In addition, he deserves notable recognition for his good sense in bringing Jill, Oliver, and Eudora Lee into the family, all of whom have changed my life. My parents, my greatest mentors, inspired in me a curiosity for the world that made me who I am. Their unconditional support has never wavered, for which I will be ever grateful.

LIST OF ABBREVIATIONS

ACFTU	All China Federation of Trade Unions
ACTU	Australian Council of Trade Unions
AFL	American Federation of Labor
AIFLD	American Institute for Free Labor Development
AITUC	All India Trade Union Congress
ANC	African National Congress
CIO	Congress of Industrial Organizations
CITU	Centre of Indian Trade Unions
COCOSA	Coordinating Committee of South Africa
COSATU	Congress of South African Trade Unions
CSR	corporate social responsibility
CTW	Change to Win
EWC	European Works Council
FOSATU	Federation of South African Trade Unions
G4S	Group 4 Securicor
GATT	General Agreement on Tariffs and Trade

GFA	global framework agreement
GMB	General Workers Union
GUF	global union federation
IAD	International Affairs Department
ICEM	International Federation of Chemical, Energy, Mine, and General Workers' Unions
ICFTU	International Confederation of Free Trade Unions
ILO	International Labour Organization
IMF	International Monetary Fund
IMF (Union)	International Metalworkers Federation
INTUC	Indian National Trade Union Congress
ISS	International Services
ISWOI	Indian Security Workers Organizing Initiative
ITF	International Transport Federation
ITS	International Trade Secretariat
IWW	Industrial Workers of the World
J4J	Justice for Janitors
LHMU	Liquor Hospitality and Miscellaneous Workers Union
Mercosur	Southern Common Market
MSF	Manufacturing, Science, and Finance Union
NACTU	National Council of Trade Unions
NAFTA	North American Free Trade Agreement
NGO	nongovernmental organization
NUM	National Union of Mineworkers
NUMSA	National Union of Mineworkers South Africa
OECD	Organization for Economic Cooperation and Development
PSGU	Private Security Guards Union
RICO Act	Racketeer Influenced and Corrupt Organizations Act
SACTU	South African Congress of Trade Unions
SARHWU	South African Railway and Harbour Workers Union
SATAWU	South African Transport and Allied Workers Union
SEIU	Service Employees International Union
SIGTUR	Southern Initiative on Globalization and Trade Union Rights
SMU	Social Movement Unionism
TGWU	Transport and General Workers Union (UK)
TINA	There Is No Alternative

UAW	United Auto Workers
UNI	Union Network International
UNIDOC	Union Development and Organizing Centers
UNI PS	UNI Property Services
UNISON	Public Service Trade Union
UNITE	Union of Needle Trades, Industrial, and Textile Employees
WFTU	World Federation of Trade Unions
WTO	World Trade Organization

GLOBAL UNIONS, LOCAL POWER

INTRODUCTION

Just over a decade ago, the reigning doxa held that neoliberal globalization was a death sentence for labor standards and worker organizations. An inevitable race to the bottom hollowed out trade unions, undermined state protections, and placed national working classes in competition with one another for scarce jobs. Whereas capital had no country, workers, it seemed, were locked in place and left behind. As Piven and Cloward (2000: 413) summarized this belief, "Globalization in turn seems to puncture the century-old belief in worker power."

But the renaissance of global labor activism that began alongside an explosion of alter-globalization[1] movements in the late 1990s has inspired a new perspective on the relationship of workers to the global economy—and a variety of substantive studies on a new dimension of labor movement activity. As a challenge to the fatalistic conception that globalization[2] necessarily undermined the power of workers, scholars, and activists formed the skeletal framework of a counter-thesis, questioning the supposed fixity of labor within the national context and its inherent weakness in the face of global capital (see Evans 2008, 2010; Herod 2001; Munck 2002). Animated by the prospect of a new "great transformation," they asserted that unions are forging a new frontier within an old tradition—global unions for the global age.

However, in the scramble to understand the increasing tendency of labor politics to "go global," scholars have overlooked many of the most critical details on the ground. This book redirects our attention to the manner in which transnational campaigns empower or inspire local movements, still the place it matters most. While some research has assessed the local *impacts* of transnational labor activism, the argument here is from the opposite direction, suggesting that local contexts determine the local strategy. Moreover, while important studies have argued that transnational labor advocacy has the tendency to undermine the autonomy and power of local movements (Seidman 2008), the campaigns examined here are inspired by global priorities and yet have empowered local struggles.

This book is about two parallel stories. First, it relates the account of the most aggressive campaign ever waged by a global union federation (GUF), a years-long effort of private security guard unions to organize against Group4 Securicor (G4S), the world's largest private employer after Walmart. What began as an isolated battle in the United States blossomed into a worldwide struggle for global unionism impacting hundreds of thousands of workers from over twenty countries. But the global effort also gave rise to deep local struggles. Consequently, the narrative moves among different scales of action, from the global arena, to the national-level context, to the local union office. Throughout the campaign, workers in different places won wage increases, union recognition, benefits, an end to abusive workplace discrimination, and, most importantly, a greater degree of control over their employer's business model. In the United States, security guard union density (8 percent as of late 2012) is now slightly higher than the national private-sector average, and the campaign settlement provides the union with a clearer path to bring more workers into the fold. Rarely have global campaigns meant more than superficial changes in workers' lives—this struggle set a new standard.

The second story describes a transition to a new spirit of transnational labor activism. The word "spirit" implies a shifting idea about how labor should best confront the problems posed by global capital. In a context of rising corporate power and declining or unenforceable worker rights (publicly enforceable claims), many of labor's tried and true strategies have proven wholly ineffective. In response, since the early 1970s unions have engaged in what I call "governance struggles," a panoply of strategies to subordinate the rules-based logic of private companies to democratic oversight by workers and their unions. The significance of the fight against G4S is the complex and contradictory ways in which those gains at the global level were articulated onto the local context, enhancing worker mobilization and transforming local union movements.

Most global union campaigns seek to assert universal labor standards and core values within a given company. But the inability to transfer any gains to the local context has often meant that workers' lives remain unchanged. Rather than insist on the incompatibility of global and local levels of activism, the findings in this book suggest a paradox—effective global unionism requires reciprocity with local actors. The conclusions also permit cautious optimism about the prospects for authentic labor internationalism where others have asserted an overriding pessimism (see Burawoy 2010). The question therefore posed here is simple: How can global unions build local power?

Backdrop

In 2008 I hosted two trade union organizers from India who coordinated global campaigns for Union Network International (UNI) Global Union, the largest of the global unions. They were on their way to a conference in Puerto Rico hosted by the Service Employees International Union (SEIU), a prominent and controversial North American union. Their job was to coordinate a campaign to raise the living and working standards of five million private security guards. They claimed to have built a coherent network of unionists sufficiently mobilized to take on the country's largest employer, a private security firm called G4S. Moreover, they were not alone. Others like them were coordinating the same campaign against the same employer in Africa, Eastern Europe, Latin America, and the United States.

As a former organizer myself, I was deeply cynical about the prospects for cross-border collaboration among unions. The obstacles always seemed insurmountable. Aside from a common employer, in some cases, what did the workers of the world truly share? It seemed wise to heed the cautionary tale of history, which suggested that hostility, in some form or another, was a far more likely response to globalism than solidarity. The brief outpouring of internationalism around the dramatic 1999 World Trade Organization protests in Seattle had come and gone rather quickly, with labor retreating into national protectionism. Besides, it was hard enough winning campaigns in New York and New Jersey—forget about New Delhi.

Moreover, at that time the US labor movement was deeply embroiled in fratricide. For example, the Puerto Rico conference ended with the dramatic takeover of the local democratically elected teachers union by the SEIU (through its cooperation with corrupt local political elites).[3] This was a disheartening finale to an event that was to ostensibly focus on building global solidarity. Given these circumstances—when leading unions were driving wedges into their own organizations, and when labor imperialism seemed to be making a surprising comeback—it seemed justifiably insane to suggest they should lead a global organizing agenda. Yet that is exactly what my houseguests were proposing.

Further inspection, however, inspired me to reconsider my position. Maritime seafarers across the globe had recently concluded one of their first rounds of global collective bargaining, realizing an unfulfilled dream of the automobile worker unions in the late 1960s (Lillie 2006). European workers seemed to be embracing the "works councils" that emerged from the post-Maastricht environment to coordinate efforts across borders (Waddington 2011). Campaigns by international nongovernmental organizations (NGOs) and watchdog groups had directed the corporate charters of some multinational garment producers toward fairer working conditions in export processing zones (Anner 2011). GUFs in Europe were winning framework agreements in an attempt to constrain management behavior so that workers could organize (Wills 2002). Overall, scholars began heralding the beginnings of an inchoate worldwide labor movement, a perspective that gained support with the 2008 merger of the American, Canadian, and British steelworker unions. Finally, the SEIU and a handful of other US unions were developing genuine cross-border coalitions with sister unions in Europe, Australia, and the United Kingdom. This upsurge in labor transnationalism inspired a scholarly interest in labor as a vital counterweight to unfettered global capitalism (Moody 1997; Gordon and Turner 2000; Bronfenbrenner 2007; Stevis and Boswell 2007a and b; Waterman and Wills 2002; Munck and Waterman 1999; Munck 2002; Webster, Lambert, and Beziudenhout 2008; Evans 2010).

Absent from these accounts, however, was the heart of unionism—campaigns by workers against bosses. Searching for cases of actually existing union transnationalism was stymied for multiple reasons. For starters, global unionism is not the product of where we would most expect it, the International Trade Union Confederation, the umbrella organization for the global labor movement. Rather, nearly all instances of labor transnationalism emerge from within individual GUFs, and many of those are driven by large national affiliates in the United States. Second, many campaigns that claimed to be "global" in scope were only one-way foreign aid efforts. And on the rare occasions when unions were able to extract promises of good behavior from employers at the global level, they had no ability to enforce the changes locally.

Most confusing of all was the seeming schizophrenia at the SEIU. Though the union seemed, on the one hand, committed to a more comprehensive and cooperative global union approach, its indefatigable leader at the time, Andrew Stern, had recently declared his intention to outsource strikes to low-wage countries. Such an interpretation of international solidarity would be comical if it did not recall the ugly history of US labor's role in the American imperium. Consequently, the most paradoxical part of the story in this book is the leading role currently played by American trade unions in the global labor movement. Why should such enfeebled unions in the United States have any solidarity to offer the comparatively stronger traditions in Western Europe and in the leading countries of the South?

The emerging scholarly literature on global unionism was as intriguing as it was filled with generalizations and hyperbole. Some scholars' accounts were wildly optimistic, full of exuberant comparisons to Marx's First International. Other perspectives were from committed pessimists—but without the critical engagement to offer anything constructive. In either case it was heavy on speculation about a new global possibility but light on how it actually worked.

In the spring of 2009 I attended UNI's global conference at SEIU's downtown headquarters in New York City, hoping to gain a greater insight into actually existing labor transnationalism. Instead, the meeting showcased a variety of campaigns that reinforced my worst fears about global unionism—bureaucratic approaches to convince transnational companies to "do the right thing," a vague and uninspiring platitude that evoked the common story of labor's weakness more than its strength. Then the talk turned toward the G4S campaign; against this backdrop, it seemed all the more incongruous.

G4S puts 650,000 security guards to work in 125 countries, keeping watch over everything from strip malls to nuclear weapons laboratories, from the tennis courts at Wimbledon to the battlefields of Iraq. It shepherds the rich and famous throughout the developing world, occasionally fighting pirate ships in the Indian Ocean.[4] It has steadily grown richer and more powerful not *despite* the global economic crisis but *because* of it, having benefited from the perceived increased need for its services given public budgetary shortfalls, crime spikes, and heightened threats of terrorism and political violence. The mostly failed attempts to unionize within the company's US-based subsidiary, Wackenhut, were well known, making the achievements of the global effort all the more perplexing. Interested in unraveling the exceptional nature of this campaign, I decided to study an example of what was possible rather than what was predictable.

Organizing the Global Security Sector

The SEIU grew into the most dynamic union in the country during the 1990s, and its momentum continued in the early years of the new century, as it organized security guards at some of the same large retail office buildings where it had begun the pioneering Justice for Janitors campaigns (see chapter 2). The union set its sights on the $34 billion security industry at just the moment when it became dominated by European companies. While some of those firms promoted high standards in their home countries, low wages, high turnover, and dangerous working conditions were endemic to the US market. Buoyed by significant early success at multiple security companies—it remains the largest labor campaign for African American workers since A. Philip Randolph organized the Pullman Car Porters in the 1920s—the decision to pursue unionization at G4S, the largest player in the market and also a European firm, made perfect sense. "I was guilty of suggesting it would be another easy win," recalled one SEIU staffer. "But I can't remember ever being so wrong."[5]

In response to the company's ardent rebuke of union recognition in the United States, the SEIU looked beyond its national borders for allies—first in Europe, then in the Global South. As part of a corporate "southern strategy," G4S dropped its unionized European clients for higher profit margins and expanding markets in the Global South, and it soon became the largest employer on both the African continent and in India. The stage was then set for a dramatic confrontation in some of the world's most anti-union climates. The campaign took on a global dimension almost immediately. As workers occupied corporate headquarters in Indonesia, struck in South Africa and Malawi, and crashed shareholder meetings in London, the SEIU and UNI worked to tarnish the company's public profile and weaken its status with potential clients. The Organization for Economic Cooperation and Development determined that the company had violated fundamental worker rights in four countries, and an investor in G4S withdrew its financial support out of moral outrage.

In 2008, after five years of battle, the company finally submitted to a global framework agreement (GFA),[6] a policy instrument guaranteeing new rules that allowed G4S employees to organize trade unions without management interference, including in some places where local law had formerly forbid unionization at all. When the threat of management reprisals was neutralized, workers went on the offensive, winning concrete economic gains in India, South Africa, Malawi, Mozambique, Indonesia, and Poland. New security guard unions emerged in Nepal, Congo, and Ghana. Security guards in the United States, who began the campaign years earlier, won a clear path to union recognition in nine major cities. This book sheds light on the South African and Indian cases because they tell different sides of the same story. In both places private security guards are poor workers in a precarious industry, though their struggles to improve conditions—wages, benefits, job security, employer misconduct—have nonetheless been very distinct.

South African guards fought to oust racist managers and build stronger workplace unions. The militancy and social movement character of trade unionism that all but disappeared in the post-apartheid era seemed reinvigorated through this campaign—a massive strike, workplace mobilization, transnational collaboration, and community involvement. In contrast, the Indian situation did not recall an old tradition; it reflected a new one. There is a growing tendency in India's labor movement toward independent unionism outside the sphere of political party control. Embracing this new movement, the SEIU and UNI spent months touring the country in search of willing coalition partners to build a new multi-union organization to organize security guards on the basis of industry and class, not politics and caste. In both places the commitment to a global strategy paid off locally, as workers won diverse gains and built stronger organizations. Margaret Keck and Kathryn Sikkink (1998), who largely ignore labor struggles, have shown that social movements in poor countries can make use of a "boomerang strategy" by enlisting the support of rich country allies.[7] That process is present here, though we also see how unions in the North were strengthened by recruiting solidarity from unions in the Global South, a "boomerang in reverse."

This book also emphasizes a less visible dimension of the campaign—the transformations of foreign union movements under the influence of the SEIU and UNI. Call it "mimetic isomorphism" or "open-source organizing,"[8] American unions are remaking some of their most powerful counterparts around the world. Critics often claim that after hiring the SEIU and submitting to an internal reorganization, unions in Europe, South Africa, and India will bear the unmistakable imprimatur of an SEIU local and continue the legacy of the AFL-CIO as a junior partner in a national effort to extend American hegemony. But so far the risk seems unfounded. The SEIU and other members of its breakaway federation, Change to Win, have found willing partners abroad who understand the benefits of learning from the US experience and translating some aspects of a new strategy. One German unionist recalled, "One day we woke up and realized we were in trouble and the next thing we know we're doing whatever SEIU tells us to do. And I hate to admit it, but they have a point."[9]

But the lessons for labor are by no means clear. Cultural friction and hostility broke out almost everywhere the SEIU went, creating discord between North American, European, and Southern union movements. The end result was a settlement that generated accolades for its scope and persistence but also doubts as to whether or not it was "worth it." Of the 35,000 security guards the SEIU claims to represent today, only a thousand work for G4S, a surprisingly miniscule figure given the extent of the campaign. Consequently, there are those within the SEIU who interpret the campaign as "too long, too expensive, too destructive, too aggressive and didn't get us what we wanted anyway."[10] To some extent, that position has won the day. Since concluding the G4S campaign the union has retreated from some of its prior commitments to global unionism.

Nonetheless, woven throughout this book is a story of the campaign largely portrayed as successful. Beyond the material gains won for workers, compared to the resources spent winning them, the real feat of the campaign is the leverage it gives the national union over the industry as a whole—now that its largest player has submitted to union rules.

Globalization and the Sources of Worker Power

How were poor security guards and their unions able to force the hand of one of the world's largest corporations?

Recently there has been great interest in reading transnational labor struggles as if they were cast in a theatrical version of the *double movement*, Karl Polanyi's term for how nineteenth-century civil society instinctively and spontaneously "protected itself against the perils of the self-regulating market system" and re-embedded it in a variety of collectivist projects. Much the way capitalism might produce its own gravediggers, globalization is said to create the very conditions that allow workers a kind of "built-in" power to fight back.[11] In other words, the new international division of labor, the geographic dispersion of production, the vertical consolidation of corporate power, the emergence of global cities, and new labor process innovations such as just-in-time production models—in short, a new cartography of economic activity—actually make global capitalism more vulnerable to disruption (see Evans 2008, 2010; Herod 2001; Webster, Lambert, and Beziudenhout 2008).[12] These circumstances, it is said, suggest that "the hour of von Hayek is gone and the hour of Polanyi has arrived" (Munck 2002: 177–178).

One variation on this general theme argues that free-trade pacts, such as the North American Free Trade Agreement, typically the bane of labor movements, provide workers certain opportunities for transnational labor activism (Kay 2005, 2011). Another suggests that the immiserating conditions of neoliberalism paradoxically lay the foundations of social movement-inspired forms of unionism (Chun 2009). Labor activists make similar claims. Stephen Lerner, a former director of the SEIU's Property Services Division and a major player in the G4S campaign, argued that "the spread of multinational corporations and the increasing concentration of capital have created the conditions that can turn globalization on its head" (Lerner 2007: 17). There is no such happy irony in this book. This line of argument is seductive, but ultimately it provides the relationship between global capitalism and worker power a coherence it does not possess. Situated awkwardly astride this optimistic theoretical outlook rests the daunting record of failed attempts to win meaningful gains through transnational activity. Power is not, as Piven (2008: 26) says, "there for the taking," and we need to more seriously consider the conditions under which workers are able to exercise it.

Building on Erik Olin Wright's (2000) terminology, Beverly Silver (2003) explains that workers utilize *structural power* when they occupy an advantageous position in a particular economic system, or *associational power*, which flows from their self-organization into unions, political parties, or other collective organizations.

The place-bound nature of service work might seem to lend security guards a degree of structural power because their work cannot be outsourced globally. Unlike auto manufacturing or garment factory work, there is no obvious point of conflict between janitors or security guards in New Jersey and New Delhi. This power is magnified when placed in the context of emerging global cities, the command and control hubs of global capitalism. Sassen (2001), whose analysis has directly inspired the SEIU's strategy, argues that global cities require a conglomeration of low-skill, low-wage, service-sector jobs, such as security guards. And precisely because the process of making a global city global is so expensive, requiring high inputs of fixed capital (Goldman 2011), it is less simple than we think for business to simply up and leave. Therefore, Manuel Castells's (2000: 506) assertion, "At its core, capital is global. As a rule, labor is local," which is intended to derive labor's weakness, is seen from this perspective as its saving grace.

The problem is that place-bound workers experience some of the same downward pressures as those whose jobs are more subject to a spatial fix by capital. Guards endure long hours of tedium, low pay, and, being a profession that requires relatively little skill, heavy competition. This is a perfect prescription for employers keen on depressing wages, given that labor is such a large factor of production. In the end, whatever power could theoretically be derived from the industrial setting is overshadowed by the negative effects of the reserve army of labor, myriad forms of subcontracting, labor brokering, and the disaggregation of trade union movements, all of which tend to militate against any kind of labor power built into the logic of globalization.

But Silver (2003: 123) says the conditions that have systematically undermined workers' structural power have placed "a renewed premium on the

importance of associational power" and that we should see low-wage service workers such as security guards increasingly rely on their collective
action to leverage gains. The catch is that the capacity to exercise associational power is embedded in state and legal frameworks guaranteeing trade
union rights, freedom of association, and so on, all increasingly rare com-
modities (Silver 2003: 14). This raises a curious problem. On the one hand,
associational power is premised on particular political opportunities. Yet the
less one's job and livelihood are protected by such frameworks, the more
necessary—and unattainable—associational power would seem to be. The
erosion of social welfare provisions everywhere and the increasing informalization of the global labor force can only mean that the growing percentage
of workers who would count on exercising associational power is less and
less likely to be able to do so. How then can associational power become
actionable?

Frances Fox Piven suggests power moves from a potential to an actionable status when collective actors break the rules that structure a given social context (Piven 2008). In other words, exercising power entails disrupting the interdependent relationships in society that are normally bound by
rules.[13] In contrast, I use Piven's concept here to connote *rulemaking*. More
precisely, this means new terms of engagement between labor and capital
that allow associational power to be made actionable. Modifying the normative framework of employment regulation and the cultural logic that
proscribed workers as submissive—in effect, new rules governing the industrial context—was the central way otherwise powerless security guards
were able to fight back.

Governance Struggles and Worker Power: The New Spirit of Labor Transnationalism

Recent shifts in power among states, corporations, and labor groups have
encouraged unions to seek gains through new kinds of *governance struggles*,
a strategy that enhances the potential for global unionism to empower workers
locally. Governance struggles seek to exert a degree of discipline and control
over the business practices of transnational corporations and free-trade
pacts. In so doing, they alter the otherwise unilinear channels of decision
making that impact workers' ability to organize. Although the governance

concept usually implies a generalized political authority vested in nonstate actors and institutions, I use it here specifically to connote worker struggles that seek to enforce new "rules of engagement" with transnational corporations. Whereas traditional union strategies seek to exert pressure on management or the state to increase wages or benefits packages, or to respect a panoply of *rights*, governance struggles target the corporation at a level removed from the workplace in the hope of creating a new field of *rules* that will enable workers to exercise power. These rules include "neutrality agreements," by which management concedes its right to actively oppose workplace organizing or any clause or conduct code that alters management's relationship with its employees in a direction that is deemed favorable to unionization.[14]

Governance struggles, explored in depth in the next chapter, constitute the heart of labor transnationalism since the late 1960s but have only recently managed to translate global gains into local possibilities beyond a superficial level. The GUFs are the latest actors to modify this general repertoire through the implementation of GFAs. GFAs are policy instruments signed by transnational corporations and GUFs that seek to create an arena for global labor relations (Fichter et al. 2012). GFAs also link unions around the world in an effort to impact the behavior of companies throughout their supply chains. GFAs have been studied from myriad directions. Many scholars have sought to demonstrate the ways in which GFAs help unions win specific demands, a process that is present in this book, too. But my analysis suggests their greater utility is as part of a larger strategy to expand the bargaining power of national unions over entire industries by forcing major companies to play by union rules.

The labor movement is in fundamental crisis almost everywhere. Shrinking union densities, increasing casualization, flexible employment regimes, and disappearing labor legislation are only the most visible symptoms of widespread decline, a telltale sign that the opportunities for unions are increasingly limited by developments outside their national contexts and sphere of influence. Governance struggles, in various forms, have emerged as a structural response to mitigate the dilemmas posed by global capitalism. The idea is to reconstruct the rules-based power of transnational corporations to assert a degree of control for local actors.

Governance struggles have come to play such a large role in global labor activism as a direct outcome of three interrelated phenomena. First, the analysis that placed transnational corporations as the motive force of the world economy, and largely outside the purview of national states, has convinced some parts of the labor movement that it cannot rely on government protections. Although it is intended to support the normative globalization thesis, Tilly's (1995: 21) maxim nonetheless captures a fundamental historic development: "As states decline, so do workers' rights." This is exactly why labor turned toward governance struggles—to fight about rules, not rights. The largest and most successful recent victories for unions have been won not through the power vested in them by the National Labor Relations Act, for example, but by circumventing it. The relatively recent failure of unions to successfully win the Employee Free Choice Act, despite massive resources spent trying, is even more of an indication that labor will be unable to depend on national legislation. Instead, the erosion of the right to organize, bargain, and win a contract has pushed some unions toward a strategy of creating new rules. This is even more crucial at the global level, where international labor rights barely exist or are unenforceable. Second, rapidly changing investment patterns and employment regimes, especially in the growing services sector, have emphasized the perceived need for labor to insert itself more firmly into the operating protocols of global business. For many unions, even those without the capacity, resources, or know-how to change, it is now clear that waging battles in one country (against a corporation in many countries) is a recipe for failure. Finally, the increasing consolidation of corporate ownership into fewer and fewer hands presents an opportunity for unions to reach more workers and apply more leverage to a sector as a whole with a single campaign.

Governance struggles are typically associated with processes of globalization because the strategy evolved from a need to regulate capital as it shifted production to places unable or unwilling to enforce labor standards. But they are not solely transnational efforts. The fight against G4S involved the hallmarks of what are now known as "corporate" or "comprehensive" campaigns, most of which happen within national borders, which I conceive of as a governance struggle as well. As the name suggests, corporate campaigns target specific companies with the intent of weakening their public image, economic stability, or political clout in order to extract concessions. A product of ideas born in the New Left of the late 1960s, corporate campaigns have become an exceptionally popular tactic in American unionism to constrain corporations, sometimes as corollaries to actual organizing drives, though many times not (Manheim 2000). As described in chapter 2, the corporate campaign was a crucial first step in the G4S fight, and a major source of inspiration and transformation for unions around the world.

None of this is to say that governance struggles offer a panacea where other strategies have failed. However, the G4S campaign was successful because it neutralized the company while simultaneously creating the conditions for workers to organize, build new organizations, renew old traditions, and experiment with new strategies. That happened because unions and workers found a way to unleash their power—not because of capitalist globalization but in spite of it and not because they won new rights but because they made new rules.

A Theory of the New Labor Transnationalism

Scholars have produced a significant body of descriptive case studies of labor transnationalism, but the facts do not speak for themselves. The insights of Polanyi and Silver and others explored in this book notwithstanding, the field lacks a theoretical lens through which to understand the complexities of new modes of cross-border worker activity. This study endeavors to formulate such a theory—first through an analysis of governance struggles and second by finding a place for the G4S campaign in the past and present attempts of unions to reach across borders. Precisely because it is so multifaceted, this campaign can help us more confidently speculate on the potential of such activity to expand in the future.

Transnationalism is not so much a *tactic* as it is a revised modus operandi, given new political, economic, and sociocultural conditions. In the chapters that follow I argue that the bleak prognostications for labor's revitalization in the global era—the polemical context for this book—can be challenged if we expand our understanding to include new experiences of transnational labor collaboration, particularly those that link struggles in the global and local arenas. From this general argument I raise three interrelated propositions.

The first is that globalization is not the death knell of worker power, as is often stated on the Left and on the Right. Globalization performs a powerful ideological function as a component of its restructuring dynamism, most famously voiced by Margaret Thatcher's triumphant TINA proclamation: There Is No Alternative.[15] But the negative forecasts that associate union decline with neoliberal globalization, or foreclose other outcomes, cannot explain the growing number of cases in which unions have generated some form of power over global companies. The emerging counter-thesis, however, has generally overemphasized and oversimplified the structural opportunities for workers and underestimated the audacious strategies of transnational capitalists. My analysis extends beyond the limits of the counter-thesis and the focus on "structural power." Instead, evidence presented in this case shows that workers can find ways to exert "associational power" in the absence of almost any structural advantage whatsoever through governance struggles. It is worth remembering at this point that for all the structured inevitability purported by the Marxist paradigm, the most revolutionary element bequeathed to us in the *Communist Manifesto* was the conscious agency of workers.

Second, I show that transnational governance struggles are a viable means to empower workers locally. Common sense tells us that workers who have the support of a global campaign behind them are necessarily more powerful in facing down global corporations. But often the very strategies that appeal to the international community end up sidelining local labor rights by redirecting the grievance resolution to a different forum of governance (Seidman 2008). Moreover, governance struggles focus their energy on undermining corporate rules, not immediately on organizing workers. But the campaigns studied in this book have empowered local organizing and have also been strengthened by local campaigns. These strategic approaches are considered the basis for a "new labor transnationalism," a wholly different conception than the one advanced in the existing literature.

Last, successful labor transnationalism may depend on a good deal of restructuring of local union movements. In all the empirical chapters there is a focus on struggles within unions to overcome their own strategic deficits—revitalization from the inside out. But nowhere is the connection between internal revitalization and transnational collaboration more important to the story than in North America. I argue against the conception of the "new labor transnationalism" as a bottom-up phenomenon emerging predominantly from movements within the Global South. In fact, one of the most striking impressions from this book is the degree to which today's global labor movement is led by unions in the United States and how much traction US strategies have around the world. By linking global labor campaigns and local union revitalization, it makes the case for rethinking the dynamics of transnational collaboration. It argues for a shift away from a top-down perspective, in which transnationalism is bound up in the institutions of the global labor movement, without surrendering to a totally bottom-up angle, which suggests that change must come from the global grassroots. If workers are going to succeed in forging transnational power, they need an approach that draws on diverse forms of governance and mobilization at the global and local levels (including information sharing, strikes, boycotts, solidarity campaigns, corporate campaigning, etc.), depending on particular constraints and opportunities.

But beyond the lessons derived from the contours of the case study, the larger story here is about new experiments in strategy and vision that are largely absent from most of the labor movement. The outcomes reveal both the horizons and the limits of such possibilities today. According to two experienced unionists and labor scholars, Bill Fletcher Jr. and Fernando Gapasin, "the future of the union movement lies in a combination of renewed internationalism and the ability of local union movements to transform themselves" (Fletcher and Gapasin 2008: 186). That is essentially the process described in this book.

Overview

This book's six chapters lay out a theoretical framework and an ethnographic narrative about a new spirit of labor transnationalism. The first chapter recasts the history of labor transnationalism from the standpoint of governance struggles. In so doing I theorize a transition to a new kind of global labor politics that appears alongside a new kind of capitalism. The complex issues surrounding global governance regimes have been at the heart of debates about globalization. Though most of this literature centers on the institutions of the global political economy, this chapter explains how unions have engaged in governance struggles "from below." In particular, I take up the strategies for codes of conduct, social clauses, and trade-labor linkages, and then I move on to address global framework agreements in detail.

The second chapter explores the antecedents of the G4S campaign through an analysis of the SEIU's global campaigns. I demonstrate that the union's internationalism emerges from both external and internal pressures, an inside out self-transformation that highlights the link between union revitalization and labor transnationalism. It further documents the wide influence that the SEIU has had on union movements across the world, and the various ways in which its strategies and its staff have come to play such a large role in the global labor movement. The SEIU's transformation into a global actor is seen here as a kind of historical preface to the campaign against G4S. This is especially true as it acts through UNI, its main GUF.

Chapter 3 begins the ethnographic narrative of the campaign to win a global framework agreement with G4S, starting with security guard organizing in 2001 in the United States. It goes on to describe the globalization of the campaign strategy into Europe, Asia, Africa, and Latin America, ending in December 2008. Furthering the story in the first chapter, it discusses the development of another kind of governance struggle integral to the campaign and so much transnational labor activity today, the corporate or comprehensive campaign. Chapters 4 and 5 transpose the global campaign onto different local contexts, Johannesburg and two Indian cities, Bangalore and Kolkata. Here we see the ways in which local dynamics shape the strategic choices and opportunities offered to the SEIU and UNI, and the ways in which governance struggles open up pathways for local union mobilization, revitalization, and social dialogue.

The conclusion suggests that workers of the world can in fact unite, if not around common demands then around common employers. I argue that scholars and unionists should more seriously consider the local dimension of global unionism in order to fully grasp the potential and limitations of labor transnationalism. Readers may be disappointed by the absence of a principled call for unions to "be more like movements" that seems to punctuate the conclusion of most books on labor. Instead, I discuss the crucial role played by union leadership in transnational campaigns. Finally, the book would be incomplete without some speculation on the future trajectory of global unionism, given the pace at which it has changed even since this fieldwork was completed.

Workers of the World . . .

The prospect of a unified workers movement that transcends national boundaries has been central to the radical imagination for almost two centuries. Today, the pragmatic position—global companies require global unions—often seems new, but this position is as old as the union idea itself. In 1897, Tom Mann, the veteran British trade union leader and communist, declared it "next to impossible to effectively organize nationally unless international effort be made concurrently" (Mann 1897: 9). And though the iterations of labor internationalism have fascinated writers since then, only recently have scholars built the semblance of a field—global labor studies—out of the disparate perspectives of geographers, economists, industrial relations experts, business writers, and the occasional sociologist.

When I began this research five years ago I was suspicious of arguments that insisted the potential for transnational unionism was living within the contradictions of global capitalism. I wanted to see the internal workings of a global campaign—how unions struggled to transcend the challenges posed not only by global political economy but also their own entrenched organizational inertia. Though I set out with a great deal of skepticism I am now convinced that in order for unions to become a force for social transformation they will need to answer the challenges posed by global capitalism—and their own institutional blinders—with the kinds of global labor organizations that can facilitate sustained cross-border collaboration. As will become clear in the pages that follow, those formations are now coming into existence for the first time.

Chapter 1

Forging the New Labor Transnationalism: Governance Struggles and Worker Power

By now we can definitively point to growing tendencies toward transnationalism within some segments of labor movements around the world. Take any large and expanding industry with a global footprint—telecommunications, automobile production, property services, retail, transportation and logistics, food and agriculture, hotels and tourism—and there are active campaigns involving workers, unions, nongovernmental organizations (NGOs), and other civil society groups in dozens of countries. This activity has increased since the mid-1990s beyond regional cooperation to develop legitimate global structures that can carry out sustained campaigns against some of the world's largest and most union-resistant corporations. But the most successful transnational labor campaigns are not bubbling up from below, as many might hope. Nor are they mere instruments for self-interested developed-country unions. In both positions, prospects for labor transnationalism are evoked rather than investigated, and we are often left with an unhelpful choice between Pollyanna or pessimism (see

Burawoy 2010; Clawson 2010; Webster 2010). Rarely do we hear *how* those uncommon occasions of successful transnational collaboration happen. In other words, how is workers' power made actionable on the global stage?

Today global union federations (GUFs) play the most decisive role, but they are only the latest incarnation, clearly built on the successes and failures of past practice. The first task then is to theorize a transition to a new kind of global labor politics. Why has labor transnationalism moved, as I have suggested, from a proletarian internationalism toward global governance struggles? When one considers the earlier—and longer—period of transnational labor history, governance struggles are an unexpected development. For all of that time workers were becoming increasingly enmeshed with their respective national states and reliant on rights-based regimes for employment protection (Tilly 1995). International cooperation among national working classes even began to break down as nation-states assumed an ever-larger role in the everyday lives of workers and their organizations.

But over the last four decades there has been a perceptible shift in emphasis as unions recognize the inordinate role that multinational corporations have come to play in shaping the lives of working people. Corporate power is invested in making public policy, but increasingly its internal rules-based power is enough to structure employment relationships to its liking, even against governmental regulatory measures that stipulate the opposite. Consequently, unions feel less compelled to rely on rights and even actively avoid existing rights-based frameworks at times. Instead we see a decisive shift toward governance struggles, as unions have fought for new rules of engagement through neutrality clauses, codes of conduct, social clauses, and framework agreements. This shift is even clearer when we map it onto a historic example. Unions had, for most of their existence, lobbied for the International Labour Organization (ILO) to regulate labor standards by sanctioning the governments of member states. But more recent history shows a widespread preference for linking labor rights and trade policy through the supranational apparatus of the World Trade Organization (WTO) instead, a primary institution of world governance. How and why a labor-backed governance paradigm developed demands recourse to the historical record of labor transnationalism. As a preamble to that question, this chapter begins with a brief assessment of the changing global landscape for labor.

Labor Transnationalism in Transition

Early Internationalism

Labor has come a long way since *la belle époque* of Marx's International Workingmen's Association of 1864, or even before, in the 1830s, when unions in Northern Europe were motivated by a "vague idea of a common bond between laboring people" (Lorwin 1953: 3).

By the onset of the twentieth century, a broad swath of worker organizations had created several International Trade Secretariats (ITSs)[1] involving millions of workers that existed primarily as vehicles for information sharing on wage rates, working conditions, and union struggles (Windmuller 1981). Although the majority of international labor groups hailed from the UK or Germany, by the early 1900s, the anarcho-syndicalist Industrial Workers of the World were both an "authentically American" and "path-breaking internationalist" organization, with branches in Europe and Australia (Moberg 2005b). Munck (2002: 135) says this nascent labor movement was "instinctively internationalist" from its inception.

However, international labor solidarity has not been continuous. Rather, it was suddenly shattered with the outbreak of World War I and the Bolshevik Revolution, when workers abandoned a common international cause to defend a national flag and killed one another by the millions on the battlefields of Europe. Thus the "Great War" is often seen as a breaking point for international solidarity. However, when it was over, it was labor's support for the war that was the most compelling argument for an institution that would offer robust protections for workers in the wake of such devastation and tragedy. Thus, the ILO was established in 1919 by disparate groups of European socialists and Laborites, and the Gompers wing of the American Federation of Labor (AFL). The mission was, among other things, to create more robust universal labor standards. Then in early 1945, after a rift began over the US-backed Marshal Plan, a group of Communist-oriented unions came together under the banner of the World Federation of Trade Unions (WFTU)[2] (Carew, Dreyfus, Van Goethem, Gumbrell-McCormick, and Van der Linden 2000). As millions of workers found support through new organizations, it seemed, for a moment, labor internationalism was in full swing again.

Strangely, however, the *end* of the Second World War may have been as detrimental to transnationalism as the *onset* of the First World War. The first divided national working classes, while the second strengthened their nationalism. Although strong states have been historically linked to strong national working classes, they are negatively correlated with instances of labor transnationalism. Since 1945, scholars have pointed to an inverse relationship between the capacity of workers to win strong gains from nation-states and their subsequent interest in transnational activity (Logue 1980). As unions found their respective states more accommodating to wage and benefits concessions, their will to internationalism was muted (Wills 1998). However, it would be incorrect to posit the complete disappearance of labor transnationalism after the war. Instead, the postwar configuration of states had a dramatic impact on the internationalist outlook of many unions.

Labor in the Age of Three Worlds: The Cold War and Trade Union Imperialism

At the end of the war the international trade union movement lined up behind their respective country interests to take sides for the "democratic" West or the "communist" East. Although there was an initial impetus within the WFTU to be nonpartisan, ideological battles quickly led to the secession of its non-communist European members, who would later form the International Confederation of Free Trade Unions (ICFTU) in 1949.

But no unionists took up the Cold War cause with more pluck than the Americans, who became strident allies to the US government's militant anticommunism. Before the Taft-Hartley Act (1947) introduced loyalty oaths to organized labor, the AFL deployed unionists to Western Europe to help establish noncommunist trade unions (Fichter 1982). Following its merger in 1955, the AFL-CIO began a more aggressive defense of "free trade unionism" through the ICFTU, which it eventually deemed insufficiently anticommunist. It preferred to pursue cold war unionism on its own terms, especially in Latin America through its own organization, the American Institute for Free Labor Development (AIFLD).

On the heels of Castro's 1959 revolution in Cuba, AIFLD became closely aligned with Kennedy's Alliance for Progress initiative and dedicated itself to the task of suppressing radical leftist forces within the international trade unions, but mostly in Latin America (Sims 1999: 56). The central figure in the Institute was the notorious Jay Lovestone, the once

Communist Party USA leader turned Central Intelligence Agency (CIA) spy. Ted Morgan's rich biography (1999) of Lovestone details both his international romantic encounters and his strident love affair with collective bargaining, which was central to his anti-communist espionage activities in foreign labor movements. His largest role was in Latin America, where, as director of the AFL's international activities, his covert campaigns were central to US foreign policy in the region (Buhle 1999). It also trained local leaders to promote workplace unionism over more political/social movement forms and spent considerable funds constructing schools, bridges, and other infrastructure to help promote the idea that "free trade unions can produce results, while Communists produce only slogans" (AIFLD 1964, cited in Herod 2009).

While the Cold War certainly divided the movement, some important instances of collaboration happened during this time as well. It was the increasing transnationalization of capital, not proletarianization, that provided the greatest rationale for cooperation and unity. It is at this point that we see the earliest incarnations of governance struggles. Beginning in the 1960s, the trade secretariats, the institutional successors to the GUFs, took significant strides toward countering the increasing globalization of capital. The idea was to mirror the structural configurations of transnational corporations, the vision of Charles Levinson, who got his start in trade union politics as the staff person for the CIO's Paris office in 1951 (Gallin 1997). Levinson went on to lead the International Federation of Chemical, Energy, Mine, and General Workers' Unions (ICEM) for two decades and was perhaps the first to recognize the deep challenges and potential for labor unions posed by globalization. He argued that transnational collective bargaining represented an inevitable approach if unions wanted to survive. This theory prompted the ICEM to establish multiple bodies similar to world company councils in major globalizing industries at the time. In many ways, Levinson may well be the progenitor of the governance struggle.[3]

In the end it was not Levinson's ICEM but the International Metalworkers Federation that began, within the auto industry, the most significant experiment with transnational unionism and the earliest approaches to labor governance. The beginning of the deindustrialization of motor manufacturing from high-wage to low-wage areas was witnessed, first within the United States and then outside of it. The United Auto Workers (UAW), operating in the classic Fordist paradigm, sought to constrain capital flight by establishing worldwide union representation through company councils. As it turns out, the theory was more successful than the practice, and the company councils yielded very little in the way of gains for unions or workers (Bendiner 1977), but it remains an important step toward a new paradigm of labor transnationalism.

Labor, Development, and the End of the Cold War

Most historians agree that two world wars, and then a cold war, significantly undermined any basis for international solidarity. Nationalism, capitalism, anticommunism, Fascism, and Stalinism—the most powerful ideas of the twentieth century—all argued convincingly against working-class unity.

When the history of labor transnationalism has been written fully, by far the most bewildering part will be explaining how sincere and legitimate transnational cooperation actually happened *despite* decades of labor imperialism, Cold War divisions, the rise of economic and cultural nationalisms, and brutal colonial legacies. Since the Cold War, the crowning achievement of labor internationalism is the campaign against apartheid in South Africa. The campaign led by Richard Trumka's United Mine Workers of America and the National Union of Mineworkers in South Africa pressured Royal Dutch/Shell to close its South African operations as part of a global boycott against apartheid. The movement was backed by churches, international NGOs, and other unions, including crucial logistical support from seafarers in the International Transport Federation who helped expose secret trade deals between oil companies and the South African government (Bronfenbrenner 2007). Shell, unlike other oil suppliers, never left the country, choosing to trade the bad publicity for higher profits as it slowly became the primary oil supplier to the apartheid state. Nevertheless, Bronfenbrenner (2007) calls the campaign "perhaps the most comprehensive and most effective example of cross-border solidarity of labor and its allies in history." Munck (2002) claims the South African campaign rekindled "the spirit of the First International." And so we are back where we began. In many ways, the role of labor against South African apartheid represents an interregnum into new modes of transnational collaboration, and especially struggles for governance.

Recasting the New Labor Transnationalism: Labor and Global Governance Struggles

To the great surprise of the participants of the 2001 World Economic Forum in Switzerland, John Sweeney, then-president of the AFL-CIO, announced the "birth pangs of a new internationalism" at a time when many on the Left were committed to promoting the doom-and-gloom forecasts of the globalization thesis (Sweeney 2001). Sweeney declared, "This movement for a new internationalism is building from the bottom up, not the top down. . . . Its forum is the public square, not the boardroom." (Munck, 2002)

Sweeney himself was building on an important *Foreign Affairs* article by Jay Mazur, chair of the AFL-CIO International Affairs Committee. Here, Mazur (2000) declared an end to Cold War unionism, labor imperialism, and narrow workplace-centered campaigning, instead suggesting that the unions had turned a corner in the international arena, inspired by the 1999 protests against the WTO in Seattle. He wrote:

> For years governments ignored demands to include labor and environmental rights in trade agreements, confident that there was no political cost in doing so. This is now changing. Unions are forging new alliances with environmentalists, human rights groups, and religious and consumer activists. After Seattle, the demand for labor rights and other social standards can no longer be ignored. . . . A social movement of potentially tremendous force has begun to gather that can affect the bottom line and the laws of the land. (Mazur 2000: 81)

Sweeney's remarks and Mazur's sentiment succinctly summarize much of what is usually considered "new" about new labor transnationalism and, indeed, for a time it was. For the time between the passage of the North American Free Trade Agreement (NAFTA) and the WTO protests it seemed that alliances between US unions and radical social movements had provided labor with a new telescope through which to view the world of work outside its borders.[4] Armbruster-Sandoval (2005) and Mark Anner (2011) show that numerous transnational campaigns arose at this time inside the Latin American maquiladora sector by unions making use of a "boomerang strategy" (Keck and Sikkink 1998) and other creative social movement tactics. While insisting that unions were paving a better future, Mazur says they had also uncovered a critical tradition in their past.

> [Unions] have *always* operated across borders; their ideological roots—and much of their early membership—grew out of the internationalist perspective of the European labor movement of the last century. When American corporations were still huddling behind tariff barriers, workers were organizing international associations based on the principles of solidarity and social justice. (Mazur 2000: 83, emphasis added)

Although the primordialism just expressed is always suspect, as an account of labor's past this story has some merit. But the idea that labor had found a long-buried treasure has given rise to some confusing historical parallels. Munck (2002) suggests that Sweeney's speech amounts to a call for a "renewal of proletarian internationalism." Waterman, a relentless champion of labor's role in the World Social Forum scene, sees the new internationalism fundamentally characterized by cross-border solidarity activities between workers at the shop floor or grassroots level. It is often inspired by and directed at large forces of international exploitation: racism, imperialism, patriarchy, militarism, authoritarianism, and so on, and it tends to complement new social movement activity, especially identity-based movements (Waterman 2001).[5] Three leading scholars of the South African labor movement repeatedly provide the example of the Southern Initiative on Globalization and Trade Union Rights (SIGTUR), an Australia-based federation of unions in the Southern Hemisphere (Webster, Lambert, and Beziudenhout 2008). For most of its existence, however, SIGTUR has organized nothing but conferences of international union leaders, and its website offers even less that might lead us to believe it can do otherwise.[6] Finally, with near unanimity the massive 1999 anti-WTO demonstrations are seen as a crystal-clear display of the US labor movement's turn toward "globalization from below" (Brecher, Costello, and Smith 2000).

It may muddy those waters considerably to remember that as police converged on protesters in downtown Seattle, the United Steelworkers of America, the most committed labor allies of the radical activist movement, were dumping beams of Chinese steel into Elliot Bay. Though couched as a protest of unfair trade agreements, the action had the distinctive nationalist flavor of protectionism. Let us also remember that at the critical hour during the WTO ministerial, as delegates were voting on trade-labor linkages, the AFL-CIO, as an ally to the then-president Clinton, fought to establish a social clause within the WTO framework that would inordinately benefit northern labor.

Delegates from India and Africa staunchly opposed such a measure as thinly veiled protectionism, what Scheuerman (2001) calls "false humanitarianism," and the clause was never included.[7] Largely as a result of the divisions caused by the social clause debate, the WTO meetings came to a draw when consensus was blocked on important trade-related issues. Once this history is brought front and center, an important aspect of Mazur's position becomes less tenable:

> Virtually every independent labor federation has endorsed the ICFTU's call for building labor rights into the global trading system. The divide is not between North and South; it is between workers everywhere and the great concentrations of capital and the governments they dominate. (Mazur 2000: 88)

The perceived erasure of the North-South divide represents an important tenet within global labor sociology. But arguments for the homogenizing impacts of capitalist globalization are old, even classical. In the *Communist Manifesto*, Marx and Engels write of the industrial worker: "Modern subjection to capital, the same in England as in France, in America as in Germany, has stripped him of every trace of national character." What was class reductionism then is even more fallacious today. In this case, Aristide Zolberg's question is more apt for modern times: "If capitalism is of a piece, why is the working class it has called into life so disparate?" (Zolberg 1986: 397)

Most recent examples of transnational labor collaboration include workers in the North and South. Much scholarly attention has focused on the cooperation of unions and NGOs (Anner and Evans 2004). European industrial relations have also excited many scholars, particularly the development of the European Works Council (EWC) (Rogers and Streek 1995; Wills 1998; Marginson and Sisson 1996). Following the explosion of anti-sweatshop activism on college campuses (Ross 1997) and the WTO protests in Seattle, scholars began assessing a new global justice movement in earnest. Much of this work involved struggles for international unionism and solidarity with new social movements (Waterman 2001; Brecher, Costello, and Smith 2000; Cockburn and St. Claire 2001). The descriptive focus on global movements gradually gave way to a more nuanced understanding of how they may exert some form of control, or governance, within the global economy, perhaps through the social clauses of trade agreements (Kay 2005, 2011; Scherrer 1998), corporate codes of conduct (Seidman 2008; Compa 2004), and, most recently, global framework agreements (Papadakis et al. 2009; Papadakis 2011; Stevis and Boswell 2007a and b). It is this trend toward global labor governance that I want to explore next, which demands a theoretical reworking of the current view about "new labor transnationalism."

Governance Struggles—Fighting for Rules, not Rights

Governance is a contested term. Having emerged alongside processes normally associated with globalization, it refers broadly to the exercise of power in the absence of an overarching political authority, usually by a constellation of institutions that make decisions and enforce compliance with norms and rules at the supranational level. If the Westphalian system and the New Deal represented the apogee of a state-based system of government, the neoliberalism of the early part of the twenty-first century marks a new era of global governance. Political scientists emphasize the significance of the Bretton Woods institutions—the World Trade Organization, the International Monetary Fund, and the World Bank—as governance bodies, especially since the end of the Cold War. International political economy, in contrast, stresses the "worldwide tilt from states to markets" and the development of a new *arena* of "governance without government." Still others focus on "soft law" (Abbott and Snidal 2000). Following Foucault, sociologists often use the concept to signify an artful and subtle power formed through networks of knowledge, communication, and control, often resting in social institutions (hospitals, schools, churches, etc.).

The concern underpinning all of these scholarly conceptions of governance is that in the face of crisis-ridden markets and failed states, democratic society needs a new basis for its continued existence. Regulating labor rights (publicly enforceable claims) across borders would seem to be an ideal test case for the governance paradigm. The dismantling of state protections for workers has increasingly subjected labor conditions to the vicissitudes of crisis-ridden markets. International labor law is nonexistent, and unions everywhere are becoming an endangered species. Instead, corporations became the new public sphere (Deetz 1992: 348). In this instance, the governance paradigm might propose to prop up labor standards through a participatory quasi-democratic process involving a variety of generic stakeholders—NGOs, unions, business and political leaders, and perhaps even an errant human rights campaigner. The underlying problem with this logic is that it creates a false equivalency between the parties, assuming there is some sort of "democracy" created by allowing business and labor to hash it out, or to have the dispute adjudicated by a body that views them as equals in a pluralist society. In that sense, the power asymmetries among the parties tend to discredit, invalidate, or render useless (take your pick) the ostensible foundation of the governance paradigm, leading to what Rodriguez-Garavito (2005) calls "governance failure."

However, several important studies have suggested that the governance institutions not only exert a pull effect on labor strategies (Anner 2011), but they also offer workers political opportunities through which to raise standards, settle grievances, and win rights (Kay 2005, 2011). But the historical record suggests that such "opportunities" are almost always bureaucratic traps. Instead, governance struggles have been most successful when they have been able to rewrite or alter the rules of engagement with capital, whether or not they have won a spectrum of rights.[8]

To highlight the distinction between rules and rights, one can imagine a scenario in which workers at a given company's supply chain are granted the right to organize without a change in management's anti-union behavior versus a global agreement that codifies a rule stating that management must apply universal standards to its full-time and subcontracted employees. Whereas Silver (2003: 14) conceives of associational power as based on the rights granted to workers through state and legal provisions, here it is theorized as the power to act in the absence of such rights. Rather than view workers as the pitiable victims of global governance institutions, I theorize here their potential as agents of governance themselves. In other words, from the perspective of governance struggles, we should not confuse the decline of worker rights with the inability of labor to defend itself.

Labor, a central factor in much debate about private regulation, has rarely been considered an agent of global governance. Nor is it common to hear of a "governance gap" with regard to labor conditions, yet such a gap is exactly what global framework agreements are seeking to fill.[9] This approach therefore joins a handful of others seeking to "bring labor in" to debates on governance, asserting their fundamental significance in shaping the world economy (Stevis and Boswell 2007a and b; Fichter et al. 2012; Papadakis et al. 2008; Kay 2011).

There are three traditional avenues through which unions have tried to exercise governance in the public and private sphere: social clauses, codes of conduct, and global framework agreements. The issue is whether or not a regime can be established that oversees the effective observance/implementation of basic rules and regulations pertaining to labor standards. One proposed method is to allow the WTO or a "free-trade" pact such as NAFTA the power to sanction those member states that are out of compliance. This is based on the idea that since trade is the main catalyst of the global economy, it should also be the mechanism through which to enforce labor standards (and, presumably, other standards as well). Such a strategy is called a "social clause." Another is to force multinational companies to agree to source their materials and employ their workers according to a voluntary standard of fairness, or a code of conduct. After addressing these two forms, I spend the bulk of the chapter discussing global framework agreements.

The Social Clause

There is a curious irony in the way in which labor unions and social movements celebrated their landmark protest against the 1999 WTO Millennial Ministerial in Seattle. On the third day of negotiations, as demonstrators declared a clear victory in chaotic streets, African and Indian delegates blocked the necessary consensus to further discussions over trade rules that would have inserted a social clause on labor standards into all WTO decisions. Such a policy, according to prevailing wisdom within the AFL-CIO, would have mandated the enforcement of minimum or core labor standards, including prohibitions against child labor and forced labor, against discrimination at work, and against violations of the freedom to organize unions.[10] The WTO's rules-based enforcement process, now widely understood as empowering transnational corporations to move investments and production freely across borders, would have ostensibly been used to protect workers' rights against the worst abuses (Bacon 2000). Although debates about trade-labor linkages were common questions of governance for decades, the issue of a social clause was never returned to the WTO agenda after Seattle.

Unions have proposed to link trade and economic agreements with labor rights since the mid-nineteenth century, when workers first began to feel competitive pressures from low-wage areas (Charnovitz 1987). The stillborn (never operational) International Trade Organization took similar approaches after the Second World War, though it was not until the 1970s that the strategy gained more urgency, as liberalization processes encouraged the creation of legislation embedded in economic agreements (van Roozendal 2002). The sea changes of capitalism in the 1970s set in motion a series of processes that restructured the global division of labor and global trade patterns.

Soon the World Bank, the International Monetary Fund (IMF), and the General Agreement on Tariffs and Trade (GATT) exercised profound discipline over the global political economy.[11] These changes prompted unions and other social movements to explore a link between trade and labor standards at the global level via economic agreements, the GATT, and/or the ILO (van Roozendaal 2002). This notion found its first concrete expression in the ICFTU's campaign to insert a social clause into the GATT. The idea was to attach the ILO's core labor conventions to the trade pact so that exporting countries that failed to observe a baseline minimum in standards could be penalized with sanctions (Haworth and Hughes 1997). Though unsuccessful, a number of its policy prescriptions were subsequently included in the influential Brandt Report of 1980 (Hampson 2004). Then the AFL-CIO of the mid-1970s, at the behest of unions in industries most exposed to international competition (automobile manufacturing and textiles), pursued a policy of attaching labor standards to US trade policies. This activity eventually developed into the Generalized System of Preferences in 1984, which allegedly enforced punishment on trading partners for noncompliance of basic labor standards. It is premised on the idea that "trade, not aid" should be the basis for economic development.

By the mid-1990s, a general consensus among the international trade secretariats had emerged in support of safeguarding labor rights through clauses in trade agreements. The only point of debate centered around enforcement mechanisms and the proper institution—the ILO versus the

WTO—to promote the strategy. The ICFTU promoted the ILO as the first body to investigate violations, referring all unresolved cases to the WTO for possible sanctions (ICFTU 2005). After the WTO's 1996 Singapore round did not reject or advance a position on the social clause, the ICFTU pursued a successful campaign to win many southern unions over to the strategy, highlighting the expanding influence of the organization in international labor politics. It did so, however, while calling for increased funding for the IMF and the World Bank and pushing the logic of, according to its general secretary, Bill Jordan, "globalization with a human face" (quoted in Greenfield 1998: 184). These kinds of empty platitudes—they were spoken in Singapore in the midst of the Asian financial crisis—could only have appealed to the most corrupt and illegitimate union bodies and did little to bolster confidence in the social clause strategy.

Which brings us back to the inability of the United States to realize the strategy in Seattle. The reigning explanation for the social clause failure is that regional solidarity by southern representatives gravitated around the perceived protectionism of their northern counterparts, as trade-based labor standards would have certainly favored northern producers more immediately, driving a North-South wedge into global labor politics (Newland 1999).[12] In particular, India led a block of developing countries to opposition. During these debates, however, the South was divided, as South African and Brazilian delegates supported the clauses, arguing that it posed an opportunity for a deeper form of protection for workers in the global economy and mitigated against a race to the bottom. These countries accused dissenters of supporting a developmental path based on the comparative advantage of cheap labor.

Perhaps a more nuanced understanding of this dilemma appreciates the power differentials between northern and southern unions more fully. Most southern unions, including some that argued against the social clause at the WTO in 1999, support it in principle but have legitimate concerns that the process will be dominated by the more powerful trade unions of the North, subordinating the interests of the South. This situation may result in conflicting "agendas that do not reflect the core concerns of those they portend to represent," what Mark Anner (2006) has called a "paradox of labor transnationalism." Ultimately, the social clause strategy is fundamentally limited by its narrow application to trade-related politics rather than the economy as a whole, though it continues to play a role in bilateral trade agreements. The impressive compromise with capital that it entails also contains an important ideological dimension that circumscribes any "activism" to a group of union leaders or NGO officials with the necessary access to global governance bodies.

Codes of Conduct

International NGOs, global governance organizations such as the United Nations (UN) and ILO, and developing states had been proposing different kinds of corporate regulation since the 1960s. Perhaps the paradigmatic examples are the Sullivan Principles, which in 1977 enforced a code of conduct on transnational corporations operating in apartheid South Africa. Developed over two decades, the principles were used by the divestment campaign that convinced over one hundred US-based companies to withdraw their operations from the country. Seidman (2003) argues that the principles were meaningless as a voluntaristic measure but became useful when defended by unions and other social movement actors. They also inspired other codes, such as the MacBride Principles,[13] which set standards for US companies operating in Northern Ireland from 1984 onward (see McNamara 2010). Beginning in the 1970s, corporate social responsibility schemes promoted a powerful argument to preempt actual governance with public relations ploys, and corporations began adopting certain core values, standards, or practices in some formal fashion en masse. This idea flourished as neoliberal governments took power in many places during the 1980s, promoting the deregulation and deindustrialization of formerly union workplaces. As a result, these kinds of codes of conduct suffered, or went into abeyance, under the new logic that business did not answer to civil society.

But slightly more than a decade later, an explosion of labor-backed governance struggles erupted, reinvigorating the codes of conduct strategy and inspiring a wide range of scholarly intrigue (see Compa 2004; Frundt 2001, 2004; Esbenshade 2004; Armbruster-Sandoval 2005; Anner and Evans 2004; Seidman 2008).[14] Such struggles sought to "shape corporate conduct" and restrain corporate power through "binding rules" (Murray 1998). The growth of codes of conduct at this time reflects a general sentiment that global production networks and value chains had surpassed trade as a form of economic interdependence (Jenkins 2001).

Compa (2004) suggests that such codes stake out a "third way" to enforce labor rights and standards to stand in for government's apparent inability to monitor the growing number of factories within its borders and to compensate for the declining success of trade unionism. Another intriguing proposal suggests putting in place a series of mechanisms to pressure companies to compete for consumer opinion on the basis of high labor standards and quality control (Fung, O'Rourke, and Sabel 2000). Rodriguez-Garavito (2005) has promoted what he calls an "empowered participatory labor regulation" that conceives as codes of conduct as a corollary to national laws or international conventions, such as ILO core labor standards. This is particularly important in that it views the state not as a victim of economic transformations but as a participant in creating a new global regulatory environment for labor and, therefore, is susceptible to pressure (Rodriguez-Garavito 2005: 213).

But codes of conduct approaches, widely conceived, emerged as the most popular tool, largely as an alternative to the undesirable and, at the time, impossible task of organizing factory by factory on the shop floor.[15] Although most codes began as principled statements on corporate behavior, they quickly evolved into long juridical documents. The privatized nature of the codes meant that the content varied considerably, but most attempted to apply a set of standards to be followed, a local implementation procedure, and a monitoring provision. Esbenshade (2001: 98–99) describes this regulatory environment as a "social accountability contract" and "new paternalism" in that it relegates worker involvement to the lowest priority level compared to other "stakeholders." However, the code strategy provided an obvious inroad toward transnational advocacy networks (Keck and Sikkink 1998) that helped establish a broad base of support and a greater degree of legitimacy and international media attention to the struggle. Almost all the successful codes were won and defended by such networks of linked activists.

The Kukdong factory is a case in point, where workers generated significant international support and eventually secured the first collective bargaining agreement ever between an independent union and a Mexican maquiladora that raised standards significantly. Other successful cases lent credence to the strategy of transnational campaigns improving labor standards. Notable among these were struggles to win improvements in the Korean-owned

Kimi plant in Honduras, the Phillips-Van Heusen plant in Guatemala, and the Mandarin plant in El Salvador (Anner and Evans 2004).

In each of these cases, traditional union organizing had failed on numerous occasions. Instead, with the help of transnational allies in the National Labor Committee,[16] it targeted the well-known multinational brands (Nike, the Gap, Macy's, etc.)[17] that contracted with these different export processing zones to pressure their clients to agree to, and abide by, codes of conduct (Armbruster-Sandoval 2005: 474–476). This highlights the importance of governance struggles to target the largest decision makers and the most powerful stakeholders in a particular interdependent relationship rather than simply a panoply of "actors," as they are the ones that can most significantly spread new norms and rules.

But even these cases proved ephemeral as management at the Kimi and Van-Heusen plants relocated after workers won wage increases (Anner 2011). One response, taken up by the US government's Apparel Industry Partnership, was to create the Fair Labor Association in order to govern capital flight and put in place an industry-wide code of conduct. It even established a "No Sweat" label for clothing that satisfied its criteria. It met a chorus of disapproval, however, due to its low minimum standards, weak enforcement mechanisms, and lack of external monitoring provisions, thereby triggering a coalition of organizations to develop a more stringent version.

In 1997 US college students formed United Students Against Sweatshops (USAS), reviving a tradition of student-labor solidarity activism and displacing the lingering perception of student radicals as antilabor since the hard hats and hippies clashed on Wall Street over the war in Vietnam. By the early 2000s, USAS boasted over two hundred chapters in the United States (Featherstone and United Students against Sweatshops 2002), built a number of spinoff campaigns (Behind the Label, Nike Truth Tour), and secured a place for speech making and leafleting on Billy Bragg's US tour. Students and their universities played a decisive role, given their position in the global supply chain of college apparel. Although universities comprise a meager 2 percent of US apparel sales (Traub-Werner 2002: 194), USAS used its leverage to insert itself into an inchoate movement. Seeking to increase the stringency of monitoring and implementation of codes of conduct, USAS and the NLC founded the Worker Rights Consortium (WRC), funded by profits from apparel sales in over one hundred US universities and colleges. The WRC played a significant role in the Kukdong case and others, and its model promoted a system of rules to hold corporations more accountable and to make their business practices more transparent.

The working assumption was that worker rights were more secure with a robust monitoring system on corporate behavior. This prompted other organizations to join the strategy, resulting in hundreds, if not thousands, of corporate codes of conduct.[18] However, the proliferation of codes, which has typically pointed to an enlarged sphere of influence by labor and other civil society actors, may in fact be related to their weaknesses. In other words, companies submitted so willingly because the regulatory sanctions were so minimal and the monitoring process voluntary (Pearson and Seyfang 2001), making a worthwhile tradeoff if it meant avoiding bad press. Jenkins (2001) suggests a number of other weaknesses, varying from an unfair perception of codes as more than they are to the possibility that they might undermine workplace organizing. This is largely because the NGOs that are usually charged with enforcing them require access rights from management or funding from employers. Seidman (2008) is definitive in her appraisal:

> Since the mid-1990s, global brands have learned that, when activists reveal child labor, worker abuse or unsafe conditions in their supplier plants, they can ward off threats of global embarrassment and transnational consumer boycotts by adopting codes of conduct . . . corporate codes of conduct offer a weak alternative to more traditional protections for labor rights—even when backed by independent monitors, however well-intentioned. (Seidman 2008: 1001)

There are some recent victories that may point to changing fortunes for the codes of conduct strategy. Workers at Russell Athletic and its parent company, Fruit of the Loom, have won significant gains for workers in Honduras through transnational activism and local organizing. The WRC has also developed the Designated Suppliers Program, which allows participating universities (there are about 50 endorsing schools) to require companies producing its logo apparel to meet criteria favorable to union organizing (See Workers Rights Consortium 2012). Ultimately, however, codes often present transnational corporations a way to *manage* the conflicting interests of their stakeholders without actually *sharing* power. Given the limitations of a bilateral or regional strategy, unions have increasingly sought global corporate governance. The global framework agreements strategy therefore demands a critical evaluation.

Global Framework Agreements

Global framework agreements (GFAs)[19] mark the first instance in the history of the labor movement that transnational companies have bargained directly with unions at the global level. Novelty aside, they represent an important strategy to impact privatized forms of global governance by large corporations. GFAs are nonbinding[20] contracts signed between GUFs and transnational corporations that attempt to secure labor standards throughout a company's operations and, in some cases, its supply chain.

New rules of conduct are thereby made viral, diffused by human resource management practices through transnational production and service delivery networks. The fiercest debates occur over their implementation, as corporations and unions invariably view GFAs as having fundamentally different ends (IOE 2007). There has been an explosion of GFAs signed in the last decade: from five in 2000 to ninety-one in early 2013. The recent popularity of the strategy has inspired a substantial academic literature devoted to its assessment.

One view sees GFAs as a new mechanism for "social dialogue" and multinational industrial relations (Riisgaard 2005; Hammer 2005; Wills 2002). These theorists note the rising power of transnational corporations and the declining effectiveness of national-level activism, forcing unions to shift to a higher scale of bargaining. A second perspective views GFAs primarily as instruments for global governance. In other words, in the absence of a regulatory apparatus that can safeguard workers at the global level, GFAs represent a mechanism to uphold basic standards and conditions that most national legal systems do not provide, especially in the Global South (Papadakis et al. 2009; Papadakis 2011).[21] Another interesting approach from a management perspective applies Szulanski's (1996) "practice transfer model" to international human resource management. Here global agreements are seen as conveyers of new business models (Fichter et al. 2011). Others focus on the potential for GFAs to assist unions that want to organize and on the application of the agreement beyond the company's headquarters and into its corporate periphery or supply chain, where labor rights generally become weaker and weaker the further one moves from the corporate center (Stevis and Boswell 2007a and b).

This book suggests GFAs are significant in three main ways. First, GFAs create a rationale and, as their name suggests, a framework for a global union campaign. Because any struggle against a global corporation will invariably be one taken up by an alliance or coalition, a GFA offers a common goal that is potentially useful to all parties. Second, global agreements are potentially part of a long-term industrial strategy to build power within a sector or region's largest players. In other words, as global employers within a particular industry agree to union neutrality (through a GFA), they provide employees potential strength beyond the workplace, as these companies can become part of an effort to pressure other industrial leaders to sign GFAs as well. Moreover, because union organizing in the services sector is usually driven by regional market imperatives, not specific corporate targets, a GFA's impact should be measured by the extent to which it expands the union's influence over the industrial landscape. Last, GFAs offer a route to challenge company power in the absence of worker rights by establishing new rules. Although it is commonly asserted that GFAs give workers *rights*, in the legalistic sense, as forms of private governance, they do not. Rather, they construct new *rules* and regulations that reorder the labor-capital relationship in ways that can benefit workers. Global agreements are seen here as an outcome of a shifting historical struggle to *govern* global capitalism and build worker power in an arena in which a more traditional approach based on worker rights in insufficient. Such a perspective contributes an understanding of GFAs as more than policy instruments but nonetheless as useful platforms for worker mobilization, solidarity, and union renewal.

However, before we judge their merits and faults today, the historical lens taken here demands we know where they came from. Stevis and Boswell (2007) offer an explanation for the development of GFAs, usefully distilled into three general categories: union internationalism, the emergence of corporate social responsibility practices, and the evolution of European industrial relations.

The Origins of GFAs

Though capital has always been global, employees have not. It was not until the 1960s that unions sought to meet corporations at the global level, driven by the Europeanization of lead sectors in the US economy. First, unions called for national policies that would restrict the degree to which companies could expand internationally, reflective of the code of conduct and social clause strategy. This largely failed in its stated mission and in the process created bitter divisions among unions in different countries (Newland 1999).

Then, in the 1960s, Walter Reuther's UAW began to pursue coordinated bargaining. The inaugural meeting of four councils met in Detroit in 1966—General Motors, Ford, Volkswagen-Daimler-Benz, and Fiat/Chrysler (Bendiner 1978). Soon after, the IMF established more company councils, until the nine largest car companies in the world participated in council structures comprising 80 percent of automobile manufacturing in the West (Gallin 2008). In the years to come, approximately sixty such councils were established in multiple sectors.

Charles Levinson became the most outspoken proponent of this new transnationalism. He envisioned the company councils as building the skeletal framework for multinational collective bargaining, which his union, the ICEM, was able to accomplish on at least one occasion (Levinson 1972). Largely, however, the theory seemed to outperform the practice. The most likely explanation for this failure of multinational collective bargaining to take off is that companies simply refused to recognize the international trade secretariats as bargaining agents, and unions were not able to exercise the power necessary to force them to the table. This inability, however, was also entwined with the political shifts unfolding during the economic crisis of the early-to-mid-seventies. As unions became more defensive, and turned increasingly toward protectionism, internationalism was more difficult to broker.

Eventually, the world company councils withered away amid corporate intransigence, outright resistance, or interunion rivalries over tactics and Cold War ideology, surviving only as shells within the metal and chemical unions. The international food workers' union, however, continued to pursue it quite doggedly. In 1988, eight years after it had established a company council with the French foods company Danone, the two parties agreed to the first ever global framework agreement. Dan Gallin's International Union of Foodworkers (IUF) represents the historic ligature between the first and most recent attempts of unions to engage corporations at the global level. It is worth noting at this point that Danone had a history of pro-union behavior, and some of its executives, including its CEO, were prominent members of the French Socialist Party. Actually, many GUFs began targeting "soft" companies first, as a testing ground for the strategy and to encourage more resistant companies to work with unions (Croucher and Cotton

2009). In other words, Danone, like a few others, was motivated to enter into a new relationship with the union for multiple reasons, some of which were inspired by its own self-image as a worker-friendly company. This brings us to the next pathway toward global agreements.

The idea of corporate social responsibility (CSR) is to embed international norms, ethical standards, and panoply of "rights" into the business model of large corporations, thereby promoting "a market for virtue" where unions are nonexistent or unable to practice the vigilant monitoring that would otherwise be required (Vogel 2006).

In the 1970s a wave of CSR targeted corruption within major corporations (Jenkins 2001). In the 1980s and 1990s, we see a shift in CSR policies focused increasingly on social issues at specific multinationals. Today CSR represents one of the most "prominent managerial developments of recent years" (Gordon and Miyake 2000), buoyed by the additional clout given the idea by the United Nations' Global Compact in 1999. The Global Compact resulted from the unlikely meeting of trade union and international business leaders at the World Economic Forum, the first time unions had been invited to Davos (Switzerland) in two decades.

In the late 1990s, the ICFTU and the global unions developed a more comprehensive agenda for taking advantage of CSR policies. It is subsequent to that strategic maneuvering that all but two GFAs came to pass. Some GFAs are identical to CSR policies, without even a reference to core labor standards or enforcement resolutions. A cynical interpretation therefore has led some to the conclusion that GFAs, like CSR, have provided corporations an "easy out" when it comes to making real changes on social issues.

Corporate leaders are usually motivated to sign GFAs because they rely on voluntary enforcement mechanisms, may promote better employee retention and more effective human resource management practices, and can act as a "public relations triumph" if they are perceived as doing the right thing (Stevis and Boswell 2007b), all of which can also enhance competitiveness or buoy investment profiles. As a result of these similarities, critics have suggested, wrongly in my view, that GFAs are simply another type of CSR (Scherrer and Greven 2001).

The first distinction is that GFAs are, generally, negotiated documents by worker representatives, as opposed to unilateral codes of conduct developed solely by management (Papadakis 2011). Further, Tørres and Gunnes (2003) differentiate the contractual mechanisms of GFAs from the voluntarism that undergirds codes of conduct. Framework agreements commit the signatories to a set of principles, paramount among them being adherence to core labor standards, which simply go unmentioned by the vast majority of CSR initiatives. Whereas most GFAs contain stipulations on wages and working hours, these decidedly economic issues are generally left out of conduct codes (Schoemann, Sobzack, Voss, and Wilke 2008). But the most compelling difference between a GFA and a CSR policy is that the former has as its stated goal a changed relationship between workers and management. In contrast, codes of conduct have often been put into practice for union avoidance, and CSR policies are only very rarely directed at working conditions.

The final pathway to GFAs grew out of the regionalization of European Union (EU) economies. As European political economy has been pushed toward liberalization, its unions have learned to react the way American unions did, by shadowing corporations as they move. In 1983, unions were on the brink of gaining "an important legislative victory in the battle for greater worker control over corporate decision-making" (Kilimink 1983). The Vredeling Proposal would have been the first binding supranational law that required corporations to "consult" their workers before making drastic decisions such as plant transfers, closings, or the introduction of labor-saving technology. Premised on the idea that rising corporate power entailed new corporate responsibilities, the Vredeling Proposal was largely geared toward sharing information about company policy with workers in the same transnational firms (Walker 1983). The proposal failed, or, rather, it was crushed, by what *The Economist* called "the most expensive campaign in the Parliament's history, mounted mainly by American-based companies" (quoted in Horn 2011). In the wake of Vredeling's failure, unions reconvened and after decades of pushing for a Europe-wide governance mechanism finally won the 1992 European Social Charter and the EWC Directive.

Largely a response to corporate restructuring during the deepening of European integration in the 1980s and 1990s, and the development of a common market, the EWC directive allows workers in European multinational companies (with more than 1,000 employees overall and more than 150 in at least two EU countries) the right to organize associations for purposes of information sharing and enforcing labor standards. Since 1994, almost fifteen million workers in eight hundred multinational companies have participated in EWC dialogues (Waddington 2010). Originally conceived as transnational bargaining councils, EWCs have been diluted by management pressure and interunion arguments over the years. Today they exist primarily as information-sharing corporatist bodies.

The other potential of EWCs is that they would benefit workers outside Europe as well. Global campaigns within companies with strong works councils could conceivably gain leverage through the solidarity of European counterparts. The potential for this kind of North-South cooperation is an important consideration, given that global agreements have so far been more or less isolated to European companies, though, as explained later, the works council within G4S was highly functional in Europe but virtually useless, and potentially negative, for its employees anywhere else.

Implementing GFAs

Understanding the development of the GFA strategy over time helps us view it as the outcome of a struggle for a meaningful way to approach multinational corporations. And what has this struggle produced? Unions generally demand, though rarely achieve, that GFA principles apply to all workers within a given company's supply chain and its subcontractors. These provisions are becoming more common (and contentious) in the agreements, however, as the rise of labor brokers tends to shrink the percentages of formal employees relative to contract labor.

In addition to the substantive issues raised by GFAs, most specify some form of procedural implementation. Typically this amounts to annual or semi-annual meetings of corporate and union leaders that comprise some sort of sanctioned committee to discuss issues related to the agreement's scope of application (countries, suppliers, part-timers, etc.). Monitoring of the agreements is done in a variety of ways, ranging from outside enforcement agencies, to internal review boards, to works councils, or, in the cases where the agreement has been more embedded into a company's human resource management policies, to home-country trade unions. Sometimes these merely extend existing structures, and sometimes they involve the creation of new institutions within unions and corporations. Nevertheless, often these provisions are very weak, with even codes of conduct occasionally providing firmer monitoring procedures.

The implementation phase of global agreements is a growing area of study (Papadakis et al. 2009; Papadakis 2011; Fichter et al. 2012; Stevis and Boswell 2007a and b; McCallum 2011 a and b; Niforou 2012). It also continues to be problematic from the position of the unions. In most cases, the "new relationship" after the GFA amounts to a regulatory environment in which basic power asymmetries have been largely, if not wholly, preserved. Theoretically, the implementation and enforcement of a GFA should be a process between partners. Management, however, generally reserves the right to do it (or not do it) with discretion, and most agreements are never implemented or used in any way. This results from a number of factors.

First, the limited resources and poor access to local unions and/or rank-and-file workers of most GUFs ensure that they must be very selective as to where they concentrate their efforts. Second, in the absence of a local union with the capacity to use and enforce the agreement, management's protocols generally prevail. Third, the headquarters' coordination of transnational corporations is often less intense than the implementation of GFAs requires, and only rarely is the corporate periphery involved or even made aware of the agreement until it has been finalized (Papadakis 2011). This makes for very little "buy-in" from the managers who directly confront workers and unions far from the oversight of the home-country leadership. Finally, the channels of communication between GUFs and their affiliates are tenuous, and often unions have no idea that an agreement has been negotiated at all. Moreover, GFAs are usually negotiated between GUFs and corporations without the input of local union affiliates, limiting their ability to understand what a GFA is, how it can be effectively used, and why it was signed in the first place (Croucher and Cotton 2009).

As a result, even the strongest GFAs rarely inspire any union activity at all and only sometimes hold employers to respect the most skeletal elements of the law. At the same time, they may provide corporations with a green-washed facade and an economic advantage through their "social" appearance to European investors. Most damning of all, because GFAs are technically joint ventures, occasionally it is the carefully crafted agreement language itself that serves to redirect worker activity toward channels that are acceptable to both union leadership and business interests, without workers ever having been consulted.

Interviews with the staff of several GUFs reveal a cynicism about prospects for GFAs to become effective union tools on a broad scale anytime soon. One GUF staffer summed up the position of many others I spoke with: "Not great, but it's the best we got. It's *all* we got, actually."[22] Likewise, Stephen Lerner (2007) has expressed deep disdain for GFAs in writing even as the union (SEIU [Service Employees International Union]) for which he was a chief strategist has made the negotiation of GFAs a basic goal. Referring to the long list of weak and unenforceable agreements that GUFs had amassed, he said, "The time for these types of global framework agreements has come and gone. These general statements of principle are too weak and it is proven that they cannot be enforced. They should be abandoned" (32).

Other unionists share his skepticism. A paper by four staffers of the International Union of Foodworkers (IUF) (Buketov et al. 2007), which pioneered the GFA strategy, later announced a moratorium on GFAs due to their perceived weakness and lack of effective implementation. A leader of the GMB, a partner union to the SEIU and UNI in the G4S campaign, published an article in the midst of the global campaign, declaring that "the first draft of every Global Agreement seems to come out of the offices of the same Wall Street legal firm." (Smith 2008: 8)

The perception of GFAs as weak, even by those whose mission it is to secure them, does not inspire confidence in the strategy. This book explains a few ways in which they are used rather well, and it builds substantially on a small literature of other cases of effective implementation. An article by Jane Wills (2002) on the IUF-Accor Hotel agreement shows that it led to organizing gains in the United States, Canada, and Indonesia. Riisgaard (2005) has shown that a GFA signed between a federation of Latin American banana workers and the Chiquita corporation facilitated worker organizing, yet noted "the overall poor use of the agreement potential" (Riisgaard 2005: 1). A report by Dimitris Stevis (2009) for the ILO on the implementation of the International Metalworkers Federation's agreement with Daimler suggests it has contributed to local unionism in the United States, Brazil, South Africa, and Germany. Agreements signed by UNI seem to lead the field in implementation. Its agreement with the Spanish telecommunications firm, Telefonica, has aided workers in Brazil, Puerto Rico, and Chile to organize and fight layoffs. A multicountry study found that implementation requires a proactive approach by unions (Fichter, Sydow, Helfen, Arruda, Agtas, Gartenberg, McCallum, Sayim, and Stevis 2012). Even in the relatively union-strong Brazil, the GFAs in existence were widely unknown. In addition to this book's focus on UNI's agreement with G4S in the United States, South Africa, and India, my own research shows that its agreements have facilitated new organizing in Ghana, Malawi, and the United States (G4S), Cameroon (France Telecom), Brazil (Telefonica), and Australia (ISS). Much of this book suggests that the negative assessment of global agreements may be premature.

Conclusion: Governance Struggles and Worker Power

Different forms of labor transnationalism have moved along an axis structured dually by external pressures of the world political economy and an oscillating ideological compass of the unions. Both of these factors were in turn greatly shaped by the violence of the "century of war" (Kolko 1994). Here we see a curious historical paradox. Most scholars see a direct link between vibrant leftist movements and labor transnationalism. Historically, however, the First World War was both a breaking point for labor transnationalism and also "became an essential precondition for the emergence of a numerically powerful Left, moving it from the margins to the very center of . . . all world affairs after 1941" (Kolko 1994: xviii). Therefore, it was not that the Left died alongside labor's global aspirations. Rather, it grew, but it replaced *L' Internationale* with a variety of national anthems as its primary hymnal. But what is a Left without "workers of the world unite"? It would not be until after the Communist and Socialist parties became isolated that labor resumed a transnational perspective. Labor transnationalism re-emerged in the 1970s, rejuvenated in the form of governance struggles.

Codes of conduct attacked a particular problem—how best to counter the sudden upsurge of maquiladora production that resulted from NAFTA, the Central American Free Trade Agreement, and other neoliberal policy instruments. We now know that codes of conduct, though a promising strategy that seemed to engage workers across borders, had a limited lifespan. The dynamic campaigns throughout apparel factories in Latin America met their decisive end as the work generated by NAFTA moved to free trade zones in Asia and Africa. Social clauses attempted to embed labor standards in those very processes that moved work out from under the feet of garment workers. But were social clauses to gain ground and actually be implemented, it would be of little immediate benefit to workers whose lives and communities were far from the internal machinations of the WTO's or NAFTA's regulatory process. Global framework agreements have solved some of these problems. First, as a global mechanism, GFAs are able to exert more governance over capital mobility and labor processes than codes of conduct. Second, GFAs hold a much greater potential than social clauses to generate worker activity, to actually bring the governance process to a local level rather than contain it to bureaucratic loopholes.

That is not to imply that simply negotiating a framework agreement is an end in itself. The long list of agreements that are completely inactive and unenforceable is evidence that it is not. Moreover, some of the agreements with the strongest contract language have absolutely no union or movement behind them to press for their implementation. However, governance struggles through GFAs hold the greatest hope for unions to create a framework for a campaign, to enlist the support of unions around the world, and to construct a mechanism to constrain the purview of management.

Even in industries with strong levels of structural power—maritime shipping, for example—seafarers benefit from the considerable innovation, strategic research, and political organizing of the International Transport Federation more than the simple possibility of disrupting the delivery of goods. Over the past few years a spate of GFAs has created the framework for transnational campaigns of workers in a variety of industries—hotel workers at Accor, garment and warehouse workers at H&M, auto workers in Brazil, janitors in New Zealand, and telephone workers in Colombia, Brazil, and Cameroon at Telefonica, and in the United States at Deutsch Telecom.. In each of these cases, the agreements have been won, implemented, or enforced by a GUF-led campaign.

A historical perspective allows us to see that today's "global turn" is more of a return to internationalism—labor's original form—than it is a dynamic new course. At its inception, labor unionism was fundamentally concerned with taking wages out of competition, which required an internationalist ethos in nineteenth-century Europe just as it does today. In this sense, labor has always been responding to globalization. But recasting these most recent efforts as governance struggles is helpful in a number of ways.

The governance struggle idea provides us with a theoretical framework to analyze the historical development of a strategy for labor in the global era. Suddenly we see that attempts to discipline or govern large corporations, in the interest of making space for associational power to be actionable, have a longer tradition and a more varied approach. This discursive shift allows us to more clearly see the way labor has generated power outside a rights-based framework by forging new rules of engagement. The distinction between rules and rights is significant for two reasons. First, the rights discourse suggests, falsely, that workers at the global level have benefitted from government intervention when in almost every instance they have not. Second, unions have had more success holding companies accountable to their own stated prerogatives, or rules, than to what states say they should do. It only makes sense unions would want a say in how such rules are made and who they affect.

However, there is a way in which governance struggles move labor a dangerous step closer toward social partnership. This is a dilemma that must be faced seriously and will only end in labor's favor if it is adequately equipped to organize across borders. That is the subject of the next chapter.

Chapter 2

The Globalization of the Organizing Model

In early 2010, Valery Alzaga, a Change to Win (CtW) organizer who had worked on the earliest incarnations of the Justice for Janitors (J4J) campaign with SEIU, was running late to a meeting of leaders from the largest German trade unions, Ver.di and IG Metal. Alzaga had mentored South African unionists during the G4S campaign and was then doing similar work in Berlin. Unlike many American unionists who have gone to Germany to learn about the successes of codetermination and political partnership, she was there to tell them it did not work anymore. And she had a way to fix it.

> SEIU is going to change the world. We *are* changing the world, for workers anyway. . . . Look, we started in LA, we picked it up in London, it worked there. We are trying it here, it's hard, it's slow but I can say that it is working. Look at the Netherlands, it's amazing what we have been able to do there. They were getting their asses kicked and now they're running campaigns, occupying buildings. Look at South Africa, they are using this model down there, you know. Lots of people are doing this with us. This is open-source organizing. And it works.[1]

In 1990 thousands of SEIU janitors in Los Angeles (LA) set in motion a process of trade union revitalization that would come to change workers' movements across the world. The dramatic street demonstrations that shook LA intermittently that year were matched by a sophisticated campaign of corporate research, in-depth worker-to-worker meetings, and a strategy to exploit the vulnerabilities of the office building ownership structure. This wide-ranging approach to rebuild labor's strength developed as a response to the legal obstacles facing workers and in an effort to neutralize corporate power so that workers could organize. New modes of social movement-inspired mobilization and rank-and-file engagement—the heart of what came to embody the "organizing model"—captured the imagination of union leaders in America.[2]

Many agree that J4J was a turning point in American trade unionism, a beacon of hope as the labor movement emerged from the "lost decade" of Reaganomics. It inspired filmmaker Ken Loach to produce *Bread and Roses* (2001), an award-winning feature based on the campaign, and a mountain of academic studies (Waldinger et al. 1998; Milkman and Wong 2000; Savage 1998; Milkman 2006). Since then scholars have demonstrated that its ripple effect has been significant, instigating wide-scale revitalization processes and a greater interest in organizing for many US unions (Voss and Sherman 2000; Adler and Turner 2001).

What is woefully understudied, however, is the deep impact that these diverse strategies have had on the rest of the world. This chapter traces the diffusion of US-based trade union organizing ideas around the world, a process I call "the globalization of the organizing model." Despite the many studies that insist on a coherent notion of mobilization-based strategies (see Carter and Cooper 2002; Bronfenbrenner, Friedman, Hurd, Oswald, and Seeber 1998; Hurd 2004), a singular "organizing model" is a fiction. Nor are the strategies employed in the J4J campaign representative of other examples of "organizing" practiced throughout the SEIU or the wider union movement. In fact, the diversity of tactics that allegedly constitute organizing unionism tends to undercut a coherent understanding of what union organizing actually is. Nonetheless, the concept of organizing as a response to labor's woes, in all its disparate murkiness, went viral. The janitors' campaign has been the most inspirational internationally, and adopting its strategies is often a starting point for internal revitalization, as the cases that follow demonstrate. In each example, "organizing" is a polyvalent concept,

[handwritten margin note: is it really an American idea?]

Organizing model involves many strategies

invoking a number of different strategic approaches—workplace committees, one-on-one meetings with workers, social movement-inspired protests, and research-based campaigning. Taken together, these varied strategies connote a more aggressive and action-oriented unionism that is at the heart of what is often meant by the vernacular of organizing.

Globalizing these ideas and practices was a crucial antecedent to the campaign against Group4 Securicor(G4S). It allowed the union several opportunities to experiment with some of the strategies in different sectors that it eventually employed in the security industry. Moreover, the ability of the SEIU to execute ambitious transnational campaigns—the battle against G4S being a prime example—was contingent upon it developing the capacities of its partner unions first.

To demonstrate this global-local reciprocity between actors at different scales, this chapter describes a two-step process. First, the SEIU undergoes a domestic restructuring that transforms it into a union more capable of conducting transnational campaigns. Then it helps its counterparts in Europe do the same. The result is a network of unions with more common goals and shared strategic capacity better prepared to take on G4S.

This process also links new modes of labor transnationalism and union revitalization in mutual interdependence. The union renewal literature emphasizes the urgency of adopting new strategies to rebuild labor's vitality. It suggests that a movement in crisis can open the door to new activist-minded leadership and experiment with social movement unionism (Turner 2005). In other cases, internal restructuring can redirect resources, staff, and other capacity toward a more effective union. Both modes are illustrated later, as the SEIU's capacity to wage global campaigns emerged from local and national renewal processes. But the reverse is also true—transnational collaboration is, in turn, a viable revitalization strategy, and global union campaigns can empower local movements. In this formulation labor transnationalism can be seen as both an outcome of, and a catalyst for, union renewal.

very good question

The growing sphere of influence of US unionism around the world raises an interesting paradox: Why should such an enfeebled labor movement—with declining union densities, rife with business unionism, in the midst of its own civil war—have anything to offer the comparatively stronger traditions in Western Europe and in the leading countries of the Global South? The answer given here is that the global economic crisis that went public in 2007 has only emphasized the fact that unions everywhere are now facing some version of neoliberalization that American unions suffered under for the last four decades. Clearly, US unions have some experience navigating a hostile industrial relations climate, and Europeans and others can learn from their mistakes and occasional successes. The SEIU, however, is especially well positioned as an exemplar, as it managed to grow stronger during a time when no other union did.

The SEIU: Growth, Crises, and Revitalization

During the two decades including Reagan's firing of the striking air traffic controllers, a stock market crash, the passage of the North American Free Trade Agreement(NAFTA), and the ascendancy of Clinton-style neoliberalism—a time when union density steadily and uniformly declined for US unions—the SEIU's membership increased by over 100 percent (Chun 2009: 88). When John Sweeney took office in 1984 as the union's president its membership stood at 600,000, but when he left it in 1996 to become president of the AFL-CIO, winning the first contested election in the Federation's history, it had increased by one-third (Fantasia and Voss 2004).

As AFL-CIO president, Sweeney and his New Voice Coalition (including Richard Trumka of the Mineworkers' Union and Linda Chavez-Thompson of the American Federation of State, County, and Municipal Employees) embarked on a series of reforms designed to prioritize organizing, the most significant of which was an internal overhaul of the union's structure. The new leadership also took steps toward a new brand of internationalism. George Meany's AFL-CIO played a substantial role as a cold war instrument. His anointed successor, Lane Kirkland, was a card-carrying hawk of the Committee for the Present Danger (Davis 1982). Against this record, Sweeney's slate rebuilt the AFL-CIO's international programs on the aegis of solidarity and collaboration. Among their first moves in office, New Voice leaders traveled to Mexico to meet with the old and new representatives of the country's independent labor movement, the National Union of Workers and the Authentic Labor Front (Moody 1998: 58–59).

Sweeney inherited a decentralized union—"more a loose configuration of urban fiefdoms" (Fantasia and Voss 2004: 101)—and benefited from a structure that permitted radical reforms to percolate without incurring the heavy hand of a centralized bureaucracy. Nonetheless, he reversed this

[handwritten margin note: maybe precisely because all the other unions could not survive...?]

dynamic by consolidating locals through mergers and expanding the staff and influence of the national office (Moody 2007). The effect was twofold. Larger locals meant that operating costs and overhead were reduced, freeing up money for organizing. The other was a massive power transfer in the direction of Washington, D.C., and the consolidation of what would become the major union in the American labor movement.

But this record of extraordinary growth in the midst of hard times for unions everywhere belies a fundamental crisis within the union. In the 1980s janitors faced the same multipronged attack that plagued many workers in America, union or not. Though nonmobile service-sector workers were less impacted by rapid deindustrialization than their manufacturing counterparts, they nevertheless lost in the race to the bottom, too. Specifically, cleaners faced declining wages and layoffs as increased competition among their companies forced bidding wars to secure contracts. Their unions, including the SEIU, lost thousands of members, and were in wild disarray, with no idea as to how to turn the tables. Similar developments were under way among other Western trade union federations, and as the employer offensive in America offered inspiration to the social welfare states of Europe, it suddenly seemed "that the malaise of American trade unionism may be contagious" (Davis 1982).

Justice for Janitors and the Organizing Model

The J4J campaign came to LA from Denver, where it began in 1985, and it quickly grew into the epicenter of change within the labor movement. Janitors are an unlikely group to reignite labor. The mostly immigrant workforce[3] found its place in the janitorial industry as low-wage replacements for black workers who had been pushed out by management seeking higher rates of exploitation. Their power to collectively bargain in the workplace had been systematically undermined or was legally denied or ambiguous. As contract laborers, their grievances were often with a group other than their actual employer. As a result of this "liminality," Chun (2009) suggests that janitors have engaged in different "classification struggles" by exercising "symbolic power." In other words, by engaging in "public dramas"—theatrical public protests that call attention to unfair labor regimes—workers craft a symbolic politics around a moral claim to justice. In turn, these dramas invoke an important logic for overturning the status determinations that have traditionally left marginalized workers without rights, power, or access to a rule of law framework. Chun asserts that symbolic power may be an effective avenue for workers with limited structural power, such as janitors, security guards, and other low-level service-sector workers. Because the J4J campaign was so widely noticed on the world stage, leveraging gains through symbolic power for marginalized workers might be instructive for other workers in similar positions or industrial contexts. Others suggested that the winning strategy drew on tried-and-true radicalism. "Justice for Janitors turned to time-tested social movement strategies—including sit-ins, militant demonstrations, and civil disobedience[4]—that physically interfered with employers' ability to conduct business" (Tait 2005: 188).

This emphasis on tactics, especially the "street heat" of the protests, has been the most common element described by scholars, but it obscures the real reason J4J was such a success: it was cheap. The SEIU targeted the clients of the large janitorial companies who contracted janitors' services, not their direct employer. For building owners, the cost of settlement with the union (in other words, for using union labor) was so miniscule that many agreed in order to put an end to the commotion outside their offices. Put bluntly by one former SEIU organizer, "The real magic of J4J, why it was successful, was not because of how it was carried out, with protests and whatnot, but because it cost the boss a few fucking pennies on the dollar."[5]

Although the moral crisis caused by public dramas was an important component of the strategy, it was the political opportunity afforded them by the industrial structure of the janitorial business that won the campaign. Rather than obstruct business, the SEIU gave the employers a way to conduct business and to be quasi union-friendly at the same time. Although the champions of J4J credit the confrontational elements of the campaign with its victory, management's hand was most forced by the "dull compulsion of economic relations."

Furthermore, to circumvent the arduous and often anti-union National Labor Relations Board elections process, the SEIU collected union cards en masse and then forced employers to agree to industry- and area-wide union recognition agreements (somewhat akin to pattern bargaining) to avoid putting any one market player at a competitive disadvantage. This involved in-depth one-on-one meetings with workers, building clandestine committees, and access to workers outside of the job site.

J4J did not reinvent an organizing model; it popularized and redefined it. What were inchoate tendencies and rumblings of experimentation even during Lane Kirkland's AFL-CIO were suddenly given successful expression. Over time, these strategies—vibrant street protests, corporate research, worker-to-worker meetings, worksite committees, community support—in some form and combination came to embody the ideal-typical definition of union organizing. This reinterpretation of organizing unionism was significant. What was once a term to denote internal rank-and-file mobilization (Banks and Metzgar 1989) the SEIU defined as a new member recruitment strategy (Fletcher and Hurd 1998). Whereas the United Farm Workers had earlier promoted a mass-organizing model, the SEIU's janitors' campaigns were led by militant minorities. The SEIU's top-down orientation tended to challenge the democratic spirit of the earlier incarnation of the organizing model as well. What began its life as an explicitly political strategy had been boiled down to a series of rationalized tactics. This brief sketch illuminates the diffuse character of the organizing concept, which makes it difficult to define and illustrates why its adoption at the global level is rarely clear or uniform. But J4J's victory was undeniable, validating the revised version of organizing unionism. In short, it provided what the wider labor movement considered impossible: an alternative.

By 1995, over one hundred J4J organizers (at a cost of $2 million) brought 35,000 new members into the SEIU (Tait 2005). Ten years after that J4J had organized 70 percent of janitors in almost half of the fifty largest US cities (Luff 2007). Standards rose across nonunion janitorial worksites as well. In the immediate aftermath of the Los Angeles actions, many service-sector unions began experimenting with new strategies and community-based campaigns. Worker centers and unions, the dynamic twin engines of what Ruth Milkman (2010) called the "LA Model," began to increase their associations.

But there are reasons to be less sanguine about all that hope and change. Five years after J4J's unequivocal success in Los Angeles, with Clinton in the White House and a Democrat-controlled Congress, 97 percent of union locals in the United States still had *no* organizing programs, and most lacked a community outreach department (Tait 2005, emphasis added). By 2000, organizing guru Richard Bensinger had been forced to resign due to a growing list of enemies made while promoting increased budgets for organizing within affiliated unions, suggesting that even the modest adjustments to strategy and tactics promoted by the Organizing Institute (OI) would be resisted internally. A decade after Sweeney's New Voice slate promised to renounce its inherited business unionism and remake the labor movement through organizing, it was all too clear that despite increased emphasis on member recruitment, and mobilization, US unions had not stemmed the tide of declining density.

Still bucking the trend, however, the SEIU's growth continued under Andrew Stern, who took the reins in 1996. Union representation rocketed by a further one million members in the subsequent decade. This number reflected the union's political prowess in the public sector, as campaigns in California brought droves of home-care workers into the union's orbit. Those new members helped fund private-sector campaigns as well. Stern, known for proclaiming his allegiance to an Alinsky-esque model,[6] continued Sweeney's practice of hiring young activists in large numbers by increasing the role of the OI and its presence on college campuses (Moody 2007). Dramatic growth, and its apparent embrace of young progressives, prompted journalist Harold Meyerson (2003) to describe the SEIU (as part of a troika, including the then-separated hotel and garment workers' unions) as the American labor movement's militant Left vanguard.[7]

Nonetheless, Stern's leadership also continued Sweeney's centralization of the national union through controversial trusteeships, replacing the elected bodies of locals with its own appointees and raising concern among many otherwise loyal supporters. Between 1996 and 2005, this process occurred at forty SEIU Locals, or 14 percent of the union's affiliates (Tait 2005).[8] To some, Stern's growth model signaled an end to the militant spirit of organizing that informed the early janitors' struggles:

> The earlier apparent consensus regarding the *organizing model* and the grassroots approach to recruitment has long since dissolved. In the context of quantitative goals, the ideal of organizing as a method of engaging members and building commitment has given way to debates about how to be cost effective and manage recruitment programs efficiently. (Hurd 2004: 18, emphasis in original)

The J4J campaign has usually been considered a model to emulate. But what too often goes unspoken is exactly how nontransferable it is. The industrial setting is rather unique and the industry is extraordinarily difficult to organize. In that sense, it is an unlikely campaign to inspire replication. Yet that is exactly what happened next.

The Globalization of the Organizing Model

The Decline and Rise of Globalism at the SEIU

Among Stern's first acts as SEIU president in 1996 was to dismantle the union's Department of International Affairs, premised on the theory that it was a lavish waste of resources for a union in the nonmobile service sector (Anderson 2008). As Stephen Lerner explained, "I was guilty of this, of arguing that globalization was a distraction for us" (cited in Meyerson 2005: 1).[9] Too many years of false internationalism (leadership junkets and wasteful union-sponsored tourism) lent credence to the view that globalism was a profligate distraction from organizing that was best left to the AFL-CIO's Solidarity Centers (Moody 1997).

But the changing political-economic geography of American service industries in the 1990s—catering, cleaning, security, and public transport—led the union to a new understanding. In the winter of 2004 the SEIU placed Christy Hoffman in Geneva as its European director to work on campaigns against Sodexho, UK-based transport companies, and Wackenhut. (Hoffman later moved to Union Network International (UNI) and led the G4S campaign.) At its annual convention later that year, the SEIU adopted "Global Strength" as one of its main positions. The majority of companies entering the American market were headquartered in countries with considerably stronger traditions of trade unionism and, more importantly, less acrimonious labor-capital relations. These companies generally practiced global favoritism, maintaining high standards and fair labor relations in their home countries while taking a far more aggressive stance in their corporate periphery. Because of lax labor laws and low union density, the United States provided fertile ground. One SEIU leader in the United States explained:

> We kept trying to organize US workers in multinational companies. We kept running up against these European companies. Bus drivers, security, janitors, you name it. It wasn't working. . . . Those companies have different

faces [across the world]. They didn't respond to our usual tactics. We realized something had to give.[10]

That *something* turned out to be a purely national approach, and it quickly became apparent that organizing was no longer enough. But it became more than a simple matter of "scaling up" or "going global." As the SEIU began to reach out to prospective partner unions with representation in companies that also had US subsidiaries, it began to realize that while those unions had amicable corporate relations, and sometimes high density rates, they did not have a history of organizing. This fact, in addition to myriad other roadblocks to transnational collaboration, created a moment of cognitive dissonance for the SEIU staff. As one organizer recounts:

> Here we thought we were the ones that needed help. Well, we did. We needed help big time. Then all of a sudden it's clear that they [European trade unions] need help too. And that we can help them. It was an amazing moment, realizing this. Here it is, we thought, new lines of flight, like Deleuze says.[11] We went from begging for help to collaborating for change. I'm telling you it was an amazing moment.[12]

Additionally, many of the largest and most powerful unions in Europe were not only ill-equipped to confront aggressive employers and the growing trends toward neoliberalization, but they were uninterested in doing so. According to Michael Crosby, who led Change to Win's global organizing for many years:

> The level of internal opposition [within European trade unions] is enormous—organizing in a campaign represents a fundamental change in the pace and type of work undertaken by union officials. Many don't want to change and don't see the reason why they should have to change.[13]

Building partner unions that were sufficiently prepared to organize and campaign was a battle in and of itself, even before anyone ever began taking on the employer. Although the SEIU initially first looked for help abroad, it suddenly found itself driving a dramatic new movement. Because it found that a collaborative working relationship with unions not oriented toward organizing was difficult, it sought to build that capacity where it found willing partners: first the Anglo-Saxon and Rhineland social democracies and then the Global South. Ironically, just as the SEIU-inspired organizing model was being declared a failure in the United States, it was gaining popularity around the world.

Australia and New Zealand

Australia and New Zealand undertook the earliest experiments with organizing unionism outside the United States after suffering years of precipitous membership decline. Delegations of union leaders to the United States inspired a deeper commitment to the organizing model and a more Americanized tactical response, as the Australian Council of Trade Unions (ACTU) created the Organizing Works program, based on the AFL-CIO's Organizing Institute (Holland and Hanley 2002).

J4J found its first international expression as Clean Start for Cleaners in Australia in the late 1990s as the Liquor Hospitality and Miscellaneous Workers Union (LHMU) fell under the influence of the SEIU when favorable union conditions began to decline. In Australia, the award system[14] helped unions enjoy solid density rates (52 percent in 1979) and guarded against most management offensives. Further, labor law prevented intercorporate competition based on labor costs, and closed shop legislation favored unions too. But the ground beneath their feet began to shift in the 1980s, and by the early 1990s decline was in full tilt, even in an environment of rising real wages (Leigh 2005). The award system and closed shop rules unraveled during the thirteen-year tenure of a Labour government. New Zealand faced similar declines in union density—41 percent in 1991 to 19 percent three years later—after the Employment Contracts Act ended the decades-old system of a wage-fixing by the state and industry-wide union membership (Oxenbridge 1999). In effect, both countries became a right-to-work[15] state overnight. As a result of years of cooperative labor relations and quiescence, unions were not oriented to go on the offensive or even stave off decline, and they began hemorrhaging members quickly. In Australia, density rates crashed by more than half by 2000 (Carter and Cooper 2002).

In 2005, the LHMU witnessed the complete collapse of its membership under the Howard government's Workchoices decrees. Workers who previously held stable jobs at decent wages were now forced to seek other employment just to piece together a minimum wage. As companies shed record numbers of members in layoff schemes, unions watched the sky collapse and the ground fall from below. The West Australia branch of the LHMU had six cleaners (repeat: six individuals) left in their ranks by the late 1990s. But the LHMU had always represented janitors. Looking to build numbers in another industry, as so many American unions did, was an undesirable option. They were forced to try something new. Michael Crosby, then leader of the Australian Council of Trade Unions (ACTU), writes:

> We need[ed] to look for a far more radical response to systemic union decline. . . . And in Australia we have looked—perhaps to our own surprise—to a North American union—the Service Employees International Union (SEIU). (Crosby 2005: 14)

Indeed, it was a strange fit. North American unionism was rarely considered applicable in Australia. The aggressive organizing tactics of US unions had little resonance in the "land of the fair go." But Crosby soon became internationally known as an expert in the subtle art of union transformation, and a prophet of the SEIU's organizing model. In his book, *Power at Work*, largely inspired by his interactions and experiments with the SEIU, he writes:

> Successful organizing depends on a remaking of the vision of what a successful union looks like. It demands a scale of organizing not seen in our country since the turn of the 19th century. . . . It ensures that the union has to relate to the community and the political system in ways not tried in our country for generations. Above all, union success depends on a complete restructuring of the union's financial system. Waste must be driven out, tight financial management of limited resources is crucial and members generally need to be prepared to spend more money to be represented by a union organization that exercises real power in their industry. (Crosby 2005: 37)

In essence, Crosby talks of a spiritual and practical rebirth of the union, with new tactics, strategies, goals, and internal operating protocols. He was struck by the success of the SEIU at a time when so many unions around the world were losing ground.

The SEIU hired Crosby in Australia to direct the Clean Start campaign, and the LHMU acquired four researchers to work under the tutelage of a lead researcher from the SEIU, who guided them through the paces of corporate campaigning. They assembled a dedicated team to the campaign that rivaled any other organizing drive in Australian history. The campaign targeted the fourteen largest building owners in Australia, many of whom were national and global real estate players. The team produced case studies of dirty bathrooms and contaminated kitchens, alluding to the risks of lawsuits based on health hazards. The SEIU sent organizers to Sydney that trained local activists to identify leadership among the rank and file and to build a militant minority rather than a broad movement.

The staid choreography of semiannual union marches was replaced by monthly rallies in ten cities across the country simultaneously. The LHMU even attempted to overcome the earnestness of so many union demonstrations with a little levity. Union activists positioned dirty toilets outside their buildings and encouraged passersby to adequately clean them in thirty-five seconds or less, the speed needed to do such a task at current worker-to-bathroom ratios. The media noticed such stunts and reported the story favorably. The SEIU encouraged not only a serious commitment to research and organizing but the creation of a counter-spectacle, a public brand of unionism that could win support of new constituencies outside even the workforce: community groups, faith leaders, politicians, mass media, and other activist allies.

What were the outcomes of the SEIU's first exported campaign? As of 2012, the strategy produced only modest membership gains across the board in Australia, though it did manage to stop the losses. The Clean Start campaign won wage increases of one-third and improvements in job security, all during a time when conservatives controlled both houses of parliament and the Workchoice laws were in effect, the ideological equivalent of Reagan's 1980s. In New Zealand, the Service Workers Union was less impacted by transnationalism than the LHMU. Its own transition to a more organizing orientation came largely from within the country. Union leaders are cautiously optimistic that, over time, with newly acquired skills and strategies, the payoff will come in the form of density increases in more areas. But the largest change clearly stood internally, with the development of a new kind of union and a new kind of strategy. With Crosby's leadership, the SEIU was able to reorient the LHMU's practical daily activities and promote a passion and penchant for organizing the unorganized. Crosby is decisive on the importance of the partnership with the SEIU: "At United Voice[16] we know what we don't know. And SEIU knows way more than we do."[17]

The partnership appears to have been viewed as a success, at least by the participants themselves. Representatives from the ACTU have made a number of trips to the United States to visit with SEIU organizers. Having absorbed much of the J4J strategy, the organizers were interested in SEIU tactics in other industrial settings as well. In 2010, eight activists toured a variety of campaigns in the United States and were reported to have been "tremendously inspired" to share the "theories of winning" they discovered when seeing the fruits of health care campaigns, lessons they say informed their "Fair Share for Aged Care" campaign back home (SEIU 1199 2010).

The United Kingdom

Similar crises were under way in Great Britain, where unions also faced new hostilities. In the mid-1990s, the British labor movement was imploding. Membership dropped as low as 19 percent in the private sector in 1995. In search of a way out of the black hole, it seemed that unions increasingly faced a series of unappealing choices: revert to the militancy of a forgotten time and place, embrace class collaborative schemes with management, or reorient from a union to a service provider, in light of the popular view at the time that workers were individual consumers first and foremost and would be attracted to a good deal above all (Heery 2002).

UK unions began searching for ways to reverse membership decline and plummeting density through union mergers and recruitment campaigns, strategies that simply proved ineffective (Carter 1997). The Trade Union Congress's (TUC) New Unionism initiative led the way with the 1998 creation of the Organizing Academy, inspired by the AFL-CIO's Organizing Institute, to inject new ideas into the movement. But it also looked to the SEIU. British unions have been pulled by the competing influences of social partnership approaches in Europe and organizing in the United States. A series of recent campaigns within the General Workers Union, the Public Service Trade Union, the Transport and General Workers Union (UK) (TGWU), Unite the Union (UNITE), and others shows increasing ties with the SEIU and other North American unions (Tattersall 2007).

The SEIU has developed its closest ties in the United Kingdom with UNITE, the giant union that resulted from the 2008 merger of the (mostly) blue-collar TGWU and the (mostly) white-collar Amicus. Contact between the two unions began during the early years of J4J when the SEIU reached out to the TGWU to help organize within the Danish-owned International Services (ISS), one of the largest players in LA's janitorial market. It was not until 2003, however, that the two unions engaged in discussions at a higher level. UNITE's Tony Woodley, known in the United Kingdom for his "love affair" with Andy Stern and the organizing model, was elected secretary general on a reformist slate and helped push the union toward the SEIU's organizing model. Before Woodley took power, UNITE had distanced itself from the UK's Organizing Academy.

However, under the close mentorship of the SEIU, UNITE significantly reversed past practices and expanded its organizing capacity, both domestically and internationally. By 2007, UNITE had hired one hundred new field organizers, an unprecedented investment by a British trade union, many of whom fell under the direct supervision of experienced SEIU staff stationed in the United Kingdom. The close collaboration between the unions is particularly evident in two comprehensive campaigns: Justice for Cleaners and Driving Up Standards. The former was directly inspired by J4J, as it involved the growing contract cleaning industry. In an article for the Open Democracy website, Valery Alzaga reported that the cleaners' campaign won a living wage for workers at the Houses of Parliament in Westminster after their first ever strike, a struggle that was backed by MPs and migrants' rights groups such as London Citizens. As news of the success spread, workers took up similar campaigns at Canary Warf and throughout the City of London. The latter began in 2004 in the transport industry, as two UK-based busing companies, FirstGroup and National Express, were expanding into the US market, thereby encouraging transatlantic collaboration (Anderson 2009). Both the cleaners' and the bus drivers' campaigns were led by SEIU staff imported to the United Kingdom (Tattersall 2007).

By the turn of the new millennium, a handful of British trade union leaders had followed UNITE's lead and developed quite an affinity for the organizing unionism practiced in the United States (Heery et al. 1998).

Today British unions are, on the whole, the most practiced organizers in Europe, where the "British version" of the US organizing model has been crucial to increasing the social movement character of campaigns for bus drivers, security guards, and janitors (Fairbrother and Yates 2003). In some cases, new organizing has been complemented, or even led, by priorities dictated by strategic research.

In a recent documentary on transnational union collaboration, a woman asks an SEIU organizer, "Why are there so many Americans here in the London union?" Grant Williams, the organizer, responds that he has been there for two years to assist UNITE, which is beginning to organize. "Just as corporations have gone global, unions have to go global, and I'm part of that effort." "See," he says, pointing to an SEIU pin on his lapel, and smiles.

Elsewhere in Europe

Mixed results in Australia, New Zealand, and the United Kingdom did not deter the SEIU from pursuing a global agenda. In fact, it became more determined, and it paid off. In 2000, it launched an ambitious campaign against Securitas, a Swedish security firm that had acquired several major US companies. On the heels of the global agreement with Securitas, the SEIU and UNI began collaborating more closely. Despite some success in moving Australian and British unions toward organizing, the SEIU's approach to its global work was still ad hoc, and limited to unions with which it already shared close personal affinities. By 2004, Lerner's assessment about the importance of global dynamics (see above) seemed utterly passé, as so many property services industries operating in the United States were foreign-owned and well prepared to resist unionization. Moreover, the union's inconsistent approach to transnational collaboration poorly assessed the necessary structure required to coordinate internationalism on such a wide scale. The changing investment patterns of European companies into the United States, mixed with the union's corporate comprehensive strategy that demanded a systematic approach to a company's corporate profile, alerted it to the need for deeper international collaboration.

In search of a way to match the industry's expanding corporate profile, and to overcome the limitations of a failing national approach, the SEIU developed the global partnerships department with the initial purpose of

furthering bilateral relationships with European unions (Tattersall 2007). It helped significantly refocus the SEIU's attention toward internationalism in its overall strategy. As one SEIU organizer put it, "We went from shying away from global companies to actively seeking them out." She continues:

> I'm not saying we need global companies, no. But they are there, so, we have to deal with them. They're actually the future. That's where our work is heading. How can we worry about twenty workers here when ten thousand work at the same company over here? We are wasting our resources. Resources are scarce. We started to realize this and, you know, we changed. Inside out.[18]

The work within the global partnerships department pushed transnational campaigning on an unprecedented scale. Lerner (2007) has suggested that unions should target forty critical global cities, urban-corporate nodes in the property services market for the largest players, which collectively employ millions of workers.

Michael Crosby responded to the creation of the global partnerships department as if being transferred to active duty. "I said, 'Let's go. Where do you want me? This thing [the organizing model] works and I'll do just about anything to prove it,'" he remarked. Crosby's Australian accent helped soften the blow of what some were beginning to feel was a rather evangelical American labor internationalism. "He's a great ambassador for us," remarked an SEIU staffer. "He thinks like us, he acts like us, but he's not really one of us. He's . . . not a threat. It works out well."[19]

Crosby's small team of organizers and researchers, now under the leadership of David Chu of Change to Win, moved quickly and aggressively. In 2007, they began by assisting the Dutch union FNV Bondgenoten to lead campaigns for janitors in Den Haag, Amsterdam, and Utrecht, Holland's three largest cities, taking workers through the longest strike the industry has seen in sixty-five years. The strike against both public and private contractors, which drew significant support from social movement allies, won a $14 an hour wage for janitors.

In 2010, janitors launched the SchoonGenoeg (Clean Enough) campaign that led to a nine-week strike that included the hallmarks of the SEIU's influence—community support, a deep communications and public relations component, and worksite mobilization. Motivated by racist employment practices, the largely immigrant workforce of Turks, Moroccans, and Latin Americans organized simultaneous actions around the country through innovative actions such as banner drops and train station occupations in order to, in the words of Alzaga (2011), "capture the Dutch national imaginary." In addition to wage and benefits increases, workers won a neutrality clause and Dutch language classes. This victory has inspired other Dutch unions to work with Change to Win as well.

Crosby can largely be credited with popularizing the strategic orientation of the SEIU in Northern Europe. Under his leadership, the Change to Win office in the Netherlands has developed a multipronged approach that offers both campaign consultative support and organizing and research sessions as well as direct assistance through staff placements, strategic research, and money. Crosby's staff members promote a "change to organize" strategy in which unions allocate increased resources to recruitment drives, particularly on initial comprehensive campaigns. To be clear, the work is not focused on winning campaigns; rather, the goal is to remake European unions along the lines of the SEIU by transforming their underlying methodology as part of a long-term industrial strategy that necessarily requires global partnerships.

A recent documentary, *I Fight for You* (*Ikvechtvoorjou*), about the service workers' union in the Netherlands, is a testament to the dramatic influence of the SEIU on the FNV. In the opening seconds of the film, the voiceover says:

"SEIU, a trade union in the US, has developed a method called 'organizing,' that they spread around the globe. With this method, SEIU did manage to successfully organize the services sector. . . . With this 'guerilla'-like tactic that is in straight opposition to our 'Polder model,'[20] the FNV tries to involve the Dutch lower social classes in its organization and to start a contemporary class struggle."

In the film, an organizer goes on to explain his disbelief the first time he encountered an SEIU organizer at a meeting in Belfast. He asked the SEIU organizer, "But how, tell me how you did that! [bring so many service-sector workers into the union]."

"They explained: 'We ride along with people to their homes, on the bus. Even to Mexico if we have to.' And we [Dutch unionists] all thought: 'That can't be true! That you ride on a bus to Mexico!' We didn't quite understand the answers and explanations the delegation provided us. And they in turn thought we weren't too serious about it. Nevertheless, it gradually evolved in that last year, we did a training here [in the Netherlands] with them [SEIU]."

> *Interviewer*:   "So you brought the Americans here?"
> *Unionist*:   "Yes, they trained my colleagues and myself intensively in organizing."

He then commented about the union's trip to London, to witness the evolution of organizing unionism there. "In London . . . organizing is in a more developed stage. . . . They have a group of active cleaners that became organizers as well. That is the next step we still need to take now. So what we learned from that [going to London] was that we got a sneak preview of what we can achieve in the future if we develop this strategy further."

Dutch service workers have shown remarkable interest in experimenting with new models (Kloosterboer 2007). Whether or not this version of organizing helps build worker power remains to be seen. The point here is that the collaboration with the SEIU has yielded quite a bit of experimentation, and a significant amount of devotion too.

Irish unions, led by the Services, Industrial, Professional and Technical Union, established the *Crosby Commission*, named for its chair, to evaluate a way to transition toward organizing unionism (Allen 2009). Gall (2009) has suggested that organizing plays a larger revitalizing role in the United States and the United Kingdom than in Continental Europe, and others claim that the multiplicity of new strategies in Germany is too varied and discreet to actually constitute a revitalization project (Behrens, Fichter, and Frege 2003). But SEIU staff has been working with Germany's largest unions, Ver.di and IG Metall, organizing baggage handlers at the Berlin airports, community-worker support campaigns based in local activist circles, and security guards in Hamburg. With the SEIU's backing, Ver.di organized security guards into a union during the hotly contested political environment of the World Cup in Germany. The codetermination model of the German industrial relations was slow to warm to the SEIU's aggressive anti-boss campaigning. "They were scared," says a researcher who worked with the SEIU in Hamburg at the time. "They were not used to fighting, to raising hell, making trouble for bosses."[21] But they soon learned. The campaign became so hostile that workers appeared at a press conference masked and hooded for fear of retaliation at work as they testified about maltreatment from management. During the lead-up to an anticipated airport strike, Change to Win staffers sent out a call to assorted labor radicals in and around Berlin to help mobilize community support. Both Ver.di and IG Metall have grown more reliant on research too. These efforts have yielded modest results so far, with small gains through organizing. However, the influence of North American strategies is quickly gaining so much ground that German unionists now commonly use the term "organizing" in English instead of the German "organisieren." "Our model is broken, you see," says a German union activist. "We cannot fix it. So we needed those guys over there [US unionists] to help us figure it out."[22]

Critique from a Global Perspective

There is no shortage of critiques of the SEIU and its organizing model from within academia and the labor movement (Moody 1997, 2007; Gall 2009; Cohen 2009; Early 2011; Bacon and Mar 2008; McAlevey 2012). Most conclude that (1) it is a growth model, not an organizing model, and a bad one at that; (2) rank-and-file workers are often uninvolved in the overly staff-driven campaigns; and (3) the top-down nature makes for deficient union democracy and, consequently, weak unions.

Outside the national arena, most criticisms are directed at the SEIU's reputation or its most audacious claims. In an article on the SEIU's global image, David Moberg (2010) points out that US unions "like SEIU" have often been seen as "brash, culturally insensitive, and interested mainly in one-way relationships that helped the U.S. unions." Stern's friendly disposition toward China's ACFTU has allegedly granted legitimacy to an organization that is only nominally a trade union federation (Gallin 2008).

Dan Gallin may be the SEIU's fiercest foe in the global labor movement because his critique is so precise and his reputation is so credible. Polish born, a self-described "good old Schachtmanite," Gallin fell under the sway of Trotskyists in the American Midwest as a student radical in the early 1950s. When his activities as an organizer attracted too much attention, he was asked to leave the country by the US government (Gallin 2012: 15). As the decades-long leader of the international union of foodworkers, he is well known for pioneering the strategy to win global framework agreements and for his fierce commitments to organize transnational campaigns against Coca-Cola in Latin America. He recounts meetings on global unionism in Washington, D.C., twenty years earlier when Stern walked out of the meeting early, insisting that international organizing was a waste of time. This helps confirm Gallin's perception of Stern today—a false prophet bent on reinventing what he missed the first few times around. He was particularly appalled by Stern's proposal to outsource strikes to low-wage areas. In an interview with the *McKinsey Quarterly* (2006: 56), a business journal, Stern remarked:

> If workers are ready to go on strike in the United States, and we are ready to pay them to strike, it would be very costly. But paying workers in Indonesia or India or other places to go on strike against the same global employer isn't particularly expensive.

Gallin replied:

> This is extraordinary. In the past, when a strike was "outsourced," it was the other way around: strong unions would put pressure on transnational corporations . . . to defend weaker unions that were unable to defend themselves because . . . they would face extreme repression. It is hard to imagine a more cynical and manipulative approach. It is also totally unrealistic. No union anywhere, except for maybe the usual, useless clients, is going to sign on to Stern's outsourced mercenary army.

Gallin's critical perspective is sharpened from decades of confronting newbies in the global labor movement. But on the last part of the aforementioned statement, he is far off the mark. Stern and the SEIU had remarkable success at mobilizing partners, allies, and supporters across the globe. While conducting research for this book, I came across numerous people critical of the role played by US unions in their struggles or those they were familiar with. Some of those dissenting voices are captured in the chapters on India and South Africa. In particular, Communist Party leaders in both countries, each with varying degrees of influence within their respective trade union movements, did not shy away from the position that any kind of "American model" would be of no use to them and may actually do harm. They associated US labor with business unionism, labor imperialism, or racism, or they suggested that their unions risked becoming bit actors in a power play by American labors leaders interested in dealing with their counterparts in international firms more so than local labor leaders.

Jeff Hermanson, who has over three decades of experience organizing internationally, especially in Latin America, offers a kind of engagement with this strain of criticism. Hermanson did not work on the G4S campaign and does not necessarily endorse or criticize the SEIU's role. His study of political history has led him to the conclusion that what passes for "organizing" in the United States is actually an inherited model from the tradition of clandestine militancy in the Russian Revolution. As no friend of the more conservative trends within the ranks of US labor, he takes an important position on the globalization of the organizing model. He says:

> I used to get resistance from leftists with a "Third World" orientation, who said I should not be teaching an American organizing model to workers and their organizations in the developing countries. I would tell them an organizing model has no country, and should be judged by its effectiveness. I would also get pushback from organizers and union leaders, both in the US and elsewhere, who said it was not possible or advisable to do home visits in their area, always with some reason: "It's too dangerous," "Workers don't want to be bothered at home," "We don't have the resources to do it," etc. I would tell them to stop making excuses, try it and see. Usually, almost always, the home visits get results, and the resistance stops.[23]

To some extent, the most common critique of the SEIU is even corroborated by the SEIU itself. As one organizer put it, "People say we are arrogant, that we don't listen to others, we come in and change everything around. There's some truth to that. But we aren't so arrogant to think we can keep it up. So, you know, well it just made sense to go through UNI."[24]

Enter UNI: From Network to Global Union

UNI is the largest of nine global union federations (GUFs), representing some twenty million skills and services workers in nine hundred unions worldwide. To date, it has concluded forty-three global framework agreements, more than any other global union. The SEIU has played an increasing role in its overall strategic orientation. The cynical interpretation of UNI as an SEIU front group, illustrated by the earlier quote, had some currency in the global labor movement during the G4S campaign. But a deeper analysis of its structure suggests it is far more autonomous.

UNI's founders, longtime friends Philip Bowyer and Philip Jennings, arrived in Geneva in the mid-1970s from the United Kingdom and rose to power within their respective trade secretariats by the late 1980s, representing postal and telecommunications workers and clerical staff. Bowyer describes the work of the global unions at that time as a "Robin Hood industry," as they largely existed to redistribute money and other resources taken from the North to trade unions in the East and the South. In the 1980s, as the UN and the International Labour Organization were encouraging a more aggressive developmentalist agenda, the international trade secretariats (precursors to the GUFs) became increasingly preoccupied with capacity building among Third World trade unions. This included educational seminars on strategy, support for pro-democracy movements, and direct engagement with particular campaigns, as in the antiapartheid movement in South Africa.

By the mid-1990s, the large public-sector enterprises that characterized the service industries—telephone and postal workers in particular—had been privatized or heavily deregulated, and the trade secretariats were behind the times. "We were in our own little fiefdoms," remembers Dan Gallin. "We were not organized strategically. That came later, hopefully not too late."[25] At a congress of trade secretariats in Montreal, the idea of a global industry-wide organization of service workers began to take shape, and even then it only partially materialized. But by early 2000, UNI was officially founded through the merger of the unions representing postal and telecommunications workers, the clerical staff's union, media workers, and graphical workers. Later that year it began a tentative dialogue with Latin American member unions that, by 2001, established its first global agreement with the Spanish-owned Telefonica. Although the Telefonica agreement happened "nearly by accident," UNI realized it needed to operationalize its activities, or, as one leader put it, "to act more like a union. . . . What makes you a union rather than a loose federation? Well, you sign agreements with employers."[26]

UNI signed a handful of framework agreements over the next few years with companies that more or less cooperated with the process, including

Securitas and ISS, two major players in the global property services market, until it met the union-resistant Quebecor, a French-Canadian publishing company. The campaign included coordinated pickets of the company's clients (Ikea) and an enlarged role for strategic research. It tested UNI's commitment to winning agreements through a fight, and it was a prelude to the campaigning style that defined its battle with G4S.

UNI is organized into relatively autonomous sectors, the fifth largest being UNI Property Services (UNI PS). Many of the SEIU's global relationships (with UNITE and FNV Bondgenoten, for example) began within UNI PS. In 2005, the SEIU donated money to begin an organizing fund at UNI PS, at that time a small and otherwise marginal sector with UNI. UNI hired Christy Hoffman from the SEIU to lead campaigns for cleaners in the Netherlands and security officers in Hamburg, Germany, which were supported by SEIU staff. UNI's decentralized structure allowed UNI PS to move forward with an organizing program without much consultation with the entire organization, without internal upheaval, and without UNI as a whole adopting an interest in organizing. In 2005, UNI officially changed its name from Union Network International to UNI Global Union, symbolizing a desire to "act more like a union." At the time UNI was, as are most GUFs today, underresourced and with little or no connection to the rank and file. Although it had proved itself capable of signing global agreements with cooperative companies, campaigning *against* transnational corporations was beyond its ability. The SEIU's influence can be seen as pivotal. A former UNI staffer says:

> Yes, it's fair to say that. None of this [G4S campaign] would have been possible without SEIU. We don't really like saying that, but we shouldn't . . . be ashamed. Of course resources matter. Experience matters. They brought that here.[27]

Conclusion: Internal Revitalization and Exporting the Organizing Model

The point of all this, of course, is not to position the SEIU as the saving grace of the global labor movement. Nor is it to argue that American unionism on the whole offers compelling answers to the labor crisis in the comparatively stronger European contexts. In fact, US unionists can learn much from the ways in which Europeans have consolidated power, in some instances, despite low densities. It would also be foolish to champion the SEIU's political strategy around the globe given its questionable domestic track record—most notably, the forcible takeover of one of its strongest affiliates in the country, now the National Union of Healthcare Workers (Winslow 2010).

However, there are positive lessons to be learned from its actions abroad, and they deserve more consideration than they are often given by global labor scholars. As an experienced German unionist said, "No other union in the world can do what SEIU can do. So we have to listen to them. Not always agree, but at least listen."[28] But the SEIU is not a pioneer. In the mid-1990s the US-based garment workers union worked with Central American unions to implement its "fishbowl model," whereby union organization begins "underwater" and includes other organizing model hallmarks as worker classification schemes and home visits. This model helped workers organize within the Honduran export processing zone known as Kimi, where previous drives had failed (Anner 2011). But, overall, the SEIU's steps toward transnationalism are far more demonstrative.

The basis for the SEIU to coordinate transnational campaigns of this scope came from local and national renewal processes. The first fruits of these new global partnerships were campaigns against security companies. I have focused on the strategic innovation and experimentation that have accompanied the changing nature of the global political economy and the structure of employment in the American services sector. As described earlier, some of the same strategies that have laid the foundation for the SEIU's renewal have inspired similar processes elsewhere. This has involved a reallocation of resources toward new organizing and an increased reliance on strategic research to drive the overall industrial strategy.

Critics would be wrong to assert that what the SEIU is globalizing is a one-size-fits-all model. It is far more opensource, as Alzaga (2011) says, appearing in different national contexts as worker mobilization, corporate campaigns, strategic research, worksite committees, social movement unionism, and so on. But allowing for such a wide interpretation may be a problem. Because "organizing" has manifest in so many ways, it is at times an empty signifier, except as a meme for whatever is deemed necessary to rebuild labor's strength. Moreover, at the global level, the SEIU has largely promoted the concept as an instrumental process of strategic implementation, not as a component in an overall political process of rebuilding power.

Though many have suggested that the vertical consolidation of corporate power has provided a built-in structural opportunity for unions to organize globally, this case suggests that an equally important—but mostly overlooked—factor was the internal restructuring process of the union itself. In other words, the centralization of control of union decisions, prerogatives, and finances was a necessary precondition for increased organizing and membership mobilization processes normally associated with bureaucratization. But it seems that a certain level of reorganization had to take place in order to mobilize the necessary resources and personnel to realize a new kind of strategy. This outcome was not accidental but also not an intended or a predetermined consequence of the restructuring process. Rather, it evolved slowly out of the experiences of struggling against larger and more global corporations.

The second half of the equation—that labor transnationalism can in turn inspire local renewal processes—is explained through the G4S campaign in the following three chapters. It begins with the advent of security guard organizing in the United States and continues through the conclusion of the global agreement with G4S.

The transformation of the SEIU into the leading force within global union politics is a significant development for workers in multiple growing industries—cleaning, catering, healthcare, and security. The circuitous diffusion of the SEIU's influence through transcontinental networks and relationships is just one way this happened. But it would take more than organizing, however defined, to beat G4S. We now turn to a deeper examination of the larger strategy to wage governance struggles at the global level.

[handwritten margin note: but can not be led by US]

Chapter 3

The Campaign against G4S:
Globalizing Governance Struggles

Although struggles to win justice for janitors were decisive points in the union's history, then president Andrew Stern says his "dawning moment" came when the Service Employees International Union (SEIU) began organizing security guards and faced a field of foreign employers. "All of a sudden we found ourselves needing to talk more to CEOs in Europe than in the US,"[1] he said.

Two things are striking about this statement. The first is the shock Stern expresses—the union's president was wholly unaware of the most significant employment trend in one of its prime sectors. This was an initial indicator that the G4S battle would not be "just like any other J4J [campaign]," as one staffer said was the general wisdom at the time. The second is that he immediately emphasizes the need to negotiate with European CEOs, not organize with European workers. In the end, both happened, but his comment betrays an important element of the campaign strategy that is explored throughout this chapter.

The comprehensive campaign strategy has been the primary mode through which the SEIU engages transnational corporations. This has been especially true in the fast-growing property services division, which includes janitorial, security, catering, and laundry services, industries that are increasingly owned by foreign companies operating in the United States. The SEIU has therefore approached international organizing with a strategy that necessarily involves heavy lifting for union staff, a large budget, and dedicated researchers in the hopes that it will provide more fertile ground for worker organizing. This chapter explores that strategy as it was employed against Group 4 Securicor (G4S), and particularly the ways in which an alliance of unions was able to constrain the company's aggressive antiunionism.

Corporate Campaigns as Governance Struggles

The sober conclusion that rank-and-file organizing alone no longer works has encouraged the most successful unions in the United States to wage corporate or comprehensive campaigns. Comprehensive campaigns are textbook governance struggles, efforts to alter the available options of a company's decision-making apparatus to create a space more conducive to organizing. Comprehensive or corporate campaigning is a research-driven approach to mass organizing that encourages unions to exploit corporate vulnerabilities in a systematic fashion. The corporate campaign model began to take form around the same time that capitalism began its sea change in the early 1970s and the transnational corporation came to be regarded as *the* decisive factor in world labor standards. Corporate campaigns were also direct responses to the ineffectiveness of labor's traditional organizing strategies. Stephen Lerner (1991) outlined the problem and the proposed solution that refer directly to struggles by janitors as well as security guards: "To succeed, we need to approach organizing in a fundamentally different fashion. Currently our organizing is driven by the question: 'How do we win a majority of votes?' Instead we need to ask ... 'How do we develop power to force employers to recognize the union and sign good contracts'" (8). As is made clear in this chapter, the answer to his question is not that labor must simply act outside the workplace, as is often asserted (alongside "community movements," for example) but that it must reconceive the workplace as one part of a larger industrial target.

Corporate and comprehensive campaigns became the primary alternative to shop floor struggles or labor law reform. Unionists have often referred to the process as "disorganizing corporations" instead of organizing workers, what Perry calls a "war of attrition" (Perry 1996: 340). The hundreds of corporate campaigns, which have received some attention in the popular press, have given rise to a limited academic treatment that is dominated by those sympathetic to business (Perry 1987, 1996; Northrup 1994; Jarley and Maranto 1990; Mannheim 2000; Northrup and Steen 1999).

Different specific historical moments are often said to represent the birth of the strategy. The campaign against the JP Stevens textile company by Ray Rogers of the Amalgamated Clothing and Textile Workers Union (Luebke and Mullins 1982), the inspirational basis for the 1979 film *Norma Rae*, or that union's earlier campaign against Farah manufacturing (Perry 1996), is often considered a definitive starting point. The SEIU's first corporate campaign was launched in 1973 against the healthcare giant Beverly Enterprises (Mannheim 2000).

There are obvious motivations for the interest in corporate campaigning—increasing management resistance to "traditional" union tactics, Reagan's gutting of the National Labor Relations Act (much of which was continued under Bush, Clinton, Bush, and Obama), the increasing vulnerability of unions to nonlabor statutes, and recent decisions to grant private entities official corporate personhood. Finally, the increasing centralization of corporate ownership has created a powerful argument in favor of targeting specific companies in the hopes of reaching more workers and applying more leverage all at once. In other words, as companies become more powerful, they also become better targets. In this context, the possibility of weakening a company before attempting to organize its workers became very seductive. As one SEIU organizer put it:

> We would be idiots not to [use corporate campaigns]. They're [corporations] out there winning hearts and minds. They make public opinion. We have lost that [ability]. These days we aren't strong enough to just say "ok let's put our heads down and fight." That doesn't work anymore. We need a way to undercut them [corporations] before we go organize.[2]

Corporate campaigns often have two interconnected goals. Ray Rogers, a pioneer of the strategy, is famous for promoting one: target a company's

board of directors and disrupt its financial interdependencies that keep it economically viable. Another is to publicly shame the company into submission through smear campaigns and by generating negative publicity. Both were clearly present in the fight with G4S. Snow and Benford (1988) have shown that social movements can make claims on power through the clever use of symbolism and "framing processes" that resonate with different actors in order to influence their decisions. As described later, different frames—human rights, worker abuse, labor law violations—produced varied results for the SEIU and UNI Global Union.

Corporate campaigning slowly gained prominence within some segments of the American labor movement in the 1970s, though it was not until the mid-1980s that the AFL-CIO officially endorsed the controversial practice in a series of pamphlets.[3] Ten years later, when John Sweeney and Richard Trumka were campaigning for leadership of the AFL-CIO, their New Voice slate prominently promoted the use of corporate campaign tactics (Bennett 1996: 327). Today the popularity of the comprehensive approach recognizes the central role that "strategic research" slowly came to play in union-organizing drives. A "know-thy-enemy" ethic means that anticorporate research on the structure of a company, its investment portfolio, its political connections and contributions, and its industrial position relative to other players in the market has become the most reliable source to determine campaign targets and organizing priorities. Juravich (2007) develops a pragmatic approach to such campaign tactics that allows unions to not only know more about their adversary but to prioritize the strategic significance of different aspects of the corporate architecture.

Corporate campaigns have provoked far greater resistance from management than have codes of conduct, social clauses, or framework agreements because they have been so explicitly interested in interrupting normal operating procedures and undermining corporate governance. Take the recent campaign against Sodexo, the French multiservices company (food services, catering, laundry). Together, the SEIU and UNITE HERE built a coalition union called Service Workers United as part of a transnational effort. The SEIU's corporate campaign was so aggressive and unrelenting that it drew the ire of its partner union, who chastised it for ignoring workers, and management, who charged it with blackmail and took it to court under the Racketeer Influenced and Corrupt Organizations Act (RICO Act). During the discovery phase of the trial, Sodexo's lawyers revealed that they had been leaked a corporate campaign manual that the SEIU had developed that advised workers on the legalities of such actions: "It may be a violation of blackmail and extortion laws to threaten management officials with release of 'dirt' about them if they don't settle a contract. But there is no law against union members who are angry at their employer deciding to uncover and publicize factual information about individual managers" (SEIU 2011: 29).[4]

The words "corporate" and "comprehensive" are often mistakenly used interchangeably to connote a particular type of union campaign, though the latter, which is the most fitting description of the G4S fight, signifies more than a focus on the corporation. It implies that the "air war," or corporate campaign, is primarily in the service of a "ground war," or organizing campaign. Although there has been doubt cast on the effectiveness of corporate campaigns (Perry 1996), it seems comprehensive approaches have, as of late, proven more fruitful (Bronfenbrenner and Hickey 2003).[5]

The emphasis on corporate research means that worker organizing generally begins well after a corporate campaign is in motion, when the union has already decided its organizing agenda, independent of a discussion with membership or the rank and file. This raises obvious questions about union democracy. It also further distinguishes the G4S case from many contemporary comprehensive campaigns, as it began not within the offices of the national union's research department but as a ground war between workers and their employer.

The Global Comprehensive Campaign against G4S

It is time to tell the story of how the campaign against G4S was won—its origins, and its impacts on workers in different places and other global unions. No other campaign by a global union federation (GUF) has matched it in terms of its scope, depth of struggle, resources utilized, and local implementation. The arduous and confusing campaign undertaken to win demonstrates both the horizon of possibility and the limitations of transnational organizing. As a guide through the variety of strategic responses to global corporations that unions have at their disposal today, it is as complete as can be. The first phase is the effort by the SEIU to organize security guards in the United States, with a focus on its fight with Wackenhut, G4S's American subsidiary. The second describes the globalization of that effort, the complex expansion of the campaign to multiple countries, involving hundreds of thousands of workers, that eventually concludes with the negotiation of the global agreement.

Phase I: Security Guard Organizing in the United States

The Legal Landscape

Attempts to organize security guards have been circumscribed by the ambivalence of their status as workers worthy of collective bargaining rights.[6] The 1935 Wagner Act declared that unionization rights of private security guards were equivalent to other workers (McCabe 1985). Despite employer opposition, courts routinely upheld the right of the National Labor Relations Board (NLRB, or Board) to determine the appropriate bargaining unit of different groups of workers. Security guards were often lumped into existing unions of workers where they worked—guards at car factories were in the auto workers union. Though, even when guards were placed in separate units by the Board, they maintained their right to choose any union, including the same one that represented other workers at the work site (Rattay 1983). This became a contentious issue as it supposedly exacerbated the potential for "divided loyalties." In other words, were security guards and their fellow workers to be members of the same union, it presented a dilemma for guards during industrial action—join their comrades on the picket line or perform their stated mission as defenders of private property (McGuiness, Abodeely, and Williams 1989: 4).

The divided loyalties problem was specifically addressed subsequent to the passage of the Taft-Hartley Act in 1947. Thereafter, the Board was denied the right to certify "mixed unions" of guards and nonguards, though employers had the right to voluntarily recognize such unions should workers petition to join them (McCabe 1985).[7] Moreover, even "nonmixed" unions were deemed insufficiently separate, and were often made ineligible for board certification on the grounds that they were *indirectly* linked to other AFL and CIO unions. In this context, the SEIU's venture into the world of guard organizing needed a robust strategy to circumvent the NLRB process and to neutralize the objections of employers to mixed unions.[8]

From Justice for Janitors to Stand for Security   (J4J)

The organizing breakthroughs among janitors in California and elsewhere left the SEIU with a choice: "go deep" or "go wide." Going deep meant to follow janitorial organizing into other client sectors such as schools, hospitals, and special events. Going wide was to delve further into the office buildings and organize other workers there, including security guards. Many of the strategists from the Property Services division of the SEIU who had been close to Justice for Janitors promoted the "go wide" idea. But they met resistance from within their own ranks.

"Did we really want to be the Pinkerton union? Is that how we are going to build power?" asked a staffer from that time. This statement belies more than the idea than a simple stigma attached to security guards. Security is a black-dominated industry. Racist sentiment played into the perception of guards as thugs, undeserving of protection, making it more difficult to build a campaign like the one that won gains for janitors, which included wide clergy and community support. "Race had a lot to do with why some people didn't want to go there [focus on security workers]," said one SEIU staffer. "Not that people were openly racist, but they thought that they couldn't generate the necessary sympathy campaign."[9] Additionally, there was much confusion generated by the law regarding "mixed unions," and the majority opinion within the union considered the security industry a losing proposition.

Around the same time, however, Swedish-owned Securitas went on a buying rampage and took control of five large US security companies, driving it from an insignificant company to the largest player in the market. This move triggered similar actions by the Danish-owned Group 4 Falk (a parent company of G4S), which also bought up small American firms. Within two years, the US security market had been greatly consolidated and was increasingly comprised of Europe-based global companies, creating a virtual replica of the janitorial industry in the late 1990s that produced such extraordinary gains for the union. It was this corporate activity that proved to be the most forceful argument in favor of guard organizing.

The $34 billion-a-year private security industry in America, as elsewhere, is highly precarious, characterized by high turnover, low pay, few regulations, and almost no training (Gamiz 2008). In the United States, between eleven thousand and fifteen thousand security companies employ just over one million private security guards, outnumbering public police officers 2 to 1 (Strom et al. 2010), at a median income of $21,000 annually.[10] Nicholas Kristoff writes that in major cities with high levels of economic inequality, such as New York and Los Angeles, 1 percent of employees work as private security guards (Kristoff 2012). G4S guards are typically better paid than most because its market niche at private nuclear facilities delivers higher wages, and their government job sites have been buoyed by union-sponsored legislation in the past.

In June 2001, the SEIU launched a national campaign to organize security workers at Argenbright, a US subsidiary of the British-owned Securicor, in order to link the safety of air passengers to the pathetic working conditions of airport screeners. Three months later, when it became public that Argenbright employees performed the screening of two of the hijacked planes on September 11, the SEIU's campaign took on an air of prophecy (Bahadur and Koen 2009). Though airport security was nationalized in the wake of the attacks, the SEIU was the sole union to publicly speak out against deprivatization because the law precluded the right to organize. Nonetheless, the public outcry around safety and standards created a new opportunity to organize security guards. With airport guards out of reach, the SEIU simultaneously launched other security campaigns in eleven states in late 2002 under the banner of Stand for Security to begin organizing guards at several of the largest providers.

Securitas

From the beginning, the fears of those who doubted the feasibility of strong security campaigns were proven to be unfounded. In Minnesota, for example, a large Somali immigrant workforce at Securitas fell victim to overt anti-Muslim racism from white employers in the immediate wake of September 11, triggering the "Hate Has No Home" campaign that connected clergy and community groups with workers. The campaign message targeted the Swedish ownership of Securitas, insisting that the company take immediate action against racism and uphold the comparatively high standards that Securitas workers enjoyed in Europe. Battles over the nature of industrial relations erupted inside the company between its Swedish and American managers.

Initially, the US business model prevailed. The reluctance of the US-based management to concede union demands pushed the SEIU to reach out to the Securitas union in Europe, the Swedish Transport Workers Federation (STWF). Because of its history as primarily a transport and seafarer union, the STWF had a long history of transnationalism, and it greatly aided the SEIU's campaign to apply cross-border pressure. Their collaboration helped Securitas management consider the problem in detail, after it was taken up by the company's European Works Council.

Months after the Minnesota incident, UNI organized a delegation of Securitas managers, including then CEO Thomas Berglund, to tour US facilities to see firsthand how different conditions were in the US context. "Securitas was appalled when they found out what was happening in America," said a STFW leader. "They were disgusted, and to their credit they took action."[11] US Securitas managers who were found to be complicit in racist attacks were fired and soon after replaced by a European staffer. By 2003, the SEIU and Securitas had signed an agreement granting organizers access to Securitas work sites. The agreement granted the SEIU union recognition in ten cities, although it was not until the majority of guards in each market were organized into the union that bargaining was triggered (Moberg 2010). Three years later, UNI signed a global framework agreement (GFA) with the company as well. "The Securitas campaign taught us how to go global," said one SEIU representative.[12]

Maguire Properties

As Joshua Bloom (2010) describes, security officers in Los Angeles built a similar campaign around antiracism by connecting prominent members of the black community, clergy, and unionists in late 2002, an effort constructed largely on the momentum and comprehensive strategy of Justice for Janitors. This was a significant victory, given the longstanding distrust of the janitorial campaign within LA's African American community.[13]

Like the dispute in Minnesota, the LA struggle developed an unexpected global dimension after campaign research discovered that Maguire Properties was pursuing corporate partnerships with Australian firms.

The SEIU was at this time in the early stages of collaboration with the Liquor Hospitality and Miscellaneous Workers Union (LHMU) to organize security officers as well, a happenstance that proved to be especially provident. The LHMU, having already been through an SEIU-led training program in strategic organizing, became a critical global partner (see chapter 2). The unions jointly produced reports damning the company's reputation in the *Australian Financial Review* and the *LA Business Journal*. They held demonstrations outside Maguire's LA headquarters timed to coincide with visits from Australian investor delegations. When the financial backers began asking questions, Maguire contacted the SEIU to discuss unionization (see Bloom 2010: 182–183).

G4S/Wackenhut (diff. from Securitas)

Until 2008, G4S operated in the United States under the brand Wackenhut (it is now called G4S Secure Solutions USA), which grew into an industry leader in the United States through important contracts with government agencies and nuclear facilities. The decision to organize Wackenhut workers was directly tied to the perceived success of the Securitas campaign. It had given the SEIU the confidence—or false optimism—that it could take on large global players, and there was still one of those left. "The Securitas campaign was easy," said an SEIU leader. "I was guilty of suggesting it [G4S] would be another easy win. But I can't remember ever being so wrong."[14]

Union activity began in late 2003 in a few midwestern states, and it quickly became hostile. There was initial skepticism within the SEIU that the campaign could be built around worker rights abuses. Instead, it targeted the poor quality of Wackenhut's services and its unsustainable business model through a corporate campaign. Costs were high during the first three years of the campaign due in some part because the SEIU retained the services of a London-based public relations firm to assist the corporate campaign strategy, contributing to the cynical implication that the SEIU had

[margin note: framing/angle]

outsourced the campaign to the United Kingdom. (The firm later quit due to a conflict of interest when it was found it also represented G4S, evidence of how large the company's footprint had become.) Preliminary air war tactics attempted to discredit the company with its investors by noting that over $300 million of Wackenhut's portfolio was at risk by proposed legislation that would nationalize nuclear facilities. The company distributed disposable cameras at work and ordered guards to photograph SEIU organizers' license plates if they approached company property (Selby 2004). The company also pursued a lawsuit under the RICO Act,[15] alleging that the SEIU designed an extortion campaign to organize its employees. The SEIU later responded with a series of hit pieces in the media intended to undermine the company's public image, usually related to its poor performance on expensive government contracts.

After a whistleblower prompted a series of damaging news stories by releasing a video depicting Wackenhut guards sleeping on the job at Pennsylvania nuclear facilities, Exelon, the country's largest power plant operator, canceled its contract with the company (NYT 2007).[16] The SEIU and allied activists convened theatrical protests outside corporate offices where human alarm clocks tried to rouse sleeping Wackenhut CEO Gary Sanders from his bed as part of the "Eye on Wackenhut" campaign. Soon after, Sanders was forced to resign amid an investigation alleging that the company had overcharged the City of Miami (Mufson 2008).[17]

The number of Wackenhut workers within reach of the SEIU was always comparably small, and some at the SEIU thought expanding the fight to the global level was not worth the resources. Others within the union argued convincingly that taking on Wackenhut was essential to organizing the industry as a whole. For example, a deal with Wackenhut would also raise the percentage of union guards necessary to trigger organizing at Securitas, allowing the SEIU to more easily organize within the largest player in the US industry. A neutrality deal with G4S, the world's largest player in the industry, would therefore have a ripple effect beyond the prospect of organizing within that company specifically. But that would take longer than anyone thought. Instead, despite the pressure and negative publicity, G4S carried on fighting the SEIU and used its position outside the union sphere of influence to underbid competitors on contracts. It was this intransigence that eventually propelled the SEIU to abandon a purely domestic strategy, setting the stage for a dramatic confrontation.

Phase II: The Security Campaign Goes Global

In 2004, the UK-based Securicor and the Danish-owned Group 4 Falk merged to form G4S, the second largest company in the world (only Walmart is bigger), the world's largest private security employer, and the largest firm on the London Stock Exchange. Today, approximately 657,000 G4S employees work in 125 countries, securing a diversity of enterprises. The company grew to a global giant through strategic mergers in low-income countries and war zones. During the birth pangs of the new company, the British-based leaders succeeded in retaining control of the organization and its new public image. Consequently, the hallmarks of UK industrial relations philosophy were, from the beginning, clearly the driving force of the corporation's attitude toward its employees.

On the opening day of trading of G4S on the London Stock Exchange, the SEIU publicly announced its intention to organize all the company's security guards around the world. At that time the "campaign" existed primarily on the Internet after UNI Global Union launched a website dedicated to promoting security guard campaigns and anti-G4S propaganda.[18]

Then, in April 2005, without prior warning, hundreds of formerly full-time Indonesian G4S security guards were converted into temporary employees, an aftershock of the corporate merger. This sparked what became a fifteen-month strike, making Indonesia the first battleground of the global campaign outside the rich countries. International solidarity by the SEIU and UNI began as media announcements in support of the Securicor Indonesia Labour Union, affiliated to the Association of Indonesian Labour Unions. Then, over five thousand letters of support, coordinated by the transnational solidarity website, Labourstart.org, flooded G4S, demanding the reinstatement of the fired workers. The SEIU and UNI coordinated solidarity actions at Indonesian embassies around the world, causing some prominent politicians to take note of the dispute and back the workers. Unphased, the company fought back with death threats to unionists, criminal charges against union leaders (for vague violations, including "unpleasant acts"), and, eventually, retaining the same lawyer who defended the dictator Suharto, appealed the case all the way to the Supreme Court (Champagne 2007).

The SEIU responded by deploying a researcher from Washington, D.C., who spoke Bahasa and mentored local union activists in US-style organizing.

It also encouraged the Indonesian union to dedicate one of its organizers to support a research-based campaign, a move that first demonstrated the cultural barriers to labor transnationalism in the campaign. "The very idea of assigning a leader to research and communication to this campaign was an odd and new one to Indonesian security workers. The union was excellent at mobilizing troops and marching into battle, but hadn't given much thought to the propaganda side of this 'war'" (Champagne 2007: 29). Drawing much international attention, the picket lines were consistently staffed with local unionists and supporters from around the world. Slowly, a coherent campaign emerged to challenge the intransigent management.

As the Indonesia strike unfolded, the SEIU began to collaborate with UNI more significantly. The two unions widened the campaign against G4S to include unions of private security guards in Poland, Nepal, Zimbabwe, Uganda, Mozambique, South Africa, India, Malawi, and the Democratic Republic of Congo. Through visits with international unions, the SEIU gained a better understanding of G4S's modus operandi around the globe and built relationships with potential allies at the same time. In June 2005, UNI coordinated a protest involving workers from Indonesia, South Africa, the United Kingdom, and the United States at G4S's annual general meeting in London. Protest delegates delivered G4S shareholders an alternative annual report, *The High Cost of the Low Road,* which described the mistreatment of workers and the impact such industrial relations practices could potentially have on the public image and financial stability of G4S.

Solidarity in the North

In October 2005, the UK-based General Workers Union (GMB), which had built a constructive relationship with G4S, won union recognition for thousands of security guards. In recent years, the GMB has undergone an internal transformation, overturning years of corrupt leadership and stagnation to form a democratic union committed to organizing, with demonstrated respect for much of the SEIU's approach in the United Kingdom. Between Paul Kenny's appointment and then his election as general secretary in late 2005, the union had grown by 15 percent (GMB personal communication). Nevertheless, the GMB's entry into the campaign marked another cultural challenge for collaborative unionism as well.

The GMB became involved in the campaign when it felt that the SEIU's confrontational attitude began to push the company further from the bargaining table, threatening its own positive relationship with the company at home. This perspective aligns with that of G4S as well: "It is unarguable that managers directly touched by the campaign are left deeply cynical about unions, often more determined than ever not to concede anything" (Myles 2009: 56). The GMB claims that the company was not at first principally opposed to reaching an agreement but that regional and local G4S managers and CEO Nick Buckles as well were alienated by the aggressive tactics of the SEIU and UNI around the world. One GMB organizer described the campaign foundering on strategic miscalculations by UNI and the SEIU:

> G4S felt that they simply could not trust SEIU or UNI to act honestly and honorably and were able to cite occasions where either SEIU in the US or UNI had reached agreements with them at works councils or other meetings only to break them soon after. They were also aggrieved that local disputes in Indonesia and elsewhere had been exploited and fanned up by UNI/SEIU to the detriment of the workforce and the possibility of reaching an agreement . . . [and] that G4S had been accused of everything from corrupting politicians to abusing children by the global campaign without any opportunity of a right to reply.[19]

too militant?

Both UNI and the GMB accuse the other of opportunism: UNI wanted to punish the company into signing a deal, and the GMB wanted more members. A GMB organizer remarked:

> Working people are not pawns in a game of global power politics. They need to feel they are building their own power through their own unions. Delivering global or national union recognition for people and expecting them to join out of gratitude will never build sustainable workplace power. . . . Global structures built without democratic control and with no mandate do not deliver working class power. They deliver global companies a handy police force of global union bureaucrats to help them control their uppity workers.[20]

turf wars ✱

A UNI staffer replied:

> They [the GMB] didn't want us to keep up the corporate campaign because it damaged their relationship with G4S. That much is obvious to everyone,

including G4S. They certainly didn't want us out there organizing in G4S's biggest markets. They don't see themselves gaining from that kind of organizing, even though, of course, they do in the long run. . . . That's the thing, they benefit from having a stronger union . . . even though they don't help out.[21]

The GMB was also critical of the SEIU's approach to globalism, which it determined was based on parochial assumptions, a one-size-fits-all model of ideal-typical labor union practice, in apparent ignorance of local constraints.

SEIU organizers sometimes appear to be unaware that US corporate and industrial law is not universal. Their answer to the German unions was: "It soon will be." In India it was: "If we can organize in New York, why can't we in New Delhi?" The apparent SEIU search for client unions globally to build a sphere of influence also alienates many trade unionists who otherwise would support the SEIU organizing line. . . . [The GMB] wasn't aware UNI were involved in promoting any organizing model.[22]

In the end the GMB was included as the third signatory on the G4S agreement. Though in theory it considers itself an ally of the SEIU's general commitment to organizing, it remains highly skeptical and critical of how that process is executed. The G4S campaign reinforced its perception of the SEIU as culturally insensitive and authoritarian. "Overall," said one UNI staffer, "we are not enemies or anything, we're still comrades, but they left a bad taste in our mouth." Here the two finally agree, as one GMB official acknowledged, "It's your best friends that tell you when your breath smells."[23]

Instead of supporting the larger effort, collaboration with the GMB drove a temporary wedge into the global campaign. As UNI delegates were crashing G4S's summer shareholder meeting in 2005, the GMB distanced itself from the campaign in UK-related media. That fall, just after the GMB won a four-year wage agreement with G4S, UNI contacted British government ministers requesting that they cancel their contracts with the company in favor of a better corporate citizen. The unions clashed again when UNI attempted to block G4S from winning the lucrative security contract for the 2012 Olympic Games in London. In a press release detailing G4S's violations, Christy Hoffman of UNI said, "Global companies like Group 4 Securicor have global responsibilities. The Olympic games are a venue for global companies that respect human rights everywhere they operate" (UNI 2007). Although UNI had won the support of the transport workers' union to block G4S's Olympics bid (UNI 2008), the GMB's members stood to benefit through job creation.[24] Numerous requests were also made of G4S's European Works Council, which was unable to risk its productive relationship with the company by acting in the interests of other workers.

Southern Strategies, Shareholder Activism, and Human Rights

In 2006, the SEIU and UNI announced the creation of the G4S Alliance, the organizational body that would from then on determine the global campaign strategy. The campaign's structure and geography changed dramatically. With a tenuous solidarity in the North, UNI and its alliance partners made a strategic decision to reorient its focus on international human rights issues in the South. G4S workers were engaged in organizing in a variety of important countries in the Global South, and it made tactical sense to work alongside them. This decision coincided with the creation of the UN Principles for Responsible Investment (UN PRI)[25] in April 2006, which linked social issues to investment standards. Seven percent (94,041,450) of G4S shares were held by PRI signatory countries, many of which also controlled union pension funds (UNI 2009).[26] Compared to the miniscule percentages that most shareholder activism engages, this was a significant sum. As part of a gradual southern strategy of its own, G4S began divesting at this time from rich countries like Germany and France but showed explosive growth in Asia, Latin America, Africa, and the Middle East.

These circumstances meant two related things. First, the SEIU and UNI had found a potential point of financial leverage against the company. Investors are typically both excited and weary of companies that exhibit a kind of "entrepreneurial overreach," as the returns can be large but the risks many. Second, whereas stories of worker abuse in the United States or the economic arguments about the company's risky contracts did little or nothing to move the company's clients and financial backers, narratives about low standards and mistreatment in the Global South could potentially be used to influence investors in the Global North.[27] It was at this stage that the campaign strategy switched decisively to focus on labor rights as human

... maybe because diff. level of poverty...

rights. An SEIU researcher explained rather bluntly, "We found out that investors [in G4S] don't really care about poor workers in America. They care about poor workers in the Third World. So we went that route."[28]

In March 2006, a violent general strike broke out in South Africa. Approximately one hundred thousand security guards—one-third of the entire industry—took to the streets across the country, waging battles with rival unions and police. As many as sixty people were reported to have died in strike-related violence, making it the bloodiest battle since 1994 (Makgetla 2007). Most were alleged scabs, thrown from trains by strikers as they were caught commuting to work from the townships. Others were stabbed, shot, or beaten to death. The sensationalism of the strike gained negative press for UNI's affiliate in Johannesburg, the South African Transport and Allied Workers Union. Later that summer, during a European Works Council meeting that took place on a yacht, G4S CEO Nick Buckles claimed that UNI had indirectly murdered a security guard as a result of its financial relationship to its South African affiliate. The company also insinuated that UNI had assisted in lengthening the strike, which it considered a justification for temporarily suspending dialogue about a global agreement. In the wake of strike chaos, UNI took on a larger role there, and South Africa became a major node of the global campaign, with organizers from Europe transplanted to Johannesburg to help develop local union capacity.

In June 2006, UNI and its allies returned to G4S's shareholder meeting in London with an updated alternative report that highlighted worker abuses and human rights in poor countries. This action followed the Indonesian Supreme Court's favorable decision to reinstate the fired striking workers. Upon hearing the ruling, 150 security guards in Jakarta occupied G4S's company headquarters, refusing to leave until the court's decision was instituted. The occupation drew supportive visits from local nongovernmental organizations (NGOs) and other trade unions. The company capitulated a month later and was forced to pay Rp 4,000 million ($570,000) in back wages and twice the minimum required in severance packages. The criminal charges against union leaders were also dropped (Champagne 2007).

In December 2006, UNI filed a complaint against G4S with the UK National Contact Point of the Organization for Economic Cooperation and Development (OECD), citing violations of its guidelines on multinational enterprises in eleven countries, including the blacklisting of unionists, wage theft, union recognition, and access to bathrooms on the job (UNI Property

Services 2007). The company replied with a letter pleading with the OECD to recognize it as a "people business" and to discard the complaints of the union, which the company characterized as "unfounded and vexatious . . . simply another assault on our reputation as part of their ongoing 'corporate campaign' " (G4S 2007b). Revealingly, it relied on its corporate social responsibility commitments—a G4S school in India, assistance to homeless youth in Russia, farms in Malawi, a Chinese orphanage—as evidence that it had fulfilled its social obligations and should be absolved of the union's charges. Even without a verdict in hand, the SEIU and UNI took advantage of the opportunity to use the complaint as a vehicle to promote the image of an irresponsible global company through press releases, the Internet, and direct communication with investors and shareholders.

UNI commissioned a South African research institute in 2007 to execute a report on the record of abuse at G4S in Mozambique (see Mtyingizana 2007). To deepen the impact of this report, a fact-finding delegation of labor leaders, legal experts, and staff of the War on Want NGO toured southern Africa to produce *Who Protects the Guards?*, a magazine-format guide through the dark side of industrial relations in the private security industries of Mozambique, Malawi, and South Africa. Released on the eve of G4S's 2007 shareholder meeting, the report revealed stories of full-time workers in abject poverty, working seven days a week, unable to support their families, and denied dignities such as bathroom breaks and water (UNI Property Services 2007). In South Africa, cases of race-segregated bathrooms and verbal abuse of blacks by white G4S supervisors seemed especially appalling.

The report generated deeper activism and concessions from the company in the face of bad publicity. For example, it proved instrumental in helping Moroccan G4S workers win a holiday bonus, while Ugandan security guards signed their first collective bargaining agreement with the company after using the report to shame the company in the local media. UNI leaders were surprised to learn that unions in Ghana had made use of the report and were applying local pressure to management. "We didn't even know that union was still active," said a UNI staffer.[29]

But Malawian workers made the most significant strides through using the report. Approximately eight thousand G4S employees work in Malawi. UNI's Malawian affiliate, the Textile Garments, Leather and Security Workers Union, had been organizing security workers for five years, placing a concerted focus on G4S since approximately 2007, when the fight to pressure the company to sign the global agreement became more active in Africa. In the period immediately preceding the union's involvement with UNI, labor relations between G4S and its employees were fractured and chaotic. For its part, management occasionally felt a sense of terror arising from the ranks of its workforce. G4S leaders report that on two occasions its executives were attacked by angry groups of workers, causing one to flee the country and another to reportedly travel with a police escort for his personal protection.

The company won an injunction against a planned strike that was served by armed guards late in the evening at the home of a union officer, too late for the union to inform its membership. So when a chaotic wildcat strike broke out in the morning and the union was unable to contain it for two days, the company declared the strike illegal and requested the assistance of the government, which then joined forces to suppress it. Nonetheless, in two days the strike won a higher wage increase—of 16 percent—than the company's previous offer of 12 percent.

Although workers eventually won some form of recognition afterward, half a year later it was still operating without a union contract. Guards earned just enough to keep them above the World Bank's poverty line of one dollar a day, and they often worked twelve hour shifts seven days a week. UNI then established the Legal Aid Fund for African Unions in order to facilitate a lawsuit alleging underpay, as well as noncompliance with International Labour Organization conventions. In other countries, G4S unionists began the "It's About Time" solidarity campaign, which underscored the plight and fight of Malawian guards.

Much of the Malawi work was facilitated by a strong local union. For his near-single-handed efforts to mobilize support for Malawian security guards, MacDonald Chuma was awarded UNI's "Solidarity Award" at a celebration in New York City. In an article on the subject in Malawi's *The Daily Times*, a reporter notes, "Employers loathe him . . . [for his] tough-as-teak negotiating tactics." UNI used the Africa report and stories from the Malawian campaign to try to dissuade the FIFA Congress from awarding G4S the contract to provide security at the 2010 World Cup in South Africa.[30]

Similar developments were underway on the Indian subcontinent, G4S's largest market, where the company claims to have created as many as thirty-two jobs a day for two decades (G4S 2009). By late 2007, UNI had estab-

framing

lished three offices in India to coordinate a variety of campaigns in Hyderabad, Bangalore, Delhi, and Kochi. The private security campaign was unique among these for focusing exclusively on workers within the vast informal sector. To put a spotlight on these invisible workers, UNI exploited the popular claim of the country as an emerging capitalist democracy in its report *Inequality Beneath India's Economic Boom*. The document demonstrates that G4S guards receive poverty wages often below the legal minimum, work long hours without overtime pay, have no job security, and are denied the right to organize independent unions. UNI also hired legal experts from Columbia Law School and London University, plus NGOs, to produce similarly damning profiles and case studies of G4S that framed the debate in terms of political and human rights. These documents were fodder for the effort to steer the organizing committee of the 2010 Commonwealth Games, the $1.6 billion multisport event held in India, toward another security provider, causing uproar within the country's business community. Combined with the actions across southern Africa, these public shaming rituals raised a questionable profile of the company to European investors. At the same time, the ground war was proceeding apace. By early 2008, with the assistance of UNI funds and direct support from Europe-based staff, unions in Poland, the Democratic Republic of Congo, and Nepal had also built campaigns against G4S.

The OECD complaint was taken to mediation late in 2008, a favorable determination from UNI's perspective. As a result the company's investors began more serious inquiries into the violations. More pressing than the ethical dilemma of supporting a company with a poor human rights track record was the potential for the company to reveal an internal culture of denial, even in the face of independent verification of allegations. Other issues were raised as well. Was the company integrating its newly acquired subsidiaries with too much negative publicity? Was it risking its reputation in its most profitable markets?

The conclusion of the OECD report and the growing focus of unions around the world on G4S provided the SEIU's investor-targeted comprehensive campaign greater legitimacy. Soon it began consulting a Stockholm-based firm, GES, which analyzes corporate social responsibility and issues recommendations to asset managers wishing to comply with social initiatives. After reviewing a dossier on G4S, the firm recommended its clients either engage the company in dialogue about its labor practices or exclude

G4S from further investment portfolios based on its poor human rights track record. In June 2008, one of Norway's largest life insurance companies, Kapitalforvaltning, heeded this advice and divested from the company, citing violations in UNI's OECD complaint. Shortly after, the Danish government threatened to cancel its contract with G4S if it did not resolve issues raised in the OECD report as well (UNI 2009). One UNI representative said, "They [G4S] pretty much freaked out after the divestment stuff. They took us more seriously from then on."[31]

UNI and SEIU Win Global Framework Agreement with G4S

In December 2008, after five years of battling unionization, the company capitulated to a global framework agreement, claiming it was "a matter of time."[32] It also emphasized the crucial role the GMB played as a "go-between," a role facilitated by its decades-long constructive relationship with the company, as well as "its shared history, cultural understanding and mutual respect" (Myles 2009: 60). In contrast with the company's position, some within UNI and the SEIU are certain their comprehensive campaign had the intended effect, and that holding out to win workplace neutrality was worth it, even as it caused some dissension within the unions. As one SEIU staffer said:

> Bill [Regan] was the one [whose] head turned grey off of that campaign. . . . Bill Regan [SEIU leader] and a handful of contractors and the global unions beat the most anti-union and largest security company in the world into a global agreement with little if any help from his own division. . . . [Other leaders in the SEIU] would say different, but none of them were very engaged.[33]

The agreement required the company to respect four core conventions of the ILO, provisions against child labor, forced labor, discrimination in employment, and respect for the freedom of association. Additionally, the agreement contained five core elements that UNI was looking for. First, workers would be allowed to raise complaints of violations of their national law as grievance under the agreement. Second, the company and the union agreed to attempt to raise standards for workers, providing it did not put the company at a competitive disadvantage, a common feature of contracts won through corporate campaigns in the low-level service industries. Economic bargaining is then "triggered" when a certain percentage of industry leaders in a market agree to the campaign. Third, it included a formal dispute resolution process, to be worked out in different ways depending on the national context. Fourth, the agreement encouraged workers not to engage in "illegal industrial action," an aspect of the agreement that was inspired by both the company's desire for labor peace and the union's hope to avoid violent clashes like in South Africa and Malawi. Most importantly, the agreement provided a clear path to union recognition, employer neutrality, and access rights for local union staff to G4S work sites, and it restrained the company from antiunion campaigning when workers attempted to unionize. In essence, this changed the rules of engagement that had been established either by formal procedure or default for almost all G4S guards. The push for neutrality, the most staunchly opposed element, was predicated on UNI's belief that "the right to create a union in the service industry, in cleaning and security in particular . . . can't fundamentally be practiced without some ability to talk to workers on a regular basis" (Hoffman 2009).

*[margin note: * sustained contact (key to organizing model)]*

Had UNI been satisfied with an agreement that only stipulated core labor standards, as it had in the past, it is likely that the campaign would not have been as onerous as it was. In a letter drafted to G4S two months before the agreement was reached, Christy Hoffman, then UNI's organizing director, rejected G4S's proposed conciliation because it lacked a clear statement on a pathway to union recognition, a "bedrock principle" of UNI.

The letter also raises the key issue regarding the "phase-in" of the agreement. Both parties were worried that a sudden explosion of union activity once the GFA was signed would stretch the limits of their capacities too thin, and therefore they agreed to a process of selective implementation for three years, with a total phase-in within four. Fearing the global agreement would hamper its ability to "practically facilitate the freedom of association to take place" (Myles, Hoffman, Greenwood, and Powdrill 2009), the company tried to retain its position as the court of approval for how and when workers exercised their rights and to "make sure that growing unionization levels continue to support our customer desires for a stable operating environment" (Myles et al. 2009). To that end, G4S initially proposed that UNI abandon its campaign in India, its largest market, and that the phase-in should be dealt with at a separate time, a "loophole which engulfs the entire agreement," in UNI's opinion (UNI 2009).

So UNI fought, and eventually won, to have India be the first country to implement the agreement. South Africa was selected as the other trial-run country. North American security guards were initially excluded from the agreement altogether, but a separate deal was struck the following day to satisfy the SEIU that granted a clear path to union recognition to G4S guards in nine US cities—Washington, D.C., San Francisco, Seattle, Boston, Chicago, Los Angeles, New York, Minneapolis, and Sacramento—involving some of the same workers who had begun the organizing drive in 2003. That meant that the initial active phase of the agreement officially affected more than one quarter of the company's employees.

Not everyone was satisfied with this outcome. Some suggested that the union still signed the agreement too soon, out of fear of how the RICO suit might affect its ability to continue the campaign. Stephen Lerner, a major SEIU figure and a leader of the G4S campaign at the time, said, "When they [Wackenhut] sued the union on RICO, the union essentially had . . . a less robust settlement demand than they had previously demanded. The RICO suit was dismissed soon after settlement . . . I think that the union should have held out in the US longer. It would have gotten more," he said.[34]

Whether or not it was "enough," the union spent more time, resources, and expertise fighting G4S than it had ever put into a single campaign. The result was a global agreement that surpassed all others in terms of its scope and implementation. The campaign set a new standard for how to beat a union-resistant company at the global level.

Conclusion: Global Unionism as Governance Struggle

Most examples of global unionism stop here—a transnational corporation vows to uphold and defend the rights of its employees in its corporate periphery around the world. The signed pledge is declared a victory. But without unions or other organizations to monitor the process, or implement whatever changes were agreed upon, very often the only change is that the company suddenly has a stronger corporate social responsibility portfolio. The important development in this campaign then is the degree to which the larger gains were interpreted locally and the leverage it provided over the industry globally.

But the campaign is also a landmark in and of itself, a vindication of those within the SEIU and UNI who pursued a comprehensive strategy and a long-term industrial vision. A number of factors contributed to UNI's ability to execute the campaign. First, the SEIU's influence was critical. Aside from seeding UNI's organizing fund, the SEIU provided important resources that allowed UNI to place staff into the field and to hire the personnel necessary to carry out some aspects of the corporate campaign. UNI's property services strategy was also driven by campaigning ideas and leaders from the SEIU, particularly Christy Hoffman. But the resources the SEIU donated were significant beyond enabling UNI to carry out the day-to-day aspects of the campaign. The vision of a campaign that sought to govern the industry, not simply organize members into the union, was launched in Washington, D.C. Without the ideological commitment to the G4S campaign of several SEIU leaders, UNI's efforts would have been confined to the modesty that dooms so many union struggles.

Second, UNI's atomized sectoral structure (an internal anatomy rare among other GUFs) insulated the campaign from cumbersome bureaucracy, allowing it to make choices and take decisive action without broad consultation outside of the G4S campaign Alliance. Third, the Alliance structure facilitated a campaign involving a wide swath of unions with and without successful preexisting bargaining relationships. In other words, in a campaign this long and confrontational, those with positive relationships with G4S, such as the GMB, required a campaign structure that could push them to take risks without alienating them from the collective process. It also allowed UNI to tolerate a certain amount of internal dissension without a large risk of Alliance partners completely breaking rank.

Fourth, the most decisive element of the campaign that forced G4S to capitulate was the pressure applied to its financial backers by the corporate campaign. In correspondence with the SEIU, UNI, and OECD, the company routinely insisted that corporate campaigns are illegal and vowed to never surrender. But the comprehensive campaign was composed of narratives of repression and struggle from Global South, and it proved to overpower the company's intransigence. One SEIU activist explained, "Suddenly you had these fires being lit in India, South Africa, Malawi, ya know, and it was undermining their [G4S] credibility."[35] Unionists are fond of having workers tell their stories as a way to illustrate the struggle. Given the nature of global campaigning, any opportunity to "give voice" to common workers is essential, which is why in this case guards' stories filled at least seven reports that lent critical legitimacy to the corporate campaign effort.

Comprehensive campaigns are first and foremost top-down endeavors, as their critics are quick to point out. But they are not only that. Governance struggles, as I have described them here, attempt to provide a space for the disempowered to exercise associational power—for workers to organize, activists to mobilize, civil society to protest, and so on. The corporate campaign clearly disciplined the company, but UNI's commitment to organizing was also sincere, and it showed. In its past, UNI had signed global framework agreements with companies without any provisions about organizing. Moreover, although the SEIU's top-down orientation had produced gains for some guards in the United States, it also undermined others.[36] In this case, however, corporate obstinance, as well as the length of the fight, was directly related to a global struggle over new rules about organizing, access rights, and neutrality. Over the course of the campaign to win the global agreement, workers won union recognition with G4S in the United Kingdom, Poland, Uganda, Malawi, Nepal, and the Democratic Republic of Congo, plus strike settlements in Panama and Indonesia and a clearer union recognition pathway in the United States. It would take a greater fight, however, to win gains in South Africa and India.

Chapter 4

Transnationalism, Mobilization, and Renewal: The Battle with G4S in South Africa

In the summer of 2009 a group of security guards and union activists from across South Africa gathered in the basement of a hotel on Durban's coastline. The Service Employees International Union (SEIU) organizers screened a short documentary about the recent Justice for Janitors campaign in Houston, Texas. The struggle in Texas was significant because it had been the first victory for janitors in the heart of the Republican-controlled South.

"We went global here," explains a Change to Win staffer. "We had support from other janitors around the world, other movements, other campaigns." Indeed, the Houston janitors enjoyed broad solidarity from immigrants rights groups in Germany, the United Kingdom, and Italy. In one of the most significant transnational support campaigns between unions and social movements, ten cities in Europe mobilized coordinated actions to help pressure the two largest building owners in Houston, Chevron and Hines Real Estate, to capitulate. The SEIU organizer continued: "That's what we are doing here too, with G4S. Except now it's even bigger."

During the lunch break a group of unionists struck up a conversation about where dead bodies had been found during the infamous 2006 security strike. A man from Durban said that he had heard that a young guard, a suspected scab, had been killed at his girlfriend's house during the night. One organizer in Johannesburg described the scene when he saw a mob of workers descend on a group of three security personnel who had dared to cross a picket line at an intersection in the Braamfontein area of Johannesburg. "It was horrible. We lost control, you know. We lost control during the strike. That was our mistake. But we learned from it."

"I have heard people say that [the] SEIU extended the strike," I suggested.

"That is crazy. Americans aren't very fond of striking," he said, to much laughter at the table. "Why would they extend it? Absolutely not. They wanted to end it. We were going down, you know, way down, before we began working with UNI and SEIU. COSATU [Congress of South African Trade Unions] was going down too. It is still going down. But this has changed so many things," he said, spreading his arms wide to indicate the international meeting.

Turbulence and Instability in the South African Working Class

After a decade of steady decline toward a period of quiescence, the South African labor movement has lost its luster and some of its sociological intrigue. Eclipsed by larger problems in the post-apartheid era, the labor question has been largely abandoned by scholars as a central factor in South African life.

During the embattled days of the apartheid years, COSATU occupied a coveted place in the radical imagination. Vindicated by Mandela's release—he was escorted from prison by Cyril Ramaphosa, a prominent unionist—its particular brand of social movement unionism seemed all the more compelling. In fact, many credit the influx of anti-apartheid activists into the US labor movement in the 1980s and 1990s for injecting the ideas, aspirations, and practices that promoted union revitalization and new mobilization-based strategies.

Then, suddenly caught in the whirlwind of the African National Congress's (ANC's) quick and much-celebrated adoption of IMF-imposed austerity measures and World Bank loans, labor's weakness—relative to the

state it had in fact helped bring into being—became the lead story. Despite its status as a member of the ruling tripartite coalition, the union movement has steadily drifted away from its central position in the South African political economy. New dramas have replaced the old narratives about race and class struggle—the rise of a black economic elite strata, the massive influx of foreign direct investment into Johannesburg, political scandals and, Jacob Zuma's public persona, and the seemingly indefatigable HIV/AIDS epidemic.

South Africa's union movement is still intensely political, even as the class struggle discourse that once constituted its center more closely resembles sanctimonious cant at COSATU conventions. Nevertheless, it is in fact grappling with serious questions of organization and politics that both perplex and discomfit many American unionists. This context helps underscore the point that in 2005, when the SEIU began courting the South African Transport and Allied Workers Union (SATAWU) to take part in its global campaign, one union was on the offensive while the other was gasping for air. But it also suggests that an easy alliance was not possible, given the cultural and political legacies of both union movements.

In an effort to recoup some aspects of its former vitality, the South African unionists have responded to the structural changes of national and global political economy with a handful of strategic innovations. The federation's 1997 September Commission Report urged a return to social unionism and an internal reorganization that included the formation of "mega-unions"[1] in each sector. However, as COSATU affiliates operate with considerable autonomy, the federation does not have the power to enact such reforms that, for example, the Sweeney administration was able to accomplish in the United States around the same time (see chapter 2). Bezuidenhout (2000) suggests a renewal strategy aimed at building "global social movement unionism" though at present it is unlikely to inspire. Webster and Buhlungu (2004) note a series of strategic responses to changing conditions by unions, arguing correctly that these responses do not constitute a coherent revitalization program, a view similar to how Behrens, Fichter, and Frege (2003) assess renewal in Germany. The authors position renewal efforts as fundamentally aligned against specific changes in exogenous factors of political economy and social structure.

SATAWU, UNI's primary local affiliate in the country, was first and foremost concerned with redressing its own internal deficiencies in order to move toward a new kind of organizing unionism. During the course of the global campaign, UNI and the SEIU sought to redirect the conversation about union weakness away from the structural conditions of capitalism and toward the subjective choices, decisions, and organization of the SATAWU itself. In other words, they believed that strategy *matters*. By examining the global and local collaboration of the SATAWU, UNI, and SEIU, we get a sense of the changing strategic orientations of each union under the influence of the other, though primarily here I am concerned with the SEIU's and UNI's impact on SATAWU.

Labor Transnationalism Then and Now in South Africa

South African labor history is rich and closely tied to the story of the nation as it looks today. Throughout that history we can identify three moments of labor transnationalism, which I refer to as *communist/syndicalist*, *social movement*, and *institutional* to identify the dominant influences in each period.[2] The first, roughly from the early 1900s to 1960, refers to the period of worker organization that was influenced by American, Australian, British, and Scottish trade union traditions. The second period, from 1960 to 1994, largely reflects the deep analysis done by South African labor scholars on social movement unionism, a brand of militant community-based activism so fierce it has its own acronym, SMU. However, the most important point of departure for our purposes is the transition to the next phase, which takes us to the present, called "institutional internationalism," and in my opinion it is representative of what is "new" about labor transnationalism, especially in South Africa. This is an important distinction since what is commonly referred to as "new" by South Africa scholars—grassroots or proletarian internationalism—is actually more indicative of the "old" models described earlier (see chapter 1). Institutional internationalism refers to numerous collaborative efforts by various unions and nonunion labor organizations but most significantly the case study under examination here.[3]

Central to the campaign against Group 4 Securicor (G4S)—because it helps explain what the SEIU and UNI were doing in South Africa in the first place—is the demobilization of one of history's most audacious union movements. Why did the South African trade unions become more quiescent? As a starting point, it makes sense to consider some of the phenomena

that explain the same historical trends in other labor movements—
institutionalization, bureaucratization, corporatism—as an antecedent to
today's transnational activism.

Syndicalist/Communist Internationalism

With few exceptions historians have portrayed early twentieth-century
southern African (Namibia, South Africa, Botswana, Zambia, Zimbabwe,
Swaziland) labor history as if the context of the nation-state made analytic
sense, but during this time it did not (Van der Walt 2007). Such a perspective projects national borders onto a landscape of colonial or imperial rule,
ignoring the significance of regional political economies, massive immigra-
tion, networks of activists, and especially the vital role of international labor
markets. According to Van der Walt (2007):

> Transnational influences played a critical role in shaping working-class
> movements, which straddled borders and formed sections across the region
> and beyond it. Furthermore, ideological, ethnic and racial divides within
> the working class across southern Africa played a more important role in
> constituting divisions than state borders. (223)

Cycles of union and protest movements by blacks were born and reborn
throughout the 1880s, when speculative capital came searching for gold
along the shale beds of the Witswatersrand. But none were strong enough to
resist the repression of the apartheid regime (Bezuidenhout 2000). In contrast, white unions made significant inroads. White workers in South Africa
developed a local tradition of white labor supremacy by the early twentieth
century, which combined social democratic demands with bans on blacks
for certain jobs, segregation, and the repatriation of Asians. Other early
models of predominantly craft unionism were imported from Britain, which
laid foundations of a socialist Labor Party, a racist organization that affiliated to the Second International.

Inspired by anarcho-syndicalist currents around the world, however,
other whites helped build a labor internationalism that was racially inclu-
sive and class-based. Van der Walt (2007) documents the diffusion of the
Industrial Workers of the World's syndicalism from the United States' to

Britain's settler colonies via Scottish anarchists and European Kropotki-
nites. In his estimable history, radical unions were "less the scions of Marx
than the heirs of Bakunin" (67).

The first prominent union to organize only blacks was the Industrial
and Commercial Workers Union (ICU), influenced heavily by white syndicalism and the Pan-African teachings of Marcus Garvey that became popular in southern Africa. Lasting for eleven years, it essentially collapsed under its own weight, unable to deal with the demands of massive influxes of
aggrieved members (Southall 1995). When war broke out in Europe, the
splits in the socialist movements elsewhere also worked their way through
South Africa. A minority group left the party to eventually form the core of
the Comintern-affiliated Communist Party of South Africa, which argued
class, rather than race, should be the basis of trade union organization. Communist internationalism played a significant role in mobilizing black workers and promoting the idea of a nationalist liberation movement, though it
isolated itself with the turn toward armed struggle (Southall and Bezuidenhout 2004).

Political-legal apartheid began in 1947 with the electoral victory of the
National Party, which codified the racial segregation that had been central
to South African culture for more than a century. This extended the
decades-long system of "influx control"—the geographic containment of
blacks to the homelands, or *Bantustans*—by their systematic deployment to
the most arduous and dangerous kinds of work outside the majority white
cities (Kraak 1996). After the upsurge of wartime militancy, ending in the
bloody mineworkers' strike, the law conspired to drive black union leaders
underground with the 1950 Suppression of Communism Act (Southall and
Bezuidenhout 2004). Segregation was further enforced by white trade
unions that excluded blacks from their industries, and the 1956 Labor Relations Act that classified particular jobs as race-specific (Bendix 1996), ensuring that blacks and other nonwhites occupied the precarious and unskilled
sectors. Without a voice in a white supremacist country, the apartheid workplace constituted a bifurcated system of "racial despotism" (Burawoy 1985)
that enforced profound inequality. In this environment, the South African
Congress of Trade Unions (SACTU) emerged in the mid-1950s as the most
energetic organizers of the black working class. Ideologically Communist,
politically oriented toward the national struggle, the SACTU picked up
most of the slack when the ANC was banned following rising unrest in the

townships that culminated in the civil disobedience against passlaws and the Sharpeville Massacre in 1960.

Social Movement Union Internationalism   1960-1994

Massive unrest swept across Africa as national liberation movements gained momentum in the 1950s and early 1960s. South African protests against racism took the form of nationwide anti-apartheid *stayaways* organized by the SACTU in 1957, 1958, 1960, and 1961 (Silver 2003). This activity initially deflected foreign direct investment in South Africa. However, when the apartheid state proved a worthy adversary, crushing opposition and sending the SACTU into exile—and pushing many of its leaders toward underground armed struggle in the ANC's military wing, Umkhonto we Sizwe (Spear of the Nation)—the successful protection of cheap labor signaled a green light for foreign capital, which rushed in during the late 1960s and early 1970s.

This flood of foreign capital helped incubate a renewed working class that doubled in population between 1950 and 1975 inside an expanding Fordist[4] sector (Silver 2003), which contributed to the rise of black trade unionism. But as a result of open racial hostilities at work, and the relative inability for unions to take hold, black unions also grew through informal social networks outside the workplace (Webster and Adler 1999). The geographic location of these unions outside the factory provided an opportunity to include class-wide and community demands in their struggles.

In late 1972, a small strike of Durban longshoremen broke out against racist managers, which spread in 1973 to waves of strikes after Durban's Coronation Brick and Tile failed to pay the legal minimum wage, involving as many as one hundred thousand workers (Wood and Harcourt 1998). Emboldened by the success of their decisive action, blacks joined so-called independent unions by the thousands, which declared their autonomy from the control of white unions and the apartheid state. Because the workplace was so hostile toward the new unions, they deepened their ties with community organizations beyond the workplace to build a movement oriented toward radical social transformation and democracy, embodying what came to be known as "social movement unionism."

In the mid-1970s, the International Confederation of Free Trade Unions (ICFTU) established the Coordinating Committee of South Africa to aid the emerging industrial unions with legal strategies and to recoup their operating costs to fuel further action. This took the form of raising $6.6 million in the 1970s and 1980s by pressuring affiliates to give solidarity donations (Southall 1995). The ICFTU[5] also assisted the burgeoning black unions of the Federation of South African Trade Unions (FOSATU) and the unions that would come to comprise the National Council of Trade Unions as well (Lambert and Webster 2001).

Southall (1995) describes the important links that the ICFTU maintained with local unions to continue the support, as well as the relationships formed by individual South African unionists with those abroad after attending education workshops. These networks of interunion communication led to crucial forms of solidarity during recognition battles. For example, when organizing against the subsidiaries of multinationals, they were supported by unions with representation in the home country of the corporation and could call upon these unions for generalized support. During this time many unions joined their respective International Trade Secretariats as well.

During the Cold War years, unions in South Africa were more closely intertwined with the ICFTU than with the World Federation of Trade Unions (WFTU), explicitly because the basis of the affiliation was not ideological but the shared experience of a particular multinational company. Unions contained in the Soviet orbit had no such avenue to offer their support. It is hard to overlook the irony in the confluence of historical events whereby capitalism, not communism, provided a more obvious pathway to international union solidarity for a developing country.

The 1980s saw the consolidation of the black unions, the student movement, and the broader anti-apartheid struggle within coherent organizations, including COSATU. Though COSATU did not develop a coherent international strategy in the 1980s, it inherited an internationalist legacy from its predecessor, FOSATU, which was deeply enmeshed in coordinating a variety of external assistance with domestic endeavors to end apartheid. After 1985, COSATU became the primary channel through which foreign assistance flowed.

The fall of the Soviet system, the end of the Cold War, and the unbanning of the ANC and other liberation movements brought about new patterns of international union cooperation. At this point COSATU still pursued "active nonalignment" regarding affiliation to the ICFTU or the WFTU.

Some saw the ICFTU as an imperial wing of Europe, whose member unions' politics more or less mirrored the foreign policy objectives of their governments. At the same time, many COSATU leaders distrusted the efficacy of the Communist WFTU, as its members were officially state-run front groups for the Soviet bloc. In other words, COSATU saw ICFTU affiliates as defacto objects of northern imperialism, and WFTU unions as de jure subjects of oppressive puppet states. When the ICFTU finally merged with the World Confederation of Labour in 2006, COSATU heralded the new organization (the International Trade Union Confederation) with false praise as "the second coming of the international union bureaucracy."

As early as 1985, banks began pulling investments out of South Africa. Global boycotts and declining business confidence contributed to decreasing investments as well. Ultimately, a failing economy and political isolation from the world rendered the continuation of apartheid impossible. With legislative reforms on the table, but rising discontent, Adam and Moodly (1993) noted that power-sharing soon became the only viable option. Despite the existence of a strong mass movement against apartheid, the "double transition"—a process of simultaneously consolidating democracy and restructuring the economy—happened by an elite compromise that kept "the fundamental structures of capitalist society in place, thereby ensuring the loyalty of the propertied classes" (Webster and Adler 1999).

Connect w/ comment on p. 105

Institutional Internationalism

The post-1994 agreement the ANC struck with the World Bank required that South Africa phase out tariffs in twelve years. Instead, it voluntarily accomplished it in eight (Desai 2002), reducing import taxes by almost two-thirds between 1994 and 1998 alone (Desai and Bond 2008). The state attained competitiveness in automobile manufacturing and steel production, the heavily unionized Fordist sectors, through a transition to a leaner production model. After one year of the ANC's neoliberal growth program (GEAR), the news media reported the unofficial conclusion of the "Honeymoon with the West" as the rand fell 25 percent against most other foreign currencies (Koelble 1999: 11). While GEAR was popularly described as a reform of the Keynesian model, it turned out more like a grotesque perversion, including the hallmarks of the World Bank and International Monetary

Fund influence: inflation targeting, tax cuts, liberalized trade, the sale of state assets, and an expanding export-led growth sector (Marais 2001; Bond 2009). Labor unrest was widespread immediately following 1994. Resistance to both economic liberalization and political reforms happened through wildcats as well as sanctioned strikes and street protests by the new social movements. Therefore, it would be wrong to claim that the mere existence of corporatism was solely responsible for the demobilization of the unions. On the contrary, COSATU and the South African Communist Party (SACP) undertook a deep realignment of priorities to accommodate itself to participation in government that was not at all consistent with pursuing a working-class agenda. In short, the political incorporation of COSATU was not enough.

To discipline COSATU, the ANC made concessions to win over the federation to the side of championing a new vision for South African capitalism. Lehulere (2003) charts COSATU's decade-long "road to the right," including its "zigzagging" responses to GEAR, that moves the federation from a socialist orientation in 1985 to classical Keynsianism in the early 1990s to right-Keynsianism and supply-side economics by 1996. Even its stated opposition to massive privatization in 2001, which included successful nationwide stay-aways (van Driel 2003), betrays evidence of this drift, as COSATU resisted following other allied social movements to broaden the struggle to an anti-GEAR campaign in general. In this context, COSATU gained a reputation for "talking left, walking right," an arguably worse position than the one taken by Thabo Mbeki's stated preference for talking right, acting right, with his oft-quoted remark, "Just call me a Thatcherite." The SACP's deteriorating authority within the tripartite alliance since Mbeki's rise to power signaled to its party apparatchiks the need to play it safe, an internal bait-and-switch so extensive "it soon got to the point where you could get expelled from the South African Communist Party for advocating communism" (Desai 2002).

As apartheid ended and the ANC era began, COSATU realized its dependence on northern unions was shortsighted, and it began to seek out more "local" international linkages. South African unions came to occupy a dominant—almost hegemonic—position within the region, much like the global role of US and European unions. But despite decades of work in the international realm, COSATU never laid out a coherent foreign policy agenda.

At times, COSATU unions have used their influence within global union federations (GUFs) to push for radical reforms and take decisive action The National Union of Mineworkers South Africa pressured the International Metalworkers Federation to adopt a principled stance in support of international sympathy strikes. COSATU's international activities have taken a variety of forms over the last decade. Through conferences and "exchange programs," COSATU encourages the cross-pollination of ideas between unions from neighboring countries. These junkets continued to grow in popularity among leadership, gradually giving way to the rank-and-file perception today that union dues still underwrite too many bureaucratic shindigs to major European and US cities (COSATU 2009).

Though Webster, Lambert, and Beziudenhout (2008) argue that COSATU has not taken advantage of the potential global linkages with GUFs, the federation has demonstrated hostility toward the global unions for reasons not dissimilar from its on-again, off-again animosity for the ICFTU. A 2009 COSATU document suggests that disagreements abound over issues of political ideology, the popular support of no-strike clauses in agreements signed by global unions, and a lukewarm approach to unionism that privileges activism (letter-writing, lobbying) over organizing (union growth). The document refers to GUFs as "individualist" and too narrowly focused on a sectoral approach. It concludes, "Although many unions are quiet in terms of the problems in the Global Unions, when reading between the lines it is clear that there is a general problem of different orientations amongst most South African unions and their respective Global Unions" (COSATU 2009: 24).

The Industrial Context of Private Security

The system of "weak states" in postcolonial Africa pressured leaders to utilize private security companies to maintain order in the absence of an underfunded public police force. The result has been a continent-wide proliferation of private policing, with almost no regard for actual security threats. "Economic gain is the only reason why private security actors are operating in Africa; the continent's peace and stability have no place on their agenda" (Gumedze 2007: 5).

Even compared to conflict-ridden Sierra Leone, Liberia, DRC, and Angola, the South African industry has seen exceptional growth. The overall value of the industry exploded from 1.2 billion in 1990 to 30 billion in 2007, making it the fastest growing industry in the country at 13 percent annually, with the guarding sector leading the way for the past decade (Minnaar 2007: 129). Hiring freezes, followed by massive retrenchments and voluntary resignations of public police officers after 1994, created a vacuum that had to be filled, given extraordinary levels of violent crime and a heavily armed civilian population. Many former police officers then started private security ventures. Today, the 1.7 million private security officers outnumber the public police and national military personnel combined (Goitom 2012).

Widespread violence in the cities and the townships, especially after 1994, contributed to insecurity as well as a fear of crime that has driven an increase in the use of private policing solutions for wealthy and middle-class neighborhoods. The number of registered private security companies in South Africa doubled from 2,200 in 1996 to 4,763 in 2006, and many experts believe that there are many more operating below the radar of the regulatory agency, the Private Security Regulatory Authority. Most are tiny companies, employing, as one company executive quipped, "three men, two guns, and a bakkie" (Bell and Pantland, quoted in Makgetla 2007). This proliferation of so many companies is impressive, given how many are swallowed up in mergers and acquisitions.

Labor costs account for 70 percent of the average South African security company, far outweighing other factors of production. Employers therefore have a deep interest in keeping wages low, which is conveniently facilitated by an impressive reserve army to choose from—between 2005 and 2006, security guard job applications increased by 400 percent (Makgetla 2007).

Lastly, the industry is characterized by "triangular" forms of employment such as "labor brokering." Twenty years ago, most security guards were employed by the company they guarded, just like janitors in LA. But then large security providers disrupted the direct employment link, adding a level of complexity to the relationship. The real test, however, has come with the advent of labor brokers, which *hire*—though not *employ*—low-skilled workers by placing them in temporary jobs with other employers. Labor broker services have prospered in the last two decades alongside a perceived need for a more flexible workforce. The practice has aroused considerable controversy since its inception, but especially since it was recently banned in neighboring Namibia. Unions have compared the practice, which originated in the United States, to indentured servitude and human trafficking, and the workers to "modern-day slaves."

In this environment G4S has grown into the largest employer on the African continent, employing sixty thousand personnel in South Africa alone. The country is seen as an investment gateway into the rest of Africa, making it an important market for any multinational. Guateng, for example, the area of the country containing Johannesburg, has a regional economy valued at 10 percent of the GDP of all of Africa. It is obvious why a company would want a stable business climate there, and equally understandable why a union with a strategy centered on major economic hubs would also need to establish itself in Johannesburg.

The Case of the SATAWU: Labor Transnationalism and Union Mobilization

SATAWU was formed in 1998 in response to COSATU's "one industry-one union" call for affiliates to consolidate through mergers between unions of different federations. In that sense it is itself the product of a revitalization scheme. Today the union represents workers in maritime shipping, aviation, cleaning, and security, where it is the majority union in the industry with 8 percent density.

SATAWU inherited a militant tradition of social movement unionism in the public sector. One of its parent unions, the South African Railway and Harbour Workers Union (SARHWU), led a historic upsurge in public-sector wildcats and slowdowns against National Party privatization schemes toward the end of 1989. These strikes encouraged new workers to join public-sector unions in droves. SARHWU also notably stood out amongst COSATU affiliates for consistently opposing the federation's lukewarm stance against privatization and cooperated with the International Transport Federation during coordinated solidarity protests and boycotts during apartheid (van Driel 2007). However, faced with new challenges, SATAWU made a break with its forerunners' propensity for social movement unionism, and in a short time it succumbed to stagnation.

SATAWU's plan to organize the fast-growing private security industry has been remarkably unstrategic, relying primarily on its reputation as a militant union to lure individual workers from any firm. As a result of its

failure to organize
(servicing model does not work)

failure to organize effectively, it has drifted inexorably toward a textbook servicing model in which it seeks to preserve its existing membership through one-on-one legal assistance and direct aid by union organizers. This is emblematic of a shift in the overall philosophy of what it means to be a union member and union organizer that is characteristic of so many South African unions—from an emphasis on mass mobilization to the juridical determination of contracts and labor law, a shift that sees workers not as *participants* in a movement but as *recipients* of a service.

Though in 2003 SATAWU resolved to bring 100,000 members into the union each year thereafter, between 2000 and 2006 its membership instead fell by one-third, including a loss of 28,913 members alone in 2002, more than any other COSATU affiliate that year (COSATU 2003). The union attributes this falloff to the usual assortment of labor market variables, but also its "failure of providing an effective service" (COSATU 2003). Declining membership and fewer dues meant self-imposed "belt-tightening" measures, including hiring freezes, and an economic situation in which it barely paid its primary expenses. Finally, in its resolutions to COSATU, SATAWU affirmed that they had a committed team of officials in the union. However, they addressed the need for COSATU and affiliates to allocate more resources toward servicing membership. Local unionists also report that increased servicing to membership has also been at the heart of COSATU's official renewal program for years, topping its list of ways to reverse declining power.

Changing roles of paid union staff, a greatly enlarged role of the trade union bureaucracy, and an increased dependence on the legalese of industrial relations suggest a shift to business unionism. Many in SATAWU claim that transformations in the roles of their officers mirror those in other unions as well. Interviews with representatives of other unions confirm this. For many unions in South Africa, this is where the story has recently ended. However, the campaign to win and implement a global agreement with G4S has provided a framework for SATAWU to transform itself and win significant gains in multiple ways.

Phase I: Campaigning for a Global Framework Agreement

SEIU and SATAWU began collaborating in 2005 at a time when both unions needed help. SATAWU was searching for a way out of its morass, and UNI needed partners for its global campaign against G4S. SATAWU had achieved some important victories in its security campaigns through mass demonstrations and protests. By 2005, it had won improvements in training regulations, a national provident fund, and a governmental determination of wage increases for security guards. Membership nevertheless declined steadily, and the union was pushed toward financial insolvency.

SEIU leaders traveled to South Africa in early 2005 to meet with SATAWU and other COSATU unions, a trip that served the dual purpose of seeking alliance partners and a dirt-digging mission on G4S to produce fodder for the global campaign. At this stage, SEIU was still focused primarily on whipsawing gains elsewhere to win against Wackenhut in the United States. In June 2005, SATAWU joined a delegation of other G4S workers in London at the company's annual general meeting of shareholders. The meeting served as a coming-out party for the global grassroots attack on G4S. Workers distributed Alternative Annual Reports highlighting worker abuses, racial discrimination, and other violations. One South African delegate was able to gain entry to the floor of the meeting and asked questions from the floor regarding the mistreatment of security guards in the Global South. The union returned from London energized. However, after its next bargaining session collapsed amid intra-union rivalry, it found itself mired in a brutal strike.

Historical disunity among the fifteen unions in the private security industry made bargaining difficult. Dissatisfied with the industry's offers, and having been undercut by fellow unions, SATAWU called an open-ended general strike in March 2006. The strike was the flashpoint of a crisis for SATAWU, one that clarified some of its failures and provided a pivotal point for renewal. About one hundred thousand security guards—one-third of the entire industry—took to the streets across the country, waging battles with rival unions and police. As many as sixty people are reported to have died in gruesome acts of strike-related violence, making it the bloodiest battle since 1994 (Makgetla 2007). Many observers therefore worried that the security strike foreshadowed a crisis in the new-and-improved mechanisms of labor adjudication, a view later reinforced by the violent janitors' strike in late 2006 and the Metrobus strike in 2007. Overall, the strike appeared incongruent with the promise of a peaceful, democratic, and multiracial capitalism.

Two important changes transpired after the strike ended in July 2006. First, in order to regain a semblance of order, and to sustain bargaining,

SATAWU had to discipline some of its own staff and rank-and-file activists who viewed the strike's conclusion as a capitulation. This process of internal reckoning can be seen as the first step of internal restructuring. However, union sources say the changes were not radical enough to create lasting impressions within the organization. Second, SATAWU learned to channel the frustration of its members into a new kind of activism. It began working more closely with UNI, which saw the sensationalism of the strike as a liability when constructing a transnational campaign with a high international profile.

UNI felt that the sensationalism of the strike was a liability when constructing a transnational campaign with a high international profile, and that it was crucial that SATAWU regain composure and clean up its public image. To do this, UNI helped SATAWU to redirect its anger and hostility to the company in a new way via the global campaign. After deliberation, SATAWU's daily strategy then became more closely embedded with UNI's focus against G4S. However, deep rifts soon developed about the domination of global priorities over local ones. SATAWU, for example, was steadfast in its opposition to focusing on only three strategic cities: Johannesburg, Durban, and Capetown. A SATAWU staffer explains that the work with UNI was slow to warm, and that some rank-and-file activists were skeptical of the idea:

> It's sometimes hard to get people [members] excited about those kinds of actions [international]. Especially in the beginning. Some are easy. But some people think, "That's over there. Why do I have to worry about over there when we got our own problems right here?"[6]

Still, SATAWU began to aggressively target the private security industry. UNI donated almost $100,000 of assistance to SATAWU for one year with the expectation that an additional two years would be necessary to fully develop its capacity to go it alone (UNI 2008). The money funded industry research and other component resources that laid the basis of an organizing plan, and the skills development to accomplish it. UNI-sponsored workshops on organizing, member mobilization, international solidarity, and strategic research helped build internal organization among existing members, and SATAWU established security guard worker committees in nine new sites. This activated a base of members who had become largely staff-dependent. Through these sessions, members have engaged in protests and meetings with G4S workers in other countries and have occasionally assisted SATAWU organizers in recruiting new members.

Nonetheless, new organizing largely failed, and UNI briefly considered abandoning South Africa as a site of struggle within the global campaign. SATAWU staff cite fear of management reprisals and poor access to worksites as the primary explanations for organizing difficulties. SATAWU again traveled to G4S's shareholder meeting in London, this time joined by workers from Mozambique and Malawi. As UNI had deepened its ties to developing world unions over the previous year, the action had a different character this time, focused decidedly more on human rights in the Global South, reflecting a new philosophy on framing strategies.

As described earlier, as investors began withdrawing and the OECD report came back in the union's favor, the company capitulated and the global agreement went into force in December 2008. It included access rights for SATAWU staff to G4S worksites and ostensibly restrained the company from anti-union campaigning when workers attempted to unionize. Though it provided a new arena for organizing workers, it also became a springboard for an overhaul of the union.

Phase II: Implementing the GFA and Increased Mobilization

Though SATAWU had fought to win the global agreement, and was determined to use it, the early stages of the implementation process were especially rocky. After the agreement was signed and UNI prepared for a more amicable relationship with the company, SATAWU was suddenly confronted with the prospect of collaboration, in a sense, with its historical adversary. One SATAWU organizer explained:

> Those people [G4S] called us kaffirs. Fucking guys, man. Who made us work in the rain, standing, no chairs, who we did anything for them. They're still white. It's a dangerous job and they never understand it. Then all of a sudden [after the GFA was signed] we are friends. I can tell you that people were upset. Many people were confused how this is going to work. It's not like that, I told them, but some people do not want to hear that.[7]

G4S did redress some of SATAWU's grievances (back wages, increased contribution to the pension fund), as stipulated in the agreement. However, while UNI complied with the agreement and removed its company-bashing website, G4S continued its long-standing anti-union bias in its corporate periphery, a posture that is out of line with the supposedly cooperative environment of the GFA. A G4S spokesperson in Pretoria, for example, said the GFA would not benefit the company or the workers and that she had no idea why it was signed in the first place. Implementation of the agreement in South Africa often required recourse to London, where G4S's home office was called upon by UNI to discipline its South African staff. Because UNI encouraged the dispute/resolution mechanism to happen outside the local context, it was, on occasion, charged with backroom dealing by SATAWU. During a conference on union internationalism, one SATAWU delegate, who had participated in UNI's global demonstrations in support of security guards, spoke about resentment regarding UNI:

> There's a disconnect. They [UNI/SEIU] have their priorities and we have ours. But to work together, we have to combine them . . . but we answer their demands, but they almost never answer ours. Because they drive the campaign. We do their actions. I think this is why there is the resentment sometimes.[8]

Even after years of collaboration, UNI and SATAWU were out of sync, and the global agreement risked becoming a paper exercise, as so many are. "They [SATAWU] wanted a magic bullet," explained one UNI staffer. "But the agreements don't work like that. You have to put them into practice."[9]

Nonetheless, SATAWU agreed to reorient its strategy to meet the demands of the global campaign and to continue working alongside UNI. In particular, it made several key decisions that moved it closer to the organizing ideas that UNI promoted. First, it began concentrating on the major metropolitan regions of Johannesburg and Durban, and it pulled staff from more rural or smaller cities into central offices. Here we see the influence of UNI's approach that focuses on global cities (see Lerner 2007). There was also a more intense focus on G4S as a target and a deemphasis on organizing within other firms.

Second, member leaders within the union's ranks suddenly had a job to do, and the renewed interest in building membership helped initiate workplace committees of pro-union guards. SATAWU organizers were trained to speak with member-activists one-on-one and to build a movement within worksites around the global agreement. During a COSATU conference, one SATAWU member said, "Yes, we have been talking with [other security guards] about organizing. This is new. It is a new kind [of organizing] and we are excited. It has excited others as well in our places [of work]."[10]

Organizing moved slowly, however, and the global agreement provided little assistance, as company intransigence and resistance were still high. Morale ebbed and flowed within SATAWU, as it occasionally seemed as though the agreement was pointless. But after approximately six months, through high-level talks among corporate and union leaders, UNI successfully convinced G4S to abandon much of its anti-unionism, and to respect the agreement it signed. According to UNI, G4S management pressured its leadership in Pretoria to abide by the GFA. Here we can see the impact of the global agreement strategy quite clearly.

SATAWU was granted access to G4S security guard worksites, and a handful of member activists won small amounts of paid leave for dedicated union work. As it became clear that the GFA offered access and neutrality— and thus a new means to organize workers—some of SATAWU's initial skepticism of the global campaign faded. It agreed to reorient its strategy toward building density within the three largest private security companies, and G4S in particular. This required an even greater commitment on the part of UNI to help construct an organizing program around the global agreement.

UNI staffers began more regular phone communication with SATAWU organizers, some of whom were hired specifically to work on the G4S campaign. Additionally, it held a series of trainings for leadership, staff, and member activists in South Africa. This communication opened a critical dialogue about the means to transform SATAWU from a servicing union to an organizing union. Industrial mapping research (a strategy to identify the largest, most densely populated worksites in a particular geographic area), compliments of UNI and SEIU, SATAWU was able to target the largest concentrations of guards and build up its density more quickly. Said one SATAWU staffer, "It was like a science. UNI thinks of organizing like a science. I didn't see it that way, but it is. This helped greatly."[11] Fifteen months after the agreement was signed, campaigns in Johannesburg and Durban brought an estimated three thousand security guards into the union, the majority in G4S. Given the extraordinary size of the private security industry, these gains were modest. But it represented approximately a 40 percent increase in the total number of the union's security guards members, and thus demonstrable growth.

Access to the premises has not only allowed easier conversations with workers. but it gave the union an air of legitimacy, a "right" to be there. This has gone a long way in convincing would-be members to set aside their fear of management retaliation for union activity. After a meeting with G4S representatives, a SATAWU organizer, proudly displaying the copy of the global agreement he had brandished at the meeting, said:

> This is my copy of the global agreement. It's like a bible, man. When management tells me to get out, I show them this. When workers are afraid to join, I show them this. When people tell me we don't have the right, I point to this. This this this. This is the key. But only if we use it right.[12]

Labor Transnationalism and Local Mobilization

The campaign to win the global agreement, and its subsequent implementation, provided a framework through which labor transnationalism had demonstrable impacts on local unionism. First, the global agreement restrained the company's sphere of action, thus allowing SATAWU to enter G4S worksites. But in order for any organizing to take place, SATAWU struggled to restructure its organization to accommodate an organizing ethos. Better access to workers decreased fear of management reprisals. Alongside a strategy and structure that promoted organizing, the union saw dramatic membership growth. How did this happen?

Earlier we saw that SATAWU placed great emphasis on servicing its membership base, especially in court or labor bureau tribunals. The casual observer at a SATAWU staff meeting would probably be given the impression that union organizers in South Africa were basically amateur lawyers hired by the national union to mediate disputes between workers and bosses. Explained a SATAWU leader: "We spent a lot of time in courts. We call them courts. Who knows what they are? Defending our members, sometimes winning other times losing. It's good work, yes, but it wasn't what a union was supposed to be doing."[13]

Union revitalization is a complex and open-ended process. A common dilemma in the literature has to do with the source and directionality of change: from above or below? This book sides with the middle-ground approach of Voss and Sherman (2000) that understands revitalization as interplay between leadership and the rank and file. This conclusion has particular relevance in South Africa, where the historically democratic and proletarian character of unionism was driven skillfully by ordinary workers with few paid staff, lending credence to a belief in the lower echelons as having a "historic mission" to reinvigorate social movement unionism.

Nevertheless, the account forwarded here identifies the wellspring of union change as originating *above*, and being implemented by a cohort of unionists in the *middle*, that is, the staff between union leaders and the rank and file.

> We run this place. SATAWU places a lot of emphasis on us. A lot of trust. If you have a question about SATAWU, you will get your answer from an organizer. . . . The leadership asks us what's going on, they make decisions according to what we tell them often. . . . If this place is gonna change, it will start with us.[14]

In other words, SATAWU's transformation into a union with more member activity, more internal democracy, more shop-floor organization, and more capacity to organize workers has been driven unmistakably by paid union staff, not rank-and-file workers. The middle strata of the union bureaucracy—the organizers, researchers, education specialists, representatives—have taken on a decisive role in the revitalization process. Their campaigns have led to growth in union membership in some major cities and an increased role for rank and filers on the shop floor. They have influential access to both the membership and the leadership, and they are often the route by which new ideas flow into the union, an observation consistent with Voss and Sherman's (2000) research on revitalization in the United States.

This change, however, is coming not only from *above* but also from *outside*. In the rich countries, SEIU has encountered resistance to what unions consider to be unnecessary levels of confrontation with management. In Johannesburg, it met nearly the opposite, accused of "spreading business unionism" and developing client unions that can do its bidding around the world, a biting appraisal that draws strength from the legacy of US labor imperialism in Africa. After five years of collaboration, however, it appears that UNI and SATAWU have forged an interdependent, international relationship that is in fact more symbiotic than previous examples during apartheid, many of which were one-way streets. As mentioned previously, the international solidarity of unions during the anti-apartheid struggle came largely in the form of financial support, not shoulder-to-shoulder solidarity and skill sharing.

An open question in this case is the sustainability of the reforms and the continued potential of organizing. The roles of organizers, representatives, and leadership changed throughout this campaign. Organizers have played a larger role in driving strategy than before, and leadership has redirected resources toward new organizing. Part of the rationale for better internal organization has been to train shop stewards to continue some of the necessary servicing functions. In other words, an effort has been made to accommodate a new modus operandi at the institutional/organizational level. But how do we know if these changes are cosmetic or sustainable? We cannot know, but we can make a good guess. Behrens, Hurd, and Waddington (2004) develop a framework to assess union restructuring. They argue that lasting examples of revitalization involve internal change that is motivated by environmental factors and a perceived new mission, both of which describe SATAWU's transformation.

Conclusion: Global Governance, Local Power

Complex global and local processes contributed to SATAWU's ability to organize locally. At the global level, a campaign was able to secure new rules for G4S security guards around the world. In South Africa, SATAWU combined this victory with increased mobilization at the grassroots level. New organizing victories were won by altering the rules that structure the relationship between workers and management. This chapter presents two related findings. The first is that labor transnationalism can inspire local union renewal. The second is that the consolidation of new rules—through the global agreement—is a necessary yet insufficient component of a renewal strategy. A local campaign is equally crucial. Based on the outcomes of the campaign to implement the GFA in Johannesburg, I conclude that the global agreement had *mobilization-type* impacts. In other words, the most pronounced outcome of the collaborative effort between UNI and SATAWU was that the latter transformed its internal structure and overall philosophy to encourage what it felt was a more strategic approach to organizing. Moreover, this process yielded results that quite literally *mobilized* members.

South African unions have moved through a series of different modes of transnational activity. But this case study deals with an example of what I have called "institutional transnationalism," as the GUFs, formal bureaucratized unions, and management, not the political parties or community-based unions, play dominant roles.

It is possible that the historically social movement character of South African unionism made the transition to organizing unionism far easier—or "natural"—than in other places, including in India, as we will see in the next chapter. But we can say with much confidence that the decisive factor here was the impact of the global agreement that contained management's anti-unionism and promoted the ability to organize. In this sense the global agreement helped carve out a space for SATAWU to do what UNI was training it to do.

The case of SATAWU demonstrates that the new rules structure secured in the GFA promoted the ability of SATAWU to organize more workers by restraining the company from campaigning against the union. As one SATAWU staffer put it, "The political system did not help us, our union movement did not help us, but the global agreement made a crack in the company, and let some light in."[15]

Chapter 5

Organizing the "Unorganized": Varieties of Labor Transnationalism in India

During a 2009 conference held at the Service Employees International Union's (SEIU) lower Manhattan office, a UNI Global Union staff person, speaking about the global campaign against Group 4 Securicor (G4S), said, "We thought if we can do this [organize low-wage service workers] in New York, New Jersey, New Mexico, even New South Wales, we can do it in New Delhi. But we were wrong. It turned out that we couldn't do it in any of those places without doing it in New Delhi first."

The Indian context proved to hold more obstacles to transnational collaboration than did South Africa, and the global agreement was less immediately useful there. This chapter tells the story of how those barriers were at least partially overcome through innovative campaigning, a commitment to organize, and a willingness to imagine the global framework agreement (GFA) as more than a new kind of labor contract. In this case, it was a bridge into the political realm.

Indian unions assisted in the overall struggle to win the global framework agreement, as described in chapter 3. In particular, workers in Bangalore and Kolkata used the agreement as grounds to build unions within the company, though each took a different approach, as I document later. I find that the unions' divergent approaches in the two cities are based on differing qualities of global-local union relationships, traditions of state patronage, and the legacies of labor internationalism and union imperialism. I also inquire into the possibility of union revitalization, but I conclude that the unions are indicative of the larger picture within India. That is, despite recent efforts to change union conduct, and slight possibilities emerging from structural changes, there is still much to do before unions can reverse their membership decline and substantially transform their organizations.

In South Africa we saw that global agreements can have "mobilization-type" effects by helping local unions forge new organizing campaigns. That is not the case here, where the global campaign instead provided the basis on which an important social dialogue process was able to develop, leading to potentially large-scale political reforms of the private security industry nationally. Therefore, we can say that the global agreement had "legislative-type" impacts in India. But the crux of the matter in India is not simply how the global agreement was used but the way in which Indian political economy structured a particular strategy of engagement for SEIU and UNI.

Dynamics of Indian Unionism

Some have suggested that union transnationalism is an unlikely phenomenon in India, based on the premise that the exceptional nature of Indian industrial relations makes it fundamentally incompatible with other varieties of unionism, thereby militating against successful cross-national cooperation (Kuruvilla, Das, Kwon, and Kwon 2002). Indeed, the practice of international unionism is largely absent from Indian labor historiography, except for the colonial-era union imperialism emanating from the United Kingdom. Moreover, today India is not integrated into the systems of regional trade union organization and has remained steadfast in its commitment against global trade-labor linkages. Aside from some recent ad hoc attempts, Indian unions have only a slim record of transnational collaboration. The G4S case, however, demonstrates that Indian and North American unions have been able to overcome the unique aspects of their own national systems.

Labor in Postcolonial India

Circumstances for Indian workers today are not circumscribed by colonialism, but they owe much to the legacy of industrial relations that was born prior to independence. When labor was relatively strong and committed to mobilization-based strategies, employment protection and income stability were guaranteed to labor in public works projects through the Industrial Disputes Act and the Factories Act, both of which survive today. Moreover, for six decades, except for the two-year interlude (1975–1977) of Indira Gandhi's Emergency, workers enjoyed a panoply of formal democratic rights. The political system therefore ensured worker protections despite low union densities and an erratic commitment to organizing, inscribing on trade unions a deep dependency on particular political parties and loyalty to these parties, a persistent phenomenon today. Nevertheless, despite high levels of institutional support, the Indian labor movement remains paradoxically enfeebled.

In the decades of the 1970s and 1980s, the state began retreating from the promises of "Nehruvian socialism" amid widespread restructuring of the global political economy. The addition of the Contract Labor Act to India's myriad legislative statutes introduced employment flexibility to the Indian industrial relations landscape (Hill 2009). These developments undermined union densities and set the stage for further liberalization policies in the early 1990s.

From Dirigisme to Neoliberalism

Many regard the July 1991 announcement of the New Economic Policy as a decisive moment in Indian history, a defining feature of the transition from state planning to neoliberalism.

Kuruvilla and Erickson (2002) argue that the central tendency of Indian industrial relations has been transformed since the early 1990s from an authoritarian logic of maintaining labor peace to a logic promoting labor flexibility. It is popular to stress the legacy of dirigisme as anathema today, as much has changed since liberalization, with enormous implications for unions and workers. The new policies ended the system of licensing procedures in manufacturing (the "license permit raj"), liberalized the capital markets and terms of entry for foreign investment, and increased the development of export-processing zones, which had the cumulative effect of generating new interstate rivalries for investment, precipitating a race to the bottom of labor standards inside the country and increasing work-seeking migration (Bhattacherjee 2001). The last fifteen years of reforms demonstrate a disjuncture between the perceived nature of Indian labor law as rigid and its actual flexibility. Moreover, underneath India's economic boom, the delinking of growth and employment, combined with declining unionization, has resulted in fewer prospects for upward mobility for the majority of India's people.

Collectively, these changes have increased the challenges facing Indian trade unions. Though the challenges are common to many developing countries, they are compounded in India by an institutional framework that has served to amplify labor's structural deficits rather than abridge them (Chibber 2005). A primary obstacle to the trade unions is the growing tendency of Indian employers to informalize the labor force. Against the predictions of development theory, growth has not been labor-absorbing. Rather, liberalization has actually promoted employment flexibility, so much so that today the vast majority of Indian workers fall within the "unorganized" or informal sector. It should be noted that the terms "organized" and "unorganized" are the official titles given to what most scholars typically call the "formal" and "informal" sectors of the economy, respectively. Private security guards, such as those employed by G4S, fall within this sector because their conditions of work and quality of life are highly precarious.

As so many enterprises straddle the divide between the two categories, the work lives of formal-sector laborers are anything but stable either. The data show definitively that formal-sector workers have lost jobs not to mechanization but to contract laborers (Sengupta and Sett 2000). Employer strategies have therefore skillfully structured animosity between "organized" and "unorganized" laborers at the same time that the real distinction between each sector has become blurred.

While the immediate effects of liberalization have been largely negative for unions, unanimous political support for liberalization encouraged a slight but noticeable rupture between unions and their political parties, which many in the labor movement regard as a positive development. Despite reports of declining membership, there was an increase in union action during the liberalization period. These protests, largely described as blowback against the wide-ranging support by the state, parties, and employers for neoliberal policy, took the form of strikes, mass marches, walkouts, traffic blockades, and hunger strikes. Though these actions did not succeed in blocking liberalization schemes, they did slow the process considerably, and they increased public sentiment against it: public opinion against privatization increased from 34 percent in 1996 to 48 percent by 2004 (Yadav 2004). In the middle of the market-based reforms, Indian unions also won groundbreaking legislation to benefit poor families through a massive public works program known as the National Rural Employment Guarantee Act (Bhowmik 2009).

Therefore, though they are a central part of the equation, neoliberal developments do not explain the totality of labor's weakness in India. The weakness of labor in India was in no way preordained by neoliberal constraints but, rather, owes much to the strategic choices of labor unions themselves. Today it is also important to contrast the discourse of labor flexibility and informality with the extreme structuring of work relations along a matrix of nonclass factors: caste, gender, religion, language, and age. These sociocultural identities are still strong determinants of what people do and the conditions under which they do it, and they give rise to the political formations that inhibit class formation. As Barbara Harriss-White and Nandini Gooptu (2001: 236) argue:

> If class is first a struggle over class and second a struggle between classes, we can say the overwhelming majority of the Indian workforce is still kept engaged in the first struggle, while capital, even though stratified and fractured, is engaged in the second.

These dynamics bring us even closer to an understanding of the massive fissures among workers in India, and the impact these have on unified working-class mobilization. Today, while numbers vary, approximately 2 percent of the 47 million Indian workers belong to a trade union—the vast majority of which are concentrated in the public sector—spread over five major union federations, each controlled by a political party. Therefore the Indian labor market consists primarily of the expanding unorganized sector—now up to about 94 percent of the workforce—and a tiny formal sector that exists as a protected oasis, a happenstance that has given rise to the prevailing conception of Indian union members as cardholders in an elite club who are unwilling to share their privilege with others.

As firm-level unions proliferated independently of affiliation to national federations in the 1980s, unions multiplied quickly. There are about sixty-six thousand registered trade unions today, though some estimate the actual number might be as high as one hundred thousand, organized along myriad axes. In this scenario, fierce interunion competition has militated against solidarity. Rudolph and Rudolph (1987) have referred to the Indian situation as "involuted pluralism," a term used to describe the paradoxical multiplication and simultaneous weakening of interest groups.

Even within this context of weakness and extreme labor pluralism, however, there are exceptional developments as well. First, we see a slow movement toward independent unionism outside the sphere of party control, especially embodied by the creation of the National Centre for Labor and the New Trade Union Initiative, an umbrella organization of this new movement. The Self-Employed Women's Association, a union-type formation arising from Gujarati garment unions, has since the early 1970s been a voice in the wilderness within India, though it has recently been joined by other informal-sector movements (Gallin 2001). Agarwala (2008) explains that the strategies of *bidi* (a thin cigarette) makers and construction workers have changed as their industries have become increasingly informalized. Where once these groups targeted employers and aimed for worker rights, they now make demands on the state and demand welfare benefits instead. However, whereas in Agarwala's studies this is due to the plethora of tiny employers that characterize the informal sector and are unable to really bargain with their employees, in the case of the security guards studied here it results from the company's power to resist bargaining, which encourages the union to demand that the state intervene. These trends have led some in the labor movement to assert that Indian trade unions are in the midst of a wide-scale revitalization process. While these examples highlight an important degree of restructuring, it is premature to announce the arrival of a new phase of unionism.

This brief discussion helps us situate the case study within the context of a historically weak and fragmented trade union movement and amid some experimentation for renewal led by informal-sector worker organizations. The other important context to consider when evaluating the local pressures on unionism, in this case, is the remarkable rise of the security industry.

The Industrial Context of Private Security

The eleven coordinated terrorist attacks in Mumbai in 2008 were a startling rationale for increasing private security forces. Nevertheless, more than one year later the *New York Times* reported, "In much of India the first line of defense against crime stands just over five and a half feet tall, earns less than $100 a month and is armed with little more than a shiny belt buckle . . . [and is] enamored [first and foremost] by the uniform" (Timmons 2009). Although terrorism, and its continued perceived threat, has been a boon for security giants like G4S, a local trade group, the Central Association of Private Security, says that companies have done almost nothing to improve the quality of training that new recruits receive.

The expansion of the private security industry in India has paralleled the transition to free market capitalism detailed previously, but it has also exceeded typical service-sector growth. The service sector grew quickly in the 1980s and further accelerated in the 1990s, averaging 7.5 percent growth each year, surpassing rates in industry and agriculture (Gordon and Gupta 2003). The most famous dimension of the growth in services has been in software and information technology (IT)-enabled services, although the growth in services in India has been much more broad based than just in IT.

Private security and facilities services are located at the intersection of many growth industries in India. G4S offers clients a variety of standard services for a security company: guarding, cash transit, technology-based security (cameras, radio, etc.), executive protection, armed guarding, and automobile fleet tracking. It now produces garments for both Indian and British uniformed personnel and has specially designed security solutions for the IT and IT-enabled sector. It has also started a division called "First Select," which links corporate clients with potential employees. Its "facilities management" department advertises itself as a "one-stop shop" for a variety of solutions that essentially give G4S a monopoly at work sites that require multiple service inputs.

G4S employs 150,000 people in India, making it by far the market leader and also the largest transnational employer in the country, with over twice as many employees as the next largest competitor, Topsgroup. Over the two decades for which G4S and its parent companies have operated in India, it claims to have "created a new job" every eighty minutes, or thirty-two jobs each day. Since it has grown fast by mergers and acquisitions, most of these jobs are not actually "new." However, they are impressive figures nonetheless.

Because of this expansive growth, G4S credits itself with nothing less than inventing the Indian security industry. According to a local manager, fifteen years ago a security guard in India was a "guy in a dirty lungi holding a big stick." G4S, as the largest Indian security company, has helped foster the growth of an industry that in earlier years was simply an afterthought, nurtured by the rapid growth of the IT sector in a few large cities—Bangalore, Hyderabad, Mumbai, Kolkata, and Mysore. Since the 2008 terrorist attacks in Mumbai, and with the continued tension in Kashmir, the rationale for private security has also been strengthened, as the military has been stretched increasingly thin. Filling these more serious security voids has been made possible in light of G4S's 2006 acquisition of the Armor group, a private military contractor with operations in Iraq, Afghanistan, and the India-controlled Kashmir.

G4S claims to be the most densely unionized security company in the world, with over two hundred "union agreements" in force. In the Asia-Pacific region, about 20 percent of its operations are unionized. Nevertheless, G4S security guards in India still live in brutal poverty, and guards regularly report illegally low wages, contributions to pensions being withheld, and poor treatment at work.

But the background story of Indian security guards is not only couched in political economy terms. Security professionals have strikingly different cultural significance in different parts of the country. Interview partners in Kolkata, for example, revealed that a large number of security guards lie about their profession to their families because it is seen as so lowly. "We cannot ever say we are in security. Our wives would simply not hear this. It is not a good career."[1] In other places, such as in the North East region near Darjeeling and the Nepal border, the Gurkha people project enormous pride in the security industry, stemming from their legacy as fierce warriors with the British. And though a guard for G4S is in no way the same as a highly skilled Gurkha mercenary, the job of protecting one's homeland, if an Indian private security guard can be conceived of as doing that, is a badge of honor.

This backdrop helps lay out some of the various forces weighing on the ability of the campaign to be successful in India, or even to start at all. It was an important testing ground for a union movement with little experience in transnationalism and for a strategy that had never been implemented in a context as different from the United States.

Case Study

Phase I

SEIU and UNI initially thought the global agreement would have universal applicability. In many ways they thought and hoped it would function close to the way it did in Johannesburg. But local constraints presented obstacles that forced a different kind of campaign in India. Because India is G4S's largest market, and collaborative work among the unions was facilitated by a common ability to use the English language, the campaign in India became a critical component of a multipronged pressure strategy during the global campaign.

SEIU leaders visited India in 2005 in search of partner unions in the private security industry. The labor movement's historical disunity—on the basis of political party affiliation, caste, geography, and religion—meant it was necessary to first create a new organization of the warring factions. One SEIU leader explains:

> We literally went around the country interviewing people to see if we found anyone that we could work with and that wanted to work with us. You know, we'd never done something like that before. . . . It turned out we couldn't work with the Hindu nationalists. It just wasn't going to work, right? I mean it was really really bad. But so we found others. We found some of the best people we know here.[2]

By 2007, after completing its tour of the country's seven largest labor federations—"our long strange trip," according to one staffer—SEIU settled on the Indian National Trade Union Congress (INTUC), which was affiliated with Congress, and the Communist-controlled Centre of Indian Trade Unions (CITU). Historically, the INTUC unions were successful in building density in the large public-sector enterprises in Karnataka, whereas CITU's strength had always been concentrated in the industrial belts of West Bengal.

The resultant organization, the Indian Security Workers Organizing Initiative (ISWOI), was perhaps the first of its kind in India, as it bridged deep political divides. ISWOI was composed of a ten-person governing council, consisting of UNI staff and representatives of CITU and INTUC and their affiliates in the security industry. Its quarterly meetings occasionally included management representatives as well. This deliberative body was chaired by an SEIU staffer in the United States and coordinated by an India-based UNI staffer and made all the decisions concerning the strategy of the campaign.

By late 2007, UNI had also established three offices in India to coordinate a variety of campaigns throughout the country; these offices were called Union Development and Organizing Centers (UNIDOC). The private security campaign was notable for focusing exclusively on workers within the vast informal sector. To shine a spotlight on these invisible workers, UNI exploited the dubious claim of the country to be a large democracy with a growing economy in its report, *Inequality Beneath India's Economic Boom* (2009). The document demonstrates that G4S guards receive poverty wages, often below the legal minimum, work long hours without overtime pay, have no job security, and are denied the right to organize independent unions. UNI also hired legal experts who produced similarly damning profiles and case studies of the company that framed the debate in terms of political and human rights.

ISWOI began to play a larger role in the global effort by applying pressure locally to G4S. First, local unions engaged the G4S management in a number of legislative battles, kick-starting a process aimed at a reinterpretation of the confusing array of labor laws. In June 2007, ISWOI unions also participated in global demonstrations involving dozens of security guard unions around the globe.

The 2008 decision of the company's British management to submit to the demands of the global campaign was supposed to ripple through its subsidiary branches around the world and impact all 150,000 G4S employees in India. However, when asked why his company had settled with the union, an Indian G4S manager shrugged his shoulders. "It's not my job to ask those questions," he said. "The decision was not ours."[3] The failure of the parent company to adequately inform its affiliates, especially those in its largest market, was the prelude to a confusing process of implementation.

Phase II

After the successful negotiation of the global agreement, among the first organizational decisions was to determine the scope of practice for each union in ISWOI, as it became clear that the historical divides were actually too large to bridge. It was then decided that INTUC would have sole organizing rights over G4S workers in Bangalore and Kochi, whereas CITU would operate in Kolkata and New Delhi. The strict division of labor was an essential aspect of the campaign strategy. For up to two years, however, jurisdictional battles nonetheless broke out between the two organizations in Mysore, Mumbai, Hyderabad, Pondicherry, and New Delhi.

Both INTUC and CITU began their collaboration with UNI in 2007, when ISWOI was formally adopted as the campaign's strategic framework, but its work increased after the global agreement was signed, as it offered an initial promise of work site access and employer neutrality. UNI organizers, transplanted fulltime to India, mentored local unionists in Delhi, Bangalore, Kolkata, and Kochi on the ins and outs of North American organizing unionism—strategic mapping, one-on-one conversations with workers, data collection, and an explicit focus on the market-dominant company. However, despite a common cause and a shared organization, the unions have taken markedly different approaches to implementing and defending the global agreement.

BANGALORE

In Bangalore, UNI worked with the Private Security Guards Union (PSGU), an INTUC affiliate aligned with the Congress Party. In the late 1980s, twin brothers Muthappa and Muddappa formed the first garment workers' union in the state. By 2005, security guards at union garment factories began clamoring for unionization as well, which became the inspiration for the PSGU. Muthappa has played a critical role in the construction of ISWOI and is probably the most committed Indian unionist within its ranks. Although politically he is a Socialist, he prefers the union politics of the Congress Party to those of the Communist unions.

In 2007, as per UNI's suggestion, the PSGU committed itself to building density primarily within G4S. At 4,300 members, the union roughly tripled in size since it began working with UNI. UNI paid for another PSGU staffer to work in Bangalore to help motivate G4S workers to join the union. All in all, despite significant membership gains, organizing has been difficult. The company has intensified its retaliation against organizers and member activists. On-site violence, related to union politics, has become more common as well, as the organizing environment has created divides among guards.

Frustrated by management's stance, the union activity has produced important results for security guards statewide. Union pressure obliged G4S to offer appointment letters to new hires, detailing the terms of the employment relationship, disregarding the practice of using labor brokers and other third-party entities to hire guards. The company also began to pay statutory benefits such as minimum wages, more regular contributions to workers' pensions, overtime pay, and bonuses to workers based on seniority, finally bringing the company into compliance with the Contract Labor Law. Because these gains apply to workers company-wide, not only to G4S union members, these increases will effectively double the value of the salaries of 150,000 informal-sector workers, who currently earn approximately two hundred rupees a day, or about four US dollars. Finally, thousands of identity cards have been issued to union members; this affords them an opportunity to open a bank account or to receive a loan, a gain that has been shown to be vital to other campaigns of informal workers (Agarwala 2006).

Historically, the union had built membership through mass recruitment meetings, often targeting politically radical workers, at which union leaders extolled the virtues of union membership and then passed out some union cards to sign. The meetings were advertised by militant workers or staff who handed out leaflets as workers left the job site. The union began to shift its recruitment process under the influence of UNI to focus on one-on-one meetings with guards at worksites and homes. The absorption of a North American-style "organizing model" is deep and obvious. Leaders in Bangalore credit UNI and its organizers with disseminating a new way of building the union, one that they are eager to extend to their own work. During several meetings with worker activists, for example, there were lively debates on the value of mapping and how best to carry it out. Mapping refers to the process by which unions lay out the industrial landscape of a particular place through outreach and field research in order to determine what the strengths and weaknesses of a particular company or industry may be. Factors to be taken into account include the relative density of employees to managers, financial assets, the proximity of other similar union businesses, and so forth. Admittedly, the organizing orientation has redirected the political orientation of some local organizers and replaced it with a heavy reliance on numbers, as in the US-style model.

"Now, [organizing is] a science," says one PSGU organizer. "We have a plan of action. We have a strategy. We have number goals and we must reach them. That is something new. It is a good thing."[4]

The PSGU has also incorporated the global agreement into its organizing message and has translated it into regional languages such as Kannada, Tamil, Malayalam, and Telugu. In October 2009, at a meeting in a slum on the outskirts of Bangalore, PSGU organizers spoke with security guards about the global campaign and the systematic way in which they were carrying out an organizing plan. The meeting took place in a building that houses about a hundred workers. It is a common landing pad for new migrants from Assam, Orissa, Bihar, and Andhra Pradesh, poorer states from which many security guards in Karnataka immigrate. At first, workers were hesitant, and conversation in Hindi and Kannada was stilted. But after an older worker who was already a union member spoke up in Tamil, twelve others signed cards.

The company has yet to recognize the union, has been delaying discussions over economic issues for years, and has carried out a public assault on union leaders. Reports by guards of physical and emotional abuse are common, with one union activist claiming he was pushed to attempt suicide as a result of company harassment. G4S has in fact initiated contact with rival unions, as an anti-ISWOI strategy. In this environment, the global agreement has been completely ineffective in bringing the company to a union-neutral stance, which has led some in the union, including ISWOI council members, to conclude that the global agreement is a "waste of paper that we cannot afford."

PSGU has generally relied on ISWOI council meetings to voice its concerns to high-ranking G4S management. In June 2010, however, its union leaders swore not to attend another ISWOI meeting for the purpose of discussing the global agreement with G4S, citing the company's massive intransigence, sentiments shared by local INTUC and Congress Party leaders as well.

Speaking to the frustration of local unionists, a former UNI staffer in Geneva said:

We have an issue of expectations. . . . They [the Indian unionists] thought that this thing [the global agreement] would solve all our problems. That the company would react. Well, it has, actually. It has, but not the way they'd like. We need to show them that this can work. Patience is not easy to come by here, though.[5]

KOLKATA

In Kolkata, where patience is in even more limited supply, CITU has taken a decidedly different approach to implementing the global agreement. Membership in CITU's security guard union hovers around fifteen thousand, more than the membership of the other ISWOI unions combined. It has been organizing security workers for fifteen years, longer than any of the other ISWOI unions. Approximately one-third have joined since the global agreement was signed in 2008 (UNI 2009). However, CITU has not focused its campaigns on G4S workers to any great degree, choosing to build membership within any company with willing workers.

For more than three decades, CITU had relied on its deep connection to the West Bengal's Communist-led Left Front government to secure wage gains and provide a favorable terrain for union activity. Its collaboration with UNI has not been deep, and it has generally resisted the adoption of new strategies to help it grow. Instead, it has continued to rely on its function as a labor broker, connecting unemployed workers with temporary jobs in informal industries such as security, contract cleaning, and domestic work. It has amended this strategy, however, by adding a postscript to its usual message: "We tell them [the security guards] the company wants us to be in unions; that is the strongest message of why the company signed the global agreement in the first place. Then they will join."[6]

After three decades of central planning, the Left Front government (which was finally unseated in the last election) maintained decent relationships with large employers that allowed a degree of cooperation with CITU. Though this is not its stated modus operandi, this strategy became clear during a meeting with security guards, during which many of them claimed to support CITU's security guard union because it found them work in an otherwise jobless economy. The union does this on a rotating basis to ensure fairness and to secure the loyalty of as many workers as possible. Workers sign a union card and take a number, and eventually CITU connects them with a job.

The global agreement has not been incorporated into the union's organizing strategy, and there is no real interest in anything like an organizing model. A CITU organizer explained:

> We have our way. We don't go and pretend to be from somewhere else and ask to fill in this survey and ask all these questions and then come back days later and say, "Oh, hi, I am from the union, from CITU." No, we go there and we tell the people we are the union. We tell them to join, to be united and strong. That's the way we do it. We have always done it this way.[7]

He raises two important points that pertain to the implementation of the organizing model. The first touches on the issue of how unions approach nonunion workers, the second on data collection. Many North American labor organizers understand a union-organizing drive as having distinct phases; first secret and underground and then public. For the security unions in India, the idea of beginning covertly was new and, at first, disconcerting. Though the PSGU has come to see the value of this step with time, CITU has remained skeptical.

However, CITU has slowly come to appreciate the value of detailed record keeping and data collection. It may seem like a simple activity, but in practice it was not easy to adopt. A local official explained:

> It was strange to us and strange to them [the workers]. Why do we want to know where they live? Why do we want to know how many children they have? If they are married, if they have a vehicle, if they have other jobs. What business is that of ours?[8]

None of the unions have anything resembling a dedicated research department, and the organizers, many of whom come out of the rank and file, have no experience in interviewing strangers about their lives. They do not consider detailed data collection an obvious part of union organizing. In India, the information and statistics deficit within the trade union movement is mirrored on the grand scale when one endeavors to search for reliable data from the government. However, gradually the practice of record keeping has become part of the organizing process, and all the unions claim to have benefited from UNI's insistence on having more information at its disposal. As a UNI organizer in India declared, "I counted every single damn union card that came into that office. I know how many people are there. They know. They didn't like it, but now they know."[9] A CITU organizer agreed. "Before, we knew we had workers," he said. "Now, we know who they are. It's better that way." A 2009 document shows that since the start of the organizing campaigns in 2007, union membership in ISWOI-affiliated unions *grew* by 1,300 in Delhi, 3,060 in Bangalore and Mysore, 1,800 in Kochi, and 10,435 in the state of West Bengal (UNI 2009). SEIU's sanitized history of itself, in the form of a purple coffee table book, likewise suggests the campaigns in India brought "more than 22,000" workers into the fold in roughly the same time frame (Stillman 2010). All these numbers, but especially those from Kolkata, are highly dubious and do not square with the overwhelming frustration experienced by local Indian organizers and UNI staff placed in the country. But beyond the cloudy interpretations of union membership lies a deeper question about transnational collaboration.

Except for a reluctant acceptance of record keeping, CITU's security guard union largely ignored the advice of UNI on issues of strategy. However, when its local discussions with management occasionally break down, CITU has sought help further up the chain of command, relying on UNI's global social dialogue process and the company's works council to intervene, neither of which has proven effective. At other times it has used protests at worksites, strikes, and hunger strikes to draw attention to the poor conditions under which security guards labor.

While the UNI organizers were generally welcomed in Bangalore, unionists in Kolkata were far more hostile to the idea of outsiders in the movement. After four years of UNI's presence in India, interviews conducted for this project suggest that none of UNI's staff have fared well with CITU leaders. One local Indian organizer remarked as follows on his feelings about UNI's leadership in Kolkata: "They [UNI] sent us girls. Two girls. I am a good man, nothing wrong with girls. But this is a trade union of security guards. You see what I mean?"[10] While this comment is illustrative of some of the sociocultural conflict UNI encountered, it is also evidence of a fundamental truism common to both trade unions and transnational corporations operating in India: they are both dominated, with fierce determination, by men.

In 2009, the union held a successful two-day stay-away to pressure G4S to pay pension fund contributions. Then, in April 2010, to force G4S to comply with a series of demands for job security, appointment letters, and back pay, CITU conducted simultaneous actions in Delhi and Kolkata, including a protest in front of the British Embassy, which employs G4S guards. These actions, though technically in breach of the global agreement, and organized apart from UNI, resulted in a favorable determination from G4S to distribute back pay, for wages dating as far back as three years earlier, to over one hundred workers. CITU's governing ally had been a primary partner in these local actions and had worked to pressure many companies, not just G4S, to pay the minimum wage.

In 2010, CITU officials decided that CITU would no longer accept financial support from UNI, citing "ideological differences," and an official in Delhi suggested that CITU would soon reconsider its participation within ISWOI altogether. He said, "We cannot say for sure what good [ISWOI] has done us, and maybe we might be better without it."[11] Today it is no longer a part of UNI's India campaigns.

NATIONWIDE

To this day, management in India is out of compliance with the global agreement in that it represses any instance of trade union organizing activity. But the global agreement has been effective in other ways.

In early 2009, G4S lost two contracts with large players in the Hyderabad-based technology sector (IBM and WIPRO)—with rumors about a third in the Salt Lake Area outside Kolkata—after it was forced to pay higher wages and larger pension contributions. "Do you know how difficult it is to stay competitive in India?" asked a G4S representative. "Do you know how many businesses try to do our work better and cheaper than us?"[12]

In light of these developments, where union employers are being punished in the market, UNI has shifted to a new approach. The social dialogue process between UNI and G4S has not given rise to union rights or organizing neutrality as it has elsewhere. However, after a year of lobbying the state, with the company's support, it has nearly won nationwide legislation that could raise standards for security guards across the industry, effectively extending aspects of the global agreement into India's political arena.

Such legislation will undoubtedly require vigilance on the part of unions to implement it where it does not happen automatically. And given the fierce opposition of most of the industry and the pathetically low levels of unionization, it is unlikely to be implemented easily or immediately. Regardless of this, the legislation sets an important legal and political precedent for workers in the informal sector. The prospect of such a law was nearly crushed when UNI essentially abandoned its campaigns in India in late 2010 as a result of bureaucratic and financial difficulties. Indian law briefly prohibited UNI from funding its affiliate unions, causing it to remove its full-time staff person who was responsible for running the ISWOI coalition. However, UNI has once again been able to move its resources and staff in and out of the country freely and resumed the campaign where it left off.

Varieties of Labor Transnationalism

Why have CITU and INTUC unions used the global agreement differently? The unions' divergent approaches—and varied successes—are based on (1) global-local union relationships, (2) traditions of state patronage, and (3) the legacies of labor internationalism and union imperialism.

Probably the most significant factor that determines the extent to which a global agreement is implemented is the relationship between the global union federation and the affiliate union or union group, an interaction between the global and local arenas. We can clearly understand the desperate need for "bridge builders" to span the global-local divide when we examine the Indian case. Local unionists in Bangalore were far more receptive to UNI's message and its staffers than local unionists in Kolkata for a number of reasons.

There is a strong UNI culture in Bangalore, absent from Kolkata, that exerts influence through the UNIDOC office. Though the PSGU has its own office, it holds most of its general meetings at the UNIDOC headquarters in Vasantanagar, in a spacious, clean office with a large meeting room decorated with photographs from UNI's various global solidarity actions. UNIDOC houses multiple unions, each conspicuously named "UNI," plus its corresponding trade names: UNITE (UNI-IT-Enabled Services), UNICOM (Tele-Communications), UNIFIN (Financial Services), and so on. UNI has positioned itself as the primary organizing body not only for workers in the vast informal economy but also in the fast-growing services sector in Bangalore and Hyderabad. If there is a union in India with its finger on the political-economic pulse of the country's future, it is UNI.

Though the UNIDOC structure emphasizes industrial unionism, its constituent unions in the technology-related industries organize young workers by catering to a privileged class of professionals on the basis of status, income, and knowledge-based labor. These workers, UNIDOC staffers say, are of a new era, and they do not identify with the public-sector unions that have dominated the landscape throughout Bangalore's history. One might say that the new workforce is presumed to have a different habitus than the average Indian union member, which inclines him or her to reject trade unions in favor of elite associations. UNI's IT union, for example, the only union to materialize so far in the Indian IT industry, claims twenty thousand members and makes recruitment appeals almost solely through an online portal that describes the organization as a powerful non-governmental organization. Nonetheless, UNI enjoys a positive reception within UNIDOC that is crucial to its success.

In contrast, CITU staffers report significant dissatisfaction with the UNI campaign. A CITU leader in Kolkata waves his hand dismissively in the air at the mention of UNI, as if batting away a fly. He also expresses a sense of hopelessness about the ISWOI coalition. Though he clearly states CITU's deep desire for labor movement unity, he doubts that INTUC shares his commitment to nonpartisanship, and therefore he thinks ISWOI is more a UNI-directed front group than a legitimate, heterogeneous Indian organization. He raised his hands and moved his fingers so as to suggest the movements of a puppeteer bringing life to a marionette.

This leader said membership growth has been no different since the collaboration started. But he is more troubled by the fact that CITU and the Indian unions seem to be under the influence, and direction, of UNI and SEIU. "We are not sure what good this has done," said another staffer at CITU. "We have to ask this question: 'Right now, why would workers join this union [ISWOI]?' I have no idea," he said.[13]

Second, the historical patterns of labor mobilization are embedded in the divergent political contexts of the two city-states of Bangalore and Kolkata. The CITU's close connections to the reigning Communist Party of India (Marxist) meant that for over thirty years the union faced little resistance from the state and attracted members based on their political affiliations more than for any other reason. This situation led to a lack of incentive to develop a coherent organizing program for growth, since the state's role in mediating disputes and guaranteeing wages and conditions was so dominant.

In Karnataka, in contrast, although the INTUC unions grew alongside the Congress Party and enjoyed success in their state-run enterprises, the party has never held the same degree of control over the local political economy. In fact, the political history of Karnataka is opposite to that of West Bengal, as competing parties have for decades won alternating elections. As Patrick Heller (2000) describes for Kerala, this situation impresses upon parties the need to fight for local allegiances, creating a more active political climate. This has meant that unions in Bangalore have matured and are less dependent on party-state alliances than elsewhere. Moreover, comparably rapid deindustrialization, the dramatic rise of services, and the Bharatiya Janata Party's recent electoral victories have forced the unions into a new quest for relevancy. Though union density fell as it did elsewhere, the circumstances listed above nonetheless seem to have sounded an important alarm for workers in Bangalore, where the old state-sector unions are organizing again and the new autonomous unions have found a significant reception among workers in the construction and telephone industries.

Finally, different historical experiences with transnational labor cooperation have affected the way unions in each place relate to UNI, and therefore the extent to which the global agreement has had currency. European trade unions have works council structures to help coordinate union actions and share information, even if they are sometimes dominated by management interests. Likewise, Latin American trade unions benefit from their involvement in regional politics through Mercosur (Southern Common Market), and even African unions have, at times, taken advantage of bodies such as the Southern African Development Community to coordinate regional activity. India lacks such integration into an Asian bloc or trade union association. CITU unionists were also at the forefront of the movement that successfully opposed a social clause in global trade agreements and World Trade Organization rules, preferring to bank on the comparative advantage of poor workers in attracting jobs rather than to raise standards everywhere. Indian trade unionism has therefore remained largely isolated and isolationist, despite the country's status as a emerging power in the global economy.

Despite this legacy, higher levels of direct foreign investment in Bangalore have meant that workers there, especially in major growth industries, have recently been brought into contact with campaigns led by unions outside the country. Such is the case in the construction, telecommunications, security, contract cleaning, and chemical industries. In contrast, Kolkata, as the erstwhile capital of the British Empire in India, was on the receiving end of much imperialistic union activism from the United Kingdom. This has impacted the perception of international collaboration with local unions to this day. A CITU leader spoke to his relationship with UNI staff:

> They [UNI] don't understand us. It's as simple as that. To work with people, you have to understand what they do, how they operate, what they are like. They know us only as workers, not as people. We have our way, and it is not theirs, and they are pressurizing us to change. Okay, so that is their job. But we do our job and we do not do it like they want always. So, you can say we are not in agreement at all times. It has always been like that for Indians and Europeans, you know this, right? Read, ask people, you will see.[14]

Conclusion: Governance Struggles and Making Local Unions

In *A Million Mutinies Now*, prize-winning novelist and essayist V. S. Naipaul writes:

> With industrialization and economic growth people had forgotten old reverences. Men honored only money now. In seeking to rise, India had undone itself. No one could be sure of anything; all was fluid . . . many long-buried particularities had been released. These disruptive, lesser loyalties—of region, caste, and clan—now played on the surface of Indian life. (Naipaul 1991: 5).

Naipaul is referring to the paradox of "modernization," otherwise known as "capitalist development," in India. Instead of erasing the identifications of the old world, as predicated by modernization theory, and anticipated by the captains of industry, the capitalist revolution in India has reignited them with a new bitterness. Hindu nationalism is just one popular example, though not the only one. These separations of caste, religion, status, region, and language, in addition to class, divide the Indian labor market into its various segmentations and guard so well against class-based solidarity. Also, some of these divisions were to stymie SEIU's immediate success, as it navigated a new cultural landscape.

However, Indian unions did collaborate with UNI and SEIU in varied ways to win and implement the global agreement. The unique context of Indian industrial relations—involuted pluralism, deeply politicized unions, and massive informalization—provided a particularly challenging context in which to organize and mobilize workers. The main strategic response to this situation was to attempt to overcome the deep political chasms between unions within India by building the ISWOI coalition. Imperfect and fragile, it has nonetheless acted as a reasonable framework within a country that has rarely seen sustained cross-federation union collaboration.

Regarding the implementation of the global agreement, ISWOI achieved partial success by bringing G4S into compliance with national law (the Contract Labor Act), which required that it pay the legally mandated minimum wages and pension fund contributions. Unlike the situation in South Africa, for example, where the global agreement constrained management's anti-union behavior, local G4S leaders were not asked by the UK-based leadership to act in accordance with the agreement. This fact encouraged a different tactical maneuver by UNI. ISWOI was forced to redirect its claims away from management and toward the state. The result, which was the outcome of a cumbersome yet an ultimately productive social dialogue process with management, has been the establishment of new legislation to raise standards for five million security guards in the country, in terms of higher pension fund contributions, wage increases, and mandated ID cards.

This demonstrates that the global agreement, on the surface a simple labor contract, can be used by unions to win different kinds of gains. In this instance, the power of the global agreement turned out to be the fact that it generated a social dialogue process. As one UNI organizer put it, "Now we have a place to solve problems. Without that space, none of this would have happened."[15]

The influence of local bridge builders was critical. In Bangalore, local organizers credit UNI's staff with helping develop a new kind of "scientific" unionism, whereas in Kolkata, UNI was marginalized based on perceived cultural divisions and political incompatibilities. These differences help explain why the global agreement received a different amount of attention in each city and why it was more thoroughly implemented in Bangalore than in Kolkata.

However, the challenges facing the Indian unions are still great. Massive employer repression has held much constructive organizing at bay, and the unions in both cities remain loose formations, with rotating and fluctuating membership. The UNI-ISWOI collaboration represents an important step forward in the Indian labor movement, which has heretofore had very limited experience with transnational collaboration. However, it remains to be seen whether or not it has helped develop a strong enough local structure to sustain a lengthy campaign against the largest multinational company in the country.

CONCLUSION:
LABOR'S PROSPECT

This book has sought to evaluate a new dimension of labor movement activity. It has proceeded from the position that labor's fate is not predestined by ineluctable forces of world economic restructuring, though it must confront such forces with innovative strategy to rebuild its strength. In addressing this problematic, it has taken one complex case as an exemplar of a new horizon for workers and their organizations and has outlined three interrelated findings.

First, transformations in the global political economy have shifted the bases of worker power. Unions are increasingly turning toward strategies that seek to alter the "rules of engagement" between capital and labor even before worker organizing begins. This is especially true at the global level, where worker rights are essentially nonexistent and a coherent global mass movement is unlikely to materialize. These different strategies have their most recent expression as campaigns to win global framework agreements. The agreement with G4S helped workers build power not because it won them new rights but because it made new rules.

Second, reciprocity between the global and local spheres of action is a necessary condition for building global unionism. The case studies show the intricate ways in which local struggles were woven into the global effort. What began as a struggle in the United States was expanded with the support of unions in the Global South. But after the global framework agreement was signed, it greatly aided different local struggles to translate the global-level gains into national contexts. Moreover, close attention to this dynamic suggests that global union strategies tend to reconfigure local labor movements in varied ways, yet in turn local contexts determine the type of specific strategy that global unions are able to employ, a dialectical relationship that produces different forms of transnational collaboration and worker organization. Paradoxically, although global unions place primary emphasis on labor standards and universal claims to worker rights, viable transnationalism depends on actors enforcing local rules in disparate ways. In this campaign, that happened by revitalizing union traditions and building new organizations capable of participating in the overall effort.

Third, all global framework agreements—labor's latest weapon at the global level—are not born equal. The most useful are often those won through struggle and are conceived as one part of a comprehensive industrial strategy, not simply as a standalone policy instrument. Scholars and unionists should evaluate their potential utility on the basis of their short-term and long-range impact. They can have immediate and very local significance, as the chapters on South Africa and India show. However, the future of labor organizing may require that global agreements become a larger a component of a vision for worker power, not within single companies but, rather, within regional or global markets.

A cross-national comparison of the South African and Indian cases allows us to draw other related lessons as well. In each place, legacies of the past and present local constraints and opportunities structured different strategic responses and forms of transnational cooperation. In South Africa, the changed behavior of local management after the global agreement was signed presented the South African Transport and Allied Workers Union (SATAWU) with an opportunity to organize that it did not enjoy previously. The history of social movement unionism in SATAWU also allowed for an easier shift toward an organizing orientation, which produced membership gains. In India, trade union divisiveness based on political party affiliation demanded that Union Network International (UNI) broker a semblance of labor peace by constructing the Indian Security Workers Organizing Initiative (ISWOI), a new coalition of Congress- and Communist-affiliated unions. Local management was not constrained in its anti-unionism by its parent company, and though new recruitment did take place, local unionists were often frustrated by what they thought was an ineffective process of failed governance. However, UNI successfully pressured the state to handle its grievances in the form of proposed legislation covering the entire industry.

Both cases demonstrate examples where a global campaign has inspired local activity, such as gains in organizing, union building, membership growth, internal mobilization, institutional restructuring, and legislative or political gains. Overall, the campaign was able to alter the business model of one of the world's largest corporations and reorient the strategic models of unions in different places to make them more effective.

How can we assess the outcomes of the campaign in North America? Today, after a decade of organizing against G4S, only a small number—approximately one thousand workers—of its guards are members of the Service Employees International Union (SEIU). When Stephen Lerner began an internal critique of the union in the early 1990s, one of his major targets was the low numbers it was able to organize relative to its time and resources commitment. If the primary goal of this campaign was to bring guards into the union in the United States, the only conclusion at which one can reasonably arrive is that the struggle against G4S has so far been a dramatic failure. Yet this book has argued the opposite. How can this be?

Part of the answer lies in the details of how SEIU organizes property services workers in the United States. It almost never targets a single company in a given market to avoid the possibility of putting any particular employer at a competitive disadvantage. This wards against the likelihood that the higher wages and better standards of union workers would be undercut by nonunion employers, thereby undoing any gains won through unionization. Instead, the union targets specific geographic areas, attempting to organize the majority of market leaders into a union campaign before economic bargaining begins. Economic bargaining is only triggered after a particular percentage of employers submit to the union and then raise wages together.

In this context, the G4S agreement has been extraordinarily helpful in organizing other companies with larger US workforces and in convincing other industry players to operate within the union's sphere of influence.

Although it is only the third-largest security provider in the United States, its global footprint and close ties to lucrative government contracts make it a kind of industry leader anyway. Since the global agreement was signed in 2008, SEIU has organized approximately 10,000 security guards in key markets, which union leaders say would not have happened were it not for G4S. One former SEIU leader states: "The reason we did it [the G4S campaign] is because you could not organize Securitas, Allied [Barton], and the other firms if there was a multibillion-dollar multinational not covered by the agreement that could at any point come into the market."[1]

Now that the three largest global providers (G4S, Securitas, and International Services) have agreed to respect the union's access to work sites, there is greater capacity to organize guards and pressure other companies to work with the union. From this perspective, the G4S campaign was the most important component of a long-term industrial vision to exert governance over the private security industry that could lead to mass organizing on a scale previously impossible. This book has argued that it is important to view global framework agreements (GFAs) as part of a larger industrial strategy, rather than as a standalone instrument or tactic.

The union has taken contradictory lessons from the battle with G4S. On the one hand, the campaign was the vindication of those within the union who saw the global dimension as more than a boomerang strategy to return gains to US workers. The zeal with which they pursued a global agenda, which did not always mesh with the immediate priorities of local unionism in the United States, was validated by the significant gains made by unions around the world. They are satisfied by what has so far amounted to a prolonged period of capacity building to enable the possibility of a wide-reaching industrial strategy. On the other hand, the union has significantly retreated from its former commitments to transnationalism in the wake of the G4S campaign. Lerner, one of the campaign's architects in the United States, was eventually forced out of the property services division and today no longer works with SEIU. The perception of the G4S campaign as a waste of resources that did not deliver the anticipated membership gains at home played some role in building opposition to him within the union's leadership. SEIU has reduced the number of its staff dedicated to global work and curtailed its work with UNI. Some SEIU staff have resigned in response to what they see as a lack of interest in large-scale campaigning. The G4S campaign does not seem to have had a significant spillover effect within UNI, in that the organizing mantra specific to UNI Property Services has not been widely implemented throughout the rest of the union. Critics of UNI say that it has, over the last five years, favored signing agreements with willing companies over fighting with more strategic companies, a possible sign that the era of comprehensive campaigns may be short-lived.

As this book was being written, the campaign against G4S had advanced and retreated in important ways. As many as eleven countries are currently implementing the global agreement. In Morocco and Ghana, that process inspired strikes; in Mozambique, it settled them. In Poland, the agreement has helped raise wages and standards throughout the industry. The Indonesian union that was the first to tackle G4S outside the United States has since collapsed, and workers there have seen the erosion of significant gains. But we have also seen the birth of security guard unions in Nepal and several Latin American countries. In both South Africa and India, engagement in the campaign has waned at different times due to the changing nature of UNI's role, local organizational changes, or the company's shifting attitude to the global agreement. Staff changes in SATAWU disrupted the restructuring and organizing process, which has been intermittent. In India, ideological disagreements over the nature of union work pushed the Communist-affiliated unions away from the ISWOI coalition, but UNI began forging closer ties with strong security guard unions in Mumbai.

Security guards throughout North America were grandfathered into the global agreement in December 2010, two years after it was signed, and by 2012 all G4S guards were granted neutrality. It is likely that the initial settlement agreement failed to meet the expectations of some staff within SEIU who had worked on the campaign for over five years, leading to a certain level of cynicism about the outcomes. Ultimately, the victories in the global realm were more impressive and exciting, yet the (GFA) has opened doors to organizing in the United States beyond its original goals. It helped organize thousands of security guards in G4S, Securitas, and other providers.

The global campaign shed light on the hidden abode of low-level service-sector workers who would have otherwise been forced to struggle only within a national context, isolated from the larger effort. This suggests that even nonmobile service workers are not locked in place, nor are they condemned to compete with one another for miserable jobs. Rather, where crisis in the labor movement has also been a time of creative thinking, a new spirit of globalism has tried to both empower workers locally and offer them an avenue to take place in a broader struggle.

Taken together, these conclusions suggest a role for labor as an agent of governance in the world economy in the absence of a beneficial structural position or a supportive, rights-based national framework. What were once inchoate tendencies within the global labor movement have blossomed into established practices. Global unions have now signed ninety-one GFAs (as of early 2013). Increasingly, the scope of these agreements has broadened to include countries within the Global South. There has been a perceptible movement toward sustained campaigning and strategic corporate targeting within the global union federations (GUFs), practices that replaced focusing on small companies, aid-based activism, and winning agreements for the sake of social dialogue alone. That is not to say that the G4S case is not still exceptional; for all that has changed, it remains unmatched in its scope. What can this watershed campaign tell us about labor's prospects at the global level?

Lessons in Labor Transnationalism

For labor scholars and unionists alike, arguing about SEIU is practically a national pastime. It is seen as both guiding light and global bully, which for some suggests an uncomfortable hypocrisy. This book has tried to embrace the contradiction. Though the old face of US-sponsored labor imperialism has certainly changed, SEIU's insistence on the importance of restructuring local unions in other countries has made it a bittersweet ally and an easy target for much pithy critique. But it demands a more serious appraisal than is often given because the contradictions the union presents are so real and not easily resolvable. As one European union activist put it, "If the IMF [International Monetary Fund] had a trade union wing, it would do what SEIU does. It's weird, but in a way those people [SEIU leaders] are our role models, but they are also a huge pain in the ass."[2]

This book places "those people" at the heart of a burgeoning movement and suggests its strategic outlook has much to recommend it in other parts of the world. This will undoubtedly draw the groaning disapproval from many of that union's detractors, both in the United States and abroad. A few facts, however, are incontrovertible. Since the late 1980s SEIU has been experimenting with new strategies to grow its ranks during a time when many unions simply raised a white flag. It was aided greatly by an influx of innovative activists from the social movements who helped push it in a more aggressive direction. By and large, its actions were considered inspirational to unions and labor scholars throughout the United States. In the last decade it has played an expanded role in the labor movements of the United Kingdom, Ireland, Germany, Holland, Mexico, Australia, and Denmark, in addition to its involvement in India and South Africa, detailed here.

Many of the largest and most powerful unions in Europe are ill equipped to weather the current storm of neoliberalization that is undermining the fabric of the European social model. Others are simply opposed to trying anything new. For years they have been surviving in an environment in which they did not have to organize, but now it looks as though they do. French union density hovers around 7 percent, which is the same in the United States. German unions, though still among the most politically powerful in the world, are legitimately concerned about their future in a crisis-ridden European Union (EU). For some in Europe, learning from the mistakes and occasional victories of US unions offers a sensible option. However, as described in chapter 2, the resistance to change among large European unions is a significant roadblock to global union organizing. Also, the ambiguous nature of the "models" proposed by SEIU may also make the transition difficult outside a close mentoring relationship, which can logistically only happen in very few cases.

But there are others besides SEIU to choose from. The United Steelworkers has promoted the consolidation of large trade union bureaucracies in the United States, Canada, the United Kingdom, and the Caribbean (Workers Uniting) in the hopes of coordinating bargaining and contract cycles. Since the 2005 strike at Grupo Mexico, it has also forged significant relationships with Los Mineros, the independent Mexican miners union, and it has begun working alongside IG Metal, Germany's largest union. The United Food and Commercial Workers Union has grown into an active affiliate of several GUFs. Its work with UNI against Walmart, which is still in its early stages, could blossom into the most historic global union victory of all time, and it is also developing collaborative relationships with FNV Bondgenoten to organize Ahold workers in the Netherlands, the parent company of the US-based Stop & Shop. The communication workers' union has embarked on a significant partnership with ver.di, their German counterpart, to coordinate activities against Deutsche Telekom. Communication Workers of America (CWA) staff have been brought on by UNI to help coordinate the global telecommunications campaigns. The Teamsters, which is familiar with internationalism, has been engaged in transnational battles with some of the same school bus campaigns that SEIU fought alongside British unions, such as National Express Group PLC. The union is replicating many of the same tactics that formed the G4S campaign, including shareholder activism, cross-border information sharing, and corporate-meeting crashing.

The expansion of US unions into Europe makes sense for two reasons. First, US unions understand what it means to confront an anti-union company and mobilize a campaign of workers against hostile management, a situation with which many European unions have no experience. Louis Uchitelle (2010), the renowned labor journalist, has highlighted the strategic assistance that German unions have lent those in the United States. But by far the greater trend is US unions visiting Germany explicitly to share the research- and resource-intensive organizing model promoted by SEIU and other Change to Win unions. No one thinks the US system is heading toward a codetermination model, but the neoliberalization of the EU countries is now explicitly on the agenda. It stands to reason that the union movement that has already undergone such a transition would have something useful to offer. Whether the American model that gets exported or showcased focuses on aggressive organizing or contract concessions is an important question. But so far it seems that European unions want to engage with the aspect of American unionism that is experienced in fighting corporate take-backs. Second, although capital has always been global, employers were not. The Europeanization of the American services sector means that US unions are inescapably pulled toward a transnational battle. The deeper its ties with unions in the company's home country, the better.

A renewed commitment to organizing the unorganized has for decades been at the heart of the most recent attempts to rebuild labor's strength. Sporadic attempts have successfully, if momentarily, suspended the dominant trends toward labor weakness, managing the decline with a touch of grace. But union density has steadily declined in the places where organizing has been most passionately implemented, the United States and the United Kingdom, especially in the private sector (Gall and Fiorito 2011: 234). Perhaps the most sobering conclusion we can draw from this case study then is that union organizing alone, country by country, would not have worked—it had to be a global effort.

Governance Struggles and Labor Organizing at the Global Level

One outcome of the growth of corporate power and the restructuring of employment relations over the last four decades has been the rise of a variety of labor movement strategies to discipline the business practices of large transnational companies. As part of a rebellious spirit against neoliberalism, this activism has led some to declare the birth of a Polanyian-style counter-movement. But we must move beyond the notion of a social movement as a pendulum swinging against capitalism, a Sisyphean struggle for an ever-elusive goal of actually taking power. Moreover, Munck's (2002) remark that the popular vision of today's transnationalism as a return to proletarian internationalism constitutes a "wish list" of academics could not be more astute. Instead, this book has traced the historical contours of a new kind of labor politics that evolved slowly as a shifting response to corporate global-ization and foreign direct investment trends. Transnational campaigns have largely developed as a response to common international employers and new political conditions. The European common market provided a basis for regional transnationalism first. The Europeanization of the American services sector in the last twenty years has also prompted unions to recon-sider the efficacy of "unionism in one country." SEIU's interest in global unionism emerged initially not from a principled commitment to interna-tionalism but as a coping mechanism with the industrial structure of the US services sector. The campaign against G4S is emblematic. As a reaction against the immense power of the company and the incursion of European companies into the US property services sector, it embodies many of these new organizing strategies, especially the tendency toward governance strug-gles. However, it was hardly motivated by pragmatism alone—never before or since has a campaign of this magnitude been waged without the leading union pursuing an immediate reward. Remember that G4S union mem-bers in South Africa, India, or anywhere outside the United States are not SEIU members. So what did SEIU "get"? The first fruit of the long-term industrial strategy was the global agreement. Not only did it neutralize employer opposition in key places, but it also enlarged the governance SEIU exercised over the industry globally. In the end, the campaign was largely divorced from the potential to organize a small oasis of G4S workers in the United States, most of whom were located outside SEIU's traditional areas of strength anyway. The goal was to expand the union's degree of control over the landscape of private security firms.

To accomplish such a goal, the rules-based system of the Guidelines on Multinational Corporations and the neutrality clause within the GFA were both more useful to workers than any national labor rights legislation, including the legally binding National Labor Relations Act in the United States. The limitations of the rules-based framework of global agreements are not to be downplayed. But this book offers a view of their potential through a Gorzian lens. In *Strategy for Labor: A Radical Proposal*, Andre Gorz (1967) lays out the concept of *nonreformist reforms*. These are not once-and-done alterations to the conditions of capitalism but, rather, reformist policies that leave open the potential for deeper social transformation. At their best, GFAs represent what Gorz had in mind. They offer an avenue for labor to move beyond the facile constraints of monitoring corporate power, as previous struggles sought to do, to challenging it.

To this end both the union and the company concur that targeting the corporation's ability to conduct business was central. Therefore, the conventional assessment of UNI as *the organizer* among the GUFs (Fichter and Helfen 2011) must come to grips with the top-down aspects of the comprehensive campaign, particularly the role played by strategic research.

Contrast the "organizing model" of the 1930s (a common reference point for those who view labor as a social movement) with SEIU's campaign against G4S. The former model encouraged workers to act on their righteous indignation; the latter systematically gathered information on worker abuses in poor countries in order to file a report to shareholders, hoping to engender the sympathy of European investors. If SEIU is able to position itself as the answer to a global crisis of unionism—and there certainly is one—it will mean increased reliance on strategic research within corporate campaigns. None of this is to argue that corporate campaigns should be abandoned. Rather, the point is to call attention to the considerable role that strategic research has come to play within campaigns like the one against G4S, and the implications of that phenomenon for any notion of labor organizing. Governance struggles tend to have a top-down approach, with the intention of prying open a space for worker organizing at the bottom. The globalization of an organizing model, as showcased in chapter 2, means that the nature of union renewal, not just its extent, is worth considering.

Global Unionism Reimagined

It is tempting, though ultimately misleading, to view the central tension in this book from the standpoint of strategy alone—a false top-down versus bottom-up dichotomy. Rather, we should remember the central question posed at the beginning concerning worker power at the global and local levels.

On the one hand, the structural limitations of global capitalism may enhance labor's power in the nonmobile service sector, where a spatial fix cannot easily outsource labor globally. This is especially true within the large cities studied here—Johannesburg, Bangalore, and Kolkata. On the other hand, the reserve army of labor, new forms of labor brokering and subcontracting, and the general disarray of the trade union movement overshadow whatever benefits may be derived from the vulnerabilities of global capitalism. Instead I have argued that these conditions suggest a crucial need for unions to exercise associational power through governance struggles. But the ability of this campaign to exercise such power is first and foremost the result of a historical process of institutional and organizational innovation at the local, national, and global levels, a process that many large unions in the United States and Europe have yet to begin.

And herein lies the rub. The campaign against G4S, though a bellwether for a new mode of labor transnationalism, is not easily replicable at this point in time. For exactly this reason there are those within SEIU and UNI who are reluctant to promote a strategy as comprehensive as the one against G4S, explicitly because it is so difficult to execute, and the risks of losing are so large. Having come at a cost of millions of dollars in unrecouped dues and years of vigilance, the G4S campaign is indeed exceptional in many ways. But if we take seriously the findings in chapter 2—that SEIU and UNI benefited from years of experimentation with a panoply of global campaigns before taking on G4S—we cannot expect a union to simply replicate a strategy without the organizational capacity to do so. In other words, there needs to be a fundamental transformation of trade unions, both in fact and in conception. For most unions today, the internal restructuring and revitalization process is an essential precondition for rebuilding labor's power.

Munck (2002: 169) suggests, "If the new internationalism of the global era is to be seen as distinctive it might also involve a new understanding of the 'architecture' of human society." In other words, how do the various social strata relate to each other? There is a lot of distance—culturally, economically, and politically—between trade unions in North America, South Africa, and India. The challenge for a campaign like this is to give those relationships coherence across time and space, to weave together a common story from the disparate contexts.[3]

Here we can clearly understand the desperate need for "bridge builders" to span the global-local divide. Stories of the interactions between local and global union staff are strewn throughout the case studies in chapters 2, 3, 4, and 5. Although the importance of such activists has featured heavily in accounts of labor-community coalitions (Brecher and Costello 1990; Tait 2005; Tattersall 2010), rarely have these activists been seen as crucial to global campaigns. These roles have been played by a variety of American and European staff placed into South Africa and India fulltime to translate the local priorities of the global campaign. In both places, culture clashes between local and global staff played out as arguments over strategy. Nevertheless, the unions were eventually able to overcome these divisions, and the collaborations played a vital part in the construction of a new kind of unionism.

It has become an article of faith that a basic element of that new unionism appreciates the power of globalization and the desperate need for transnationalism. Unionists within SEIU and UNI, as well as most practitioners in the global labor movement, consistently assert the normative presumption that global corporations require global unions. Moreover, there is a broad consensus that such activity should remain, at all costs, *nonideological* (see Sweeney 1998).

As cautionary wisdom that seeks to avoid another Cold War in the global labor movement, it is sound advice. But there is also a danger that the sentiment surrenders the potential for a union's political vision at the altar of economic pragmatism, a frightening resignation to the "end of ideology" thesis and neoliberal common sense. Rather, an argument can be made that if there is a context in which unions are in desperate need of a guiding set of political ideas, it is in the realm of labor transnationalism. Acting nonideologically, if that is even possible, means accepting the extant political conditions as they are and operating within an established framework, a set of ruling ideas and customs. But the most decisive recent moments at SEIU have occurred explicitly when it led workers outside the reigning ideological context created by the National Labor Relations Board, by unscrupulous political leaders, by economic crises, and by entrenched labor movement norms and practices. It was at these moments, pursuing a vision above and beyond what was deemed possible or rational, that SEIU began to write a new narrative for American labor. That includes the campaign against G4S.

The global arena provides a fitting context in which to further an alternative vision. Globalization is more than a series of processes; it represents a new *episteme*. The same is potentially true for global labor. Labor transnationalism requires a greater commitment to antiracism, cosmopolitanism, solidarity, and cooperation. More than a bleak economism, these values will determine which strategies are even attempted in the first place, and will help ensure that a new spirit for labor can truly materialize.

Jeremy Anderson (2008), research director for the International Transport Workers Federation, refers to SEIU's American organizers in the United Kingdom as *imagineers*, a term he likens to those who help construct nations in Benedict Anderson's ([1983] 1991) *Imagined Communities*. In other words, as bridge-builders between movements of different national character and political orientation, their job is to construct an imagined community out of a disparate group of workers who do not otherwise share the routines of daily life. In Benedict Anderson's usage, an imagined community "is imagined because the members of even the smallest nation will never know most of their fellow-members, meet them, or even hear of them, yet in the minds of each lives the image of their communion" (Anderson [1983] 1991: 224).

All union organizing requires a bit of imagineering, of fostering a collective consciousness among those with varied experiences and sometimes conflicting interests. But the task is even more crucial at the global level. For all the hype that globalization has transcended national borders and erased local character, we are aware of our differences now more than ever. As one former UNI researcher put it, "How do you take all these peoples' lives, all these people from different places, and build something out of it? You can't just say, 'Oh, well, they're all workers for the same giant company' and be done with it. That's shit. It's too simplistic. Not just the [global framework] agreement, the G4S campaign is trying to find ways to build a movement that lasts and really connects people."[4]

The experienced leadership at the forefront (and behind the scenes) of the campaign was critical to this process. While much has been said about the need for rank-and-file involvement and the mid-level staff that carry out orders, crediting those at the top echelons of the labor movement is utterly passé. But in this case, as in most global campaigns, it is warranted. After all, it would be presumptuous to assume that labor will naturally overcome the myriad obstacles to solidaristic action or will choose the path of long-term goals over the temptations of intermediate compromises. The possibility requires visionary leadership and careful organization with an explicit ideological orientation, in addition to all the practical necessities of such an undertaking. Local victories must be generalized and articulated in ways that meaningfully support the larger effort. A group of autonomous movements, fragmented and unconnected, each vying for its own local power, would not have beaten G4S. Leadership's job was to ensure that gains are spread fairly, and that the whole campaign was not compromised by opportunism and/or spontaneity in specific places. This is not antithetical to union democracy. In a campaign with the scope and time span such as the one against G4S, union democracy means durable structures for participation. Democracy was contingent upon union staff creating such a space somewhere between the "tyranny of structurelessness" and the "iron law of oligarchy."

Part of the imagineering process requires labor to write a new historical biography in which workers are active participants in crafting a different kind of globalization. That will depend on thoughtful and aggressive leadership more than on strategic and tactical maneuvering, and it is impossible without ideology.

Final Remarks

As the world of labor has changed, so has the world of labor studies. Three decades ago, the seemingly terminal crisis of the former challenged the explanatory power of the latter. A cottage industry emerged to bid farewell to the working class and its primary organizations, a critique based on its passivity and decline in the face of a transforming world political economy.

During a time when workers' movements seemed anachronistic, and even as the alter-globalization movement (so full of promise during the millennial craze of the late 1990s) dissolved into innumerable single-issue causes, one might not have bet on a sustainable labor transnationalism to emerge when it did.

But, today, workers are fashionable again,[5] as the labor question has resurfaced as an integral element of the globalization debate. The scholarly examination of labor and union movements is taking up more space in the social sciences, largely dedicated to an assessment, in one form or another, of prospects for renewal. There is a new journal dedicated to global labor studies and a handful of international research institutes dedicated to an interdisciplinary study of world labor politics, drawing a significant number of students from the movements themselves. Recasting labor studies in a global lens allows us to shed new light on the macro-sociological position of workers today. And a close examination of "actually existing" transnationalism opens a window into the dialectical relationship it has with local communities. It is the interstices of these dimensions that I have tried to illuminate here.

Writing amidst the explosive 1968 revolts in Paris, Henri Lefebvre (1968) remarked, "Events belie forecasts. To the extent that events upset calculations, they are historic." In this respect, the G4S campaign is already historic, having redefined the limit of possibility for labor. The lingering questions concern its future. The increasing reports of creative global campaigns are an encouraging sign that labor is charting a new course—the security guard unions being an excellent case in point. Struggles such as these remind us that victory is not as simple as winning; it is about building the power to fight in the first place.

Appendix: Comparative Research at the Global Level

This book is written from the standpoint of historical materialism. In other words, contradictions within the past are resolved through the struggle for a new present, which of course contains new contradictions. Why is this theoretical orientation important for any consideration of methodology? The overall design of this book is geared toward generating a new insight about labor transnationalism, and a more coherent and realistic conception of what such activism looks like today as compared to the past.

Rather than a bottom-up phenomenon led by workers in the South, I have suggested that the most dominant trends within the world of global unionism tend toward a new kind of organizing strategy that combines a comprehensive campaigning model with new forms of global governance. To do this I have told the story of one complex example that is simultaneously an outlier and representative at various times and places.

In effect, this has led me to examine cases within a case, or what I call "nested" case studies. Nested case studies allow us to study divergent phenomena that are contained and contextualized within a single unit of analysis.

In this case the unit of analysis is the campaign that is comprised of several parts—a historical period of renewal and strategic reorientation, a global-level campaign, and then local mobilizations.

I draw heavily on the theoretical understandings of Burawoy's (1985) global ethnographic work and Geertz's (1977) emphasis on cultural connection. Though I have not undertaken a strict ethnography, I make direct links with the local, regional, national, and global arenas under study by specifically targeting interviews and observation within each sphere. I argue that Johannesburg, for example, cannot be seen as inherently separate from the history of its nation-state, South Africa, which is also inextricably linked to the regional and global political economy. Moreover, the aspects of my study that focus on the private security industry globally are also conducted at multiple scales to account for the complications involved with studying sub-contracted employment and global supply chains. I have taken care to emphasize an understanding of my case studies as situated in discreet but related arenas of action. Most importantly, there is a historical dimension to the case study as well that involves the antecedents of the global campaign, the period of revitalization and change described in chapter 3.

Undoubtedly some critics will take issue with the biases inherent in my comparative case study methodology. I chose to focus on this campaign because it represents the frontier of an emerging practice—the cutting edge of global unionism. I focused on South Africa and India as foreign research sites because there is such a strong basis for comparison, and yet the results in each place were so different. Johannesburg, Bangalore, and Kolkata are all regionally important cities with strong links to the global economy. Both sites were also important battlegrounds in the global campaign for the employer and the unions. However, peculiarities of labor law, union history, and political structure ensure that local structures create different environments for labor transnationalism to take place. As I was interested in how the local context influenced the implementation of the global strategy, these two places provided a rather unique opportunity to study such a process as it unfolded in real time. This situation provided the basis for an analysis not only of the way in which global unionism can have local affects but also of the reason it takes different forms in different places.

These sites also were chosen for their theoretical importance. Indeed, the campaign against G4S cannot be regarded as typical, nor is the depth to which the campaign was taken up in South Africa and India. But as there are so few examples of actual global campaigns, choosing a "typical" or "representative" one is not easy, perhaps impossible. Here Burawoy's (1985) insights into case study methodology have been influential again. He argues that there are multiple "modes of generalization," not only the typical mode, which extrapolates from sample to population. A second mode conjoins the micro context with the larger social totality that shapes it, the underlying assumption being that "every particularity contains a generality" (18). My analysis aspires to expose these forces as they construct a social reality.

For example, as I argue in chapter 2, the campaign against G4S is the product of multiple sources—general revitalization efforts in the US labor movement, the incorporation of those strategies around the globe, the reactions to the Europeanization of the US service sector, and the ability of UNI Global Union (UNI) to coordinate these varied social forces and put them into action. Likewise, as the South African experience of mobilization-based reforms (as a consequence of transnational collaboration) has some relevance to that country's labor history and present conjuncture, so the campaign in India can be seen within a context of other informal-sector labor movements.

Interview Data

The majority of information about my cases comes from interviews with unionists, employers, and assorted experts such as local politicians and social movement activists. These interviews spanned three years, nine countries, and four continents, including approximately one hundred formal and semi-structured interviews with trade union organizers, government officials, corporate leaders, low-level managers, political activists, and other academics. Most interviews took place outside the United States: Johannesburg, Durban, Bangalore, Delhi, Kolkata, and Geneva. I also spoke informally with groups of workers and union organizers during meetings, at their homes, and at worksites. Where possible, I observed meetings that related to the implementation of the global framework agreement. Often these meetings included representatives from multiple trade unions, rank-and-file workers, and corporate representatives. To respect the anonymity of those who requested it, most of the interview extracts and quotations are attributed to generic terms like "staff," "organizer," or "researcher" and are cited using this generic title and the year the interview was conducted. Some people, however, are simply too high-profile or have published too well-known material to be cited anonymously.

The majority of data was collected between the middle of 2008 and the end of 2011. The chapters on South Africa and India primarily describe events that transpired between 2007 and 2011. I went through an extensive fact-checking process with leaders of UNI Global Union in the fall of 2012.

Studying Transnationalism

This book studies an emerging practice known as labor transnationalism, or sustained cross-border collaboration among trade unions. It is differentiated from past forms of cross-border collaboration. In recent years, the concept of transnationalism has gained ground as an explanatory framework to describe migration patterns, economic flows, social movement activity, and cultural exchange (see Portes 1997; Portes, Guarnizo, and Landolt 1999; Tarrow 2005). Portes et al. (1999) stress the importance of delimiting the concept of transnationalism so as not to overburden it with the necessity of having to explain everything, or diluting it until it is meaningless. My conception of the phenomena meets their three criteria for what constitutes a transnational activity:

a) the process involves a significant proportion of persons in the relevant universe (in this case, workers and their unions);
b) the activities of interest are not fleeting or exceptional but possess a certain stability and resilience over time; and
c) the content of these activities is not captured by some preexisting concept, making the invention of a new term redundant.

This last point raises an important distinction to be made between transnationalism and internationalism. I distinguish transnationalism from internationalism by the way the state functions in each concept, a demarcation borrowed from social movement studies (Tarrow 2005). In other words, whereas international activities can be seen as one-way interactions or simply collaborations between states, transnationalism implies a blurring of state demarcations and a tendency to transcend national borders, not merely cooperate within them. In truth, both phenomena operate in the book, reflecting the different positions of the various labor movements and ideological approaches to labor activism that I draw out. However, internationalism is more indicative of earlier modes of cross-border union activity than it is today.

NOTES

Introduction

1. Alternatively, this movement has been called the anti-globalization movement, the globalization movement, the anti-corporate globalization movement, and the movement of movements, more or less interchangeably, none of which satisfies a great degree of accuracy. The *anti-globalization movement*, the most popular in the mainstream press, is an inversion of the truth: the objective of the alter-globalization movement is not to stop "globalization," an impossible and undesirable goal, but to change what is being globalized. In other words, it is *for* globalizing fair labor standards and environmental protections and *against* globalizing corporate power (see Graeber 2002: 62–63).

2. Perhaps because, as Jameson and Miyoshi (Jameson, Miyoshi, Fish, and Dussel 1998) argue, "globalization falls outside the established academic disciplines," it is a highly contested concept that has a tendency to avoid a simple definition, including a late-capitalist world system developed in Kondratieff cycles of expansion and contraction (Wallerstein 1979); a neoliberal project for class power and "accumulation by dispossession" (Harvey 2005); emergent forms of supranational governance (Hardt and Negri 2001); a rise of a global informational society networked via key nodes of information exchange (Castells 2000); and a techno-ontology of governance

(Ong 2006). Most point to some distinction between a Kenysian welfare state and a Shumpeter workfare state (Jessop 1994). In this book, the first definition is the most useful, as it draws heavily on Polanyi's conceptual analysis of successive waves of embedding and disembedding, a major theoretical frame in global labor studies.

3. The situation in Puerto Rico was not black and white. I have relied mostly on discussions with conference participants and labor journalism in my determination (i.e., Early 2008; Landau 2008; Democracy Now! 2008).

4. These different work locations are cobbled together from various sources, although an article in *The Guardian* corroborates them (Taylor 2012). This article also explains the increasing role the company plays running private prisons and replacing public police.

5. Organizer interview, 2011.

6. Global framework agreements (GFAs) are explored in depth throughout this book. Occasionally I refer to "international framework agreements," "global agreements," or, simply, "framework agreements" interchangeably.

7. Keck and Sikkink (1998) devote much space to transnational advocacy networks, which are at times comparable to different types of transnational labor campaigns.

8. This term was coined by an American unionist based in the Netherlands to describe the process by which unions implement some aspects of the American "organizing model" into their own industrial and national context (see Alzaga 2011). It should not be confused with "open-source unionism," a phrase used by Richard Freeman and Joel Rogers (2002) to suggest that unions deepen their connection to Internet-based technologies to allow greater communication among workers.

9. Leader interview, 2009.

10. Researcher interview, 2009.

11. Peter Evans (2008: 273) argues that "neo-liberal globalization has created a set of socio-cultural, ideological, organizational, and even economic conditions that enhance the potential for counter-hegemonic globalization," deepening the theoretical scope of previous accounts describing "globalization from below" (see Brecher, Costello, Smith 2000),). See also the geographical literature: (Wills and Waterman 2002; Wills 2002; Herod 2001; Castree, Coe, Ward, and Samers 2004).

12. Strangely, Evans's structural power argument draws on the analysis of Cardoso and Faletto (1979), who argue for "collective action guided by political wills that make work *what is structurally barely possible*" (emphasis added). Evans (2010: 356) says, "Globalization, both as the generic shrinking of geographic and social space and in the form of the specific structures of the contemporary neoliberal capitalist political economy, stimulates and facilitates the mobilization of labor solidarity at the transnational level as well as the construction of transnational labor movement organizations and networks." Jennifer Chun argues, "Ironically, the very processes that have rendered historically disadvantaged workers such as immigrants, women, and people of color the target of cost-cutting employer practices have also laid the groundwork for social movement-inspired forms of unionism that seek to overcome the social and cultural as well as economic conditions of worker exploitation" (Chun 2009: 8).

13. Rules are different from laws. Following Tilly (2005), labor laws are sanctioned by governments, or "publicly enforceable claims." Though a law is a kind of rule, Piven's analysis, as well as my own, views rules in a broader sense. Rules are usually made first and foremost through the (formal or not) operating structures of the dominant forces in society—capital and the state. Sometimes, however, trade unions, social movements, NGOs, and others intervene, resulting in new rules. In this book, rules are considered private regulations

14. One such example is the Alliance Agreement, which SEIU pioneered in the early 2000s. The Alliance strategy involved union-management collaboration to lobby state governments for more money for underfunded nursing homes, a percentage of which would then be shared when workers organized. It also set in place pre-existing template contracts that drove the collective bargaining process. Internationally, labor and student organizations are increasingly trying to enforce policies that intervene against a multinational company's ability to use non-union labor throughout its supply chain.

15. There is a sense in which this sentiment was the felt, though unspoken, feeling of many discouraged leftists as well.

Chapter 1

1. These bodies, precursors to the GUFs, are explored later in this chapter.
2. The WFTU remains today a shell of its former role as the haven for the unions of Soviet-dominated countries
3. Levinson's work therefore drew deep criticisms from the pro-management writers (Northrup and Rowan 1979), so called Left pessimists (Ramsay 1997), and Marxists (Olle, Schoeller, and Mann 1977), who disagreed with "the implicit attempt to find a superficial economic basis for the necessity and possibility of international trade union politics" (Olle, Schoeller, and Mann 1977: 70).
4. This was most evident in its collaboration with the Alliance for Sustainable Jobs and the Environment, which brought radical ecologists and mainstream unionists into the collective fray against NAFTA, Fast Track, and the Seattle WTO Ministerial.
5. In all, Waterman (2001: 71–73) makes thirteen propositions of newness with remarkably little redundancy.
6. Long-standing participants within the global labor movement, interviewed for this project, had either no idea what it was or could not name anything it had accomplished, and SIGTUR declined repeated interview requests.
7. The numbers of southern unions opposed to the social clause gradually diminished as it slowly became a global, rather than an AFL-CIO, strategy, though Indians remained its most fervent "no" votes.
8. Almost all global agreements contain ILO core labor rights, though rarely have they been able to impact the rules of the industrial relationship. Moreover, whereas companies have often conceded to demands for more labor rights, the fight against G4S demonstrates how willing large companies are to wage fierce battles against a new relationship.

9. It is common to hear about jurisdictional governance gaps, or gaps in global "participation," referring, respectively, to a lack of judicial power to enforce basic rights and the failure to provide meaningful avenues for political participation for the marginalized communities.

10. Core labor standards technically incorporate eight basic "conventions" of the ILO into its rubric that are commonly reduced to the four general rights mentioned earlier. The complete set is as follows: No. 87 (freedom of association and the right to organize); No. 98 (on the right to organize and bargain collectively); No. 100 (on equal remuneration); No. 111 (on discrimination in employment and occupation); No. 138 (on minimum age); No. 29 (on forced labor); No. 105 (on the abolition of forced labor); and No. 182 (on the abolition of the worst forms of child labor).

11. This was not the founding rationale for the GATT. In the late 1940s, as market-based solutions were considered anathema, the GATT was established to implement a multilateral system of institutional checks and balances and slowly move toward liberalization (Ikenberry and Grieco 2002). This is in stark contrast to the "Shock Doctrine" of the late 1990s (Klein 2007).

12. Newland argues, "Workers in poorer and less-developed nations often view unions based in the advanced industrial countries as defenders of privilege. Their suspicions persist that such unions' insistence on increased wages, conformity with labour standards, and environmental safeguards for Third World workers is simply a disguised form of protectionism, designed to undercut the developing world's main source of comparative advantage: low labour costs" (Newland 1999: 56–57).

13. Both codes are named for their creators, the Reverend Leon Sullivan and the poet Sean MacBride.

14. If there is a moment of vindication for Karl Polanyi in this book, this is it.

15. Evans and Anner (2004) describe mass firings of workers when they tried to organize, and Rodriguez-Garavito (2005) emphasizes codes presented as an alternative to the fatal violence often provoked by organizing in the maquiladora sector.

16. The NLC had gained a degree of notoriety since its enigmatic leader, Charles Kernaghan, testified that clothes bearing the label of TV personality Kathie Lee Gifford were made by children in Honduran maquiladoras. Rather than apologize, Gifford appeared teary-eyed and indignant on ABC's *Prime Time Live* to clear her name. "I felt like I was being of all people, being kicked in the teeth for trying to help kids," she said. When it was made public a few days later that her clothing line also was produced in New York-based sweatshops, her husband rushed to the factory to distribute one hundred dollar bills to mistreated workers.

17. It was exactly this type of activism that inspired Naomi Klein's bestseller, *No Logo: Taking Aim at the Brand Bullies* (1999). It quickly became a bible for the global justice and antisweatshop movements.

18. These include the Social Accountability 8000 (SA8000), the Ethical Trading Initiative (ETI), the Clean Clothes Campaign (CCC), and many more (Compa 2004).

19. Also known as "global agreements," "international framework agreements," or "framework agreements."

20. The overwhelming majority of GFAs are considered nonbinding because they are not necessarily legally enforceable in court. Their status as voluntary agreements

does not make them nonbinding, as many voluntary agreements in the United States have such standing. Some lawyers believe that GFAs may be enforceable in US courts under section 301 of federal labor law, the statute that is often used to adjudicate collective bargaining agreements. While there is an obvious reason unions would desire that agreements become binding, some trade unionists suspect that, especially in Europe, where collective bargaining agreements are not binding either, the potentially legally enforceable nature of a GFA might make it harder to win from a large corporation. On the other hand, scholars and labor activists routinely show that hard law regulation simply does not work—the extraordinary prevalence of wage theft and unfair labor practice charges in the United States is ample testament. In other words, the problem is not one of soft versus hard law but one of power.

21. This should be distinguished from governance struggles, which seek to alter corporate business practices, not to fill a democratic deficit.
22. Staff interview, 2009.

Chapter 2

1. Interview, 2010.
2. This is contrasted to business unionism—in which unions are perceived as providing a "product" in the form of higher wages, legal representation, or job security—or the "servicing model," where unions approach their members as clients or customers.
3. The percentage of Latino workers in the US service economy increased from 28 percent in 1980 to 61 percent in 1990 (Prashad 2003: 40)
4. My analysis views these as tactics, not strategies. A strategy implies an overall vision for social change; a tactic is a particular set of practices that constitutes one part of a strategy.
5. Organizer interview, 2012.
6. Saul Alinsky's (1946 [1989]) *Reveille for Radicals* reflected his experience as a community organizer in Chicago's industrial ghettos of the 1930s. Alinsky thought "People's Organizations"—community institutions built by highly trained organizers—were preferable to corrupt unionists that only focused on workplace issues. The spirit of Alinsky's "model" is often credited with influencing the radicals of the 1960s and 1970s who promoted innovative organizing tactics in a variety of social movement settings. Stern's detractors, however, are quick to suggest that he was enamored as well with Alinsky's insistence on a top-down movement structure.
7. But Fantasia and Voss (2004: 116) claim that the profile of the union's senior staff "would tend to make for a closer resemblance to Silicon Valley entrepreneurs than to veteran staffers of the trade union movement."
8. Some claimed that trusteeship *diffused* the J4J ethos throughout the country. Others maintained that trusteeships are imposed only in cases of extraordinary malpractice, corruption, or irreconcilable political differences. One notable example is Sweeney's ally, Gus Bevona, who was ousted from his perch on top of the powerful

building services local (32BJ) in New York City. Bevona surrounded himself with profligate corruption of legendary proportions—including penthouses and private planes—funded by members' dues. However, we should not forget Bevona's role in the Justice for Janitors story. Under pressure from both a dissident caucus within his own union and the national embarrassment of having previously offered no form of solidarity to the Los Angeles strikers (the industry was heavily unionized in New York), Bevona contacted ISS to "threaten chaos in their [*sic*] New York buildings if a settlement was not reached in Los Angeles" (Fantasia and Voss 2004: 144). The company responded with a signed contract that day offering pay raises, vacation time, sick days, and union recognition.

9. Lerner was not a lone labor leader to dismiss the specter of globalization. Bruce Raynor, leader of UNITE HERE, said, "My thinking on this has changed. For many years I didn't see the point of international affairs, but we've learned a lot in the past few years. What's happening to unions in this country can't be separated from what's happening to unions everywhere else. We're going to rise or fall together" (cited in Howard 2007: 70).

10. Leader interview, 2010.

11. Gilles Deleuze, a French theorist, is hardly a common name in labor sociology. For an explanation as to why his positions may be of use to labor activists, see Anderson (2009).

12. Organizer interview, 2010.

13. Email correspondence, 2012.

14. In Australian industrial relations, part of the logic of compulsory arbitration is a determination, or an *award,* by the state that all workers in a particular industry receive equal wages and benefits. This has been significantly eroded and replaced by a system of enterprise bargaining.

15. In the United States, twenty-three states, mostly located in the South, have laws allowing for minority unionism. In such cases, though a union may win a contract covering all workers in a specified unit, no one is forced to join or pay dues, leading to obvious free rider problems. The laws that grant an individual the "right to work" without any obligation to join a union are largely seen in the United States as a major barrier to union organizing in the South. Some organizers dissent from this view, claiming the low union density in the American South stems more from a historical bias and fear of right-to-work laws than from the strength of the actual legislation, claiming as many southern workers desire union membership as do workers anywhere else.

16. In 2011, the LHMU changed its name to United Voice.

17. Email correspondence, 2012.

18. Organizer interview, 2010.

19. Staff interview, 2010.

20. A polder, common in Holland, is an artificial geologic formation created by reclaiming land from bodies of water. The Polder model, or polderen, connotes a high degree of corporatism in Dutch industrial relations. Historically, the corresponding union strategy has mostly been servicing unionism.

21. Researcher interview, 2009.

22. Leader interview, 2009.
23. Email correspondence, 2012.
24. Organizer interview, 2010.
25. Interview, 2010.
26. Leader interview, 2011.
27. Researcher interview, 2009.
28. Leader interview, 2009.

Chapter 3

1. From an interview with *Workforce*, a journal aimed at providing information to human resource managers.
2. Organizer interview, 2011.
3. See the *Changing Situation of Workers and Their Unions* (AFL-CIO Committee on the Evolution of Work 1985); Industrial Union Department's *Developing New Tactics: Winning with Coordinated Corporate Campaigns* (1985) and *The Inside Game: Winning with Workplace Strategies* (1986). The former Food and Allied Service Trades division of the AFL-CIO for years published a *Manual of Corporate Investigation* (Juravich 2007: 18).
4. The discovery of this document raises an important question as to the effectiveness of the corporate campaign. If management can uncover secreted information about the union and its supporters, then it inherently weakens the ability of other unions to use corporate campaigning in the future. In a related case, see the Cintas example (Von Bergen 2006).
5. According to Bronfenbrenner and Hickey (2003), "In elections with moderately aggressive employer campaigns, when the union runs a comprehensive campaign, win rates average 93 percent overall and 75 percent in manufacturing. However, win rates drop to 35 percent overall, 29 percent in manufacturing, when the union fails to run a comprehensive campaign." Juravich (2007) says that the major victories in recent memory have all employed some type of comprehensive campaign strategy.
6. In this sense they are a clearer case of a marginalized group of workers than janitors, and have in fact engaged in some of the same classification struggles that Chun describes.
7. Section 9(b)(3) also grants employers the right to withdraw their collective bargaining agreement after the contract has expired if it had been voluntarily recognized. See the case *Truck Drivers 807 v. NLRB* (McCabe 1985: 163).
8. This legal dispute continues today as security providers have invoked the divided loyalties problem to discourage unionization, and governmental offices have argued that unionized security guards represent a threat to national security. This is despite the fact that, to take one example, unionized security guards and first responders on September 11, 2001, were widely praised. A 2006 Congressional hearing explores the issue in great detail (US House of Representatives Committee on Education and the Workforce. September 28, 2006).

9. Organizer interview, 2011.

10. U.S. Department of Labor, Bureau of Labor Statistics, "Occupational Employment and Wages, May 2006." *Occupational Employment Statistic.*

11. Leader interview, 2009.

12. Organizer interview, 2011.

13. LA janitors were historically mostly black and union, until the industry restructured in the 1970s and 1980s, replacing high-paying workers with underpaid new immigrants. See Joshua Bloom's chapter in *Working for Justice* (2010) for a good history of this dispute.

14. Organizer interview, 2011.

15. Utilized by employers such as Ravenswood Aluminum in its dispute with the United Steelworkers of America in 1990 and Smithfield Foods in its ongoing battle with the United Food and Commercial Workers regarding its poultry processing plant in Tar Heel, North Carolina, suits under the RICO Act allow for private civil suits to recover damages, thus opening unions up to substantial monetary liability. The suit was eventually dropped, though some claim it provided a powerful incentive for UNI to settle with the company when it did.

16. Exelon subsequently thanked the whistleblower for alerting it to the misconduct and then fired him, prompting Exelon's inclusion in *Fortune* magazine's "101 Dumbest Moments in Business 2007" (Fortune 2007).

17. Wackenhut denied the charges. See Hyde (2009).

18. As part of the settlement with the company, the website has since been removed.

19. Organizer interview, 2009.

20. Organizer interview, 2009.

21. Staff interview, 2009.

22. Organizer interview, 2009.

23. Organizer interview, 2009.

24. In the end, G4S made worldwide headlines for vastly underemploying security guards during the games, finding just over half of the number it was contracted to supply "a humiliating shambles" in the words of CEO Nick Buckles (Adams 2012).

25. The UN-backed Principles for Responsible Investment Initiative (PRI) is a network of international investors working together to put the six Principles for Responsible Investment into practice. The Principles, which were "devised by the investment community," represent a voluntary commitment by over a thousand investor signatories to respect some level of environmental standards, social issues, and corporate governance.

26. Shares of G4S were owned by pension funds concentrated in high-income countries with traditional respect for labor rights, providing an added point of leverage—for example, approximately eight million in the United Kingdom and two million in the United States (UNI 2009).

27. In 2004, UNI filed an initial complaint with the OECD, focusing solely on US-related worker rights issues and corporate misconduct, but it failed to move the committee to act (UNI 2008).

28. Researcher interview, 2009.

29. Staff interview, 2009.

30. G4S did not, in the end, submit a bid for the contract, citing the potential difficulties associated with providing security for the event. See Bowker (2012).
31. Staff interview, 2009.
32. Leader interview, 2009.
33. Organizer interview, 2011.
34. Interview, 2012.
35. Organizer interview, 2011.
36. For example, in 2006 the SEIU agreed not to organize ten thousand security officers at the Allied Barton corporation in Philadelphia in exchange for organizing rights elsewhere (Davis 2009).

Chapter 4

1. In the early 1980s there was a brief moment of interest in mass consolidation and mega-mergers in the United States too, in the hopes of creating "cones of influence," though the plan was considered too radical, and subsequently it was abandoned (see Hurd 2004).
2. Here I am concerned primarily with the work of black workers to reach across borders. Though white racist unionism was also internationalist, it drew on such connections for entirely different reasons.
3. This is a curious distinction, since what is commonly referred to as "new"—grassroots or proletarian internationalism—is actually more indicative of the "old" models described previously (see chapter 1).
4. The importance of Fordism and Taylorism to Silver's theory on labor power cannot be overstated, where the nature of even automobile production, and other factory work, ensured that workers retained a greater degree of control and autonomy over the labor process than is normally "allowable" in Fordist analyses. Whereas Fordism and Taylorism are generally associated with deskilling, many black South Africans experienced upskilling as they filled jobs in factories. In a related point, Kraak (1996) argues that racial Fordism never died, and that the popular notion of the post-Fordist transition in the mid-1990s is similarly fraught with the problem of too many continued practices of the past to constitute a period of "post" anything. He suggests neo-Fordism instead.
5. Those relationships have been tested at times by "suspicion and animosity" as a result of Cold War politics surrounding the Soviet-backed WFTU and internal disputes about the liberation struggle (Bezuidenhout 2000). While apartheid provided the dominant basis for international relations within the trade unions, nonalignment was COSATU's primary foreign policy strategy. By remaining neutral, COSATU was able to build a broader front of allies against apartheid and attract wider interest and foreign assistance to its domestic operations. It did, however, provoke squabbles within the international union formations that were in the midst of a Cold War of their own. SACTU remained unaffiliated yet closely aligned ideologically with the WFTU, using its international links and resources to conduct a class war from afar. South Africa was temporarily expelled from the ILO when SACTU successfully used its influence within the WFTU to lobby against

ILO representation of the Trade Union Council of South Africa, a racist union federation (Southall 1995). Emboldened by this victory, it began a series of battles from exile with the ICFTU, and even the emerging independent black unions. The ICFTU began to funnel aid directly to unions in order to bypass their Communist leadership. SACTU took the stance that all economic aid—"direct links"—to South African workers should be channeled through its leadership in order to appropriately fund the most politically oriented unions. It believed that the "solidarity" of the northern countries and European federations actually subverted the potential of the South African unions. Eventually this position proved unpopular and untenable as its connections with actual workers waned from a distance.

6. Staff interview, 2009.
7. Organizer interview, 2009.
8. Organizer interview, 2009.
9. Staff interview, 2009.
10. Staff interview, 2009.
11. Staff interview, 2009.
12. Excerpt from a conversation after a meeting with G4S leader, 2009.
13. Organizer interview, 2009.
14. Organizer interview, 2009.
15. Excerpt from a conversation at a meeting on global unionism, 2009.

Chapter 5

1. Staff interview, 2009.
2. Organizer interview, 2011.
3. Organizer interview, 2009
4. Extract from a union meeting , 2009.
5. Staff interview, 2011.
6. Organizer interview, 2009.
7. Organizer interview, 2009.
8. Official interview, 2009.
9. Organizer interview, 2009.
10. Extract from a group interview, 2009.
11. Official interview, 2010.
12. Organizer interview, 2009.
13. Staff interview, 2009.
14. Organizer interview, 2010.
15. Organizer interview, 2009.

Conclusion

1. Organizer interview, 2009.
2. Activist interview, 2010.

3. In many cases of international labor cooperation, this has been accomplished through regional-level organization. However, South African and Indian workers do not benefit from a system of regional organizations as do unions in Europe and Latin America. Gallin (2008) asserts that the various southern African union organizations are corrupt puppets of local governments. India lacks the integration into an Asian bloc or a trade union association altogether, a happenstance that has tended to widen the divide between SEIU/UNI and ISWOI.

4. Staff interview, 2010.

5. Recently, articles on global unionism have been featured in the popular media and cultural forums, such as *American Prospect*, *The Nation*, *Mother Jones*, *Alternet*, and TED Talks.

References

Abbott, Kenneth W., and Duncan Snidal. 2000. "Hard and Soft Law in International Governance." *International Organization* 54(3):421–456.

Adam, Heribert and Kogila Moodley. 1993. *The Opening of the Apartheid Mind*. Berkeley: University of California Press.

Adams, William Lee. 2012. "London 2012: G4S Chief Admits Olympic Security 'a Humiliating Shambles.'" *Time Olympics*. Accessed October 3, 2012. http://olympics.time.com/2012/07/17/london-2012-g4s-chief-admits-olympic-security-a-humiliating-shambles/.

Adler, Glenn, and Eddie Webster, eds. 2000. *Trade Unions and Democratization in South Africa, 1985–1997*. New York: St. Martin's Press.

Adler, Lee & Lowell Turner. 2001. "Awakening the Giant: The Revitalization of the American Labor Movement." Cornell University, ILR School. Accessed January 30, 2012. http://digitalcommons.ilr.cornell.edu/articles/762/.

AFL-CIO Committee on the Evolution of Work. 1985. *The Changing Situation of Workers and Their Unions*. [AFL-CIO report]. Washington, DC: AFL-CIO.

AFL-CIO Industrial Union. 1985. *Developing New Tactics: Winning with Coordinated Corporate Campaigns*. Washington, DC: Industrial Union Dept.

AFL-CIO. 1986. *The Inside Game: Winning with Workplace Strategies*. Washington, DC: IUD.

Agarwala, Rina. 2006. "From Work to Welfare: A New Class Movement in India." *Critical Asian Studies* 38:419–444.

Agarwala, Rina. 2008. "Reshaping the Social Contract: Emerging Relations between the State and Informal Labor in India." *Theory and Society,* 37:375–408.

Agarwala, Rina. 2012. "The State and Labor in Transnational Activism: The Case of India." *Journal of Industrial Relations* 54 (September):443–458.

Alinsky, Saul. 1946 [1989]. *Reveille for Radicals.* New York: Vintage.

Allen, Kieran. 2009. "Social Partnership and Union Revitalisation: The Irish Case." In *The Future of Union Organising: Building for Tomorrow*, Gregor Gall, ed., 45–61. New York: Palgrave Macmillan.

Alzaga, Valery. 2011. "Justice for Janitors Campaign: Open-Sourcing Labour Conflicts against Global Neo-Liberalism." *Open Democracy.* Accessed January 30, 2013. http://www.opendemocracy.net/valery-alzaga/justice-for-janitors-campaign-open -sourcing-labour-conflicts-against-global-neo-libera.

Anderson, Benedict R. O'G. [1983] 1991. *Imagined Communities: Reflections on the Origin and Spread of Nationalism.* New York: Verso.

Anderson, Jeremy. 2009. "Labour's Lines of Flight: Rethinking the Vulnerabilities of Transnational Capital." *Geoforum* 40(6):959–968.

Anderson, John Jeremy Gouinlock. 2008 "Labour's Lines of Flight: Transnational Strategies for Transnational Corporations." Unpublished doctoral dissertation, University of London.

Anner, Mark and Peter Evans. 2004. "Building Bridges Across a Double Divide: Alliances Between US and Latin American Labour and NGOs." *Development in Practice* 14(1):34–47.

Anner, M., Ian Greer, Marco Hauptmeier, and N. Winchester. 2006. "The Industrial Determinants of Transnational Solidarity: Global Interunion Politics in Three Sectors." *European Journal of Industrial Relations* 12:7–27.

Anner, Mark. 2006. "The Paradox of Labour Transnationalism: Trade Union Campaigns for Labor Standards in International Institutions." In *The Future of Organised Labour: Global Perspectives.* Craig Phelan (editor). Bern: Peter Lang Publishing. Pp. 63–90.

Anner, Mark S. 2011. *Solidarity Transformed: Labor Responses to Globalization and Crisis in Latin America.* Ithaca, NY: Cornell University Press.

Armbruster-Sandoval, R. 2005. "Workers of the World Unite? The Contemporary Anti-Sweatshop Movement and the Struggle for Social Justice in the Americas." *Work & Occupations* 32:464–485.

Armbruster-Sandoval, Ralph. 2004. *Globalization and Cross-Border Labor Solidarity in the Americas: The Anti-Sweatshop Movement and the Struggle for Social Justice.* New York: Routledge.

Arrighi, Giovanni, Beverly J. Silver, and Iftikhar Ahmad. 1999. *Chaos and Governance in the Modern World System.* Minneapolis: University of Minnesota Press.

Associated Press. 2007. "Security Provider at Reactor to Be Fired." *The New York Times* (September 25) Accessed February 5, 2012. http://www.nytimes.com/2007/09/25 /business/25security.html.

Bacon, David, John Borsos, Stepehen Lerner, Warren Mar and Michael D. Yates. 2008. "SEIU Debating Labor's Strategy." *MR Zine.* Accessed January 30, 2013. http://mrzine.monthlyreview.org/2008/seiu140708.html.

Bacon, David. 2000. "Will a Social Clause in Trade Agreements Advance International Solidarity?" *Z Magazine.* Accessed September 24, 2012. http://www.zcommunications.org/will-a-social-clause-in-trade-agreements-advance-international-solidarity-by-david-bacon.

Bahadur, Aisha, and Michael Koen. 2009. "Case Study: Campaigning on Precarious Work at Group 4 Securicor." Unpublished, in author's possession.

Banks, Andy, and Jack Metzgar. 1989. "Participating in Management: Union Organizing on a New Terrain." *Labor Research Review* 14:1–55.

Barchiesi, Franco, and Tom Bramble. 2003. *Rethinking the Labour Movement in the New South Africa.* Aldershot, UK: Ashgate.

Barrick, Kelle, Marcus Berzofsky, Crystal Daye, Nicole Horstmann, Susan Kinsey, Bonnie Shook-Sa, and Kevin Strom. 2010. "The Private Security Industry: A Review of the Definitions, Available Data Sources, and Paths Moving Forward." Bureau of Justice Statistics, Department of Justice, prepared by RTI International under Cooperative Agreement Number 2009–BJ–CX–K045. Accessed June 11, 2012. https://www.ncjrs.gov/pdffiles1/bjs/grants/232781.pdf.

Barwell, T. 2009. "G4S Climbs as Demand, Purchases Help Resist Recession." Update3.*Bloomberg.* Accessed September 23, 2012. http://www.bloomberg.com/apps/news?pid=newsarchive&sid=avwgfbSCOXh8.

Behrens, M., Michael Fichter, and Carola Frege. 2003. "Unions in Germany: Regaining the Initiative?" *European Journal of Industrial Relations* 91:25–42.

Behrens, Martin, Richard Hurd, and Jeremy Waddington. 2004. "How Does Restructuring Contribute to Union Revitalization?" *Varieties of Unionism: Strategies for Labor Movement Renewal in the Global North* 1:117–137.

Bendiner, Burton B. 1977. "Labor Response to Multinationals: Coordination of Bargaining Goals." *Monthly Labor Review* 101:9.

Bennett, James T. 1996. "Comprehensive Corporate Campaigns." *Journal of Labor Research* 17(3):327–328. doi:10.1007/BF02685850.

Bezuidenhout, Andries. 2000. "Towards Global Social Movement Unionism? Trade Union Responses to Globalization in South Africa."International Institute for Labour Studies. Discussion Paper 115. Geneva, Switzerland.

Bhattacharjee, Anannya, and Fred Azcarate. 2006. "India's New Unionism." *New Labor Forum* 15(3):64–73.

Bhattacherjee, Debashish. 2000. "Globalising Economy, Localising Labour." *Economic and Political Weekly* 35:3758–3764.

Bhattacherjee, Debashish. 2001. "The Evolution of Indian Industrial Relations: A Comparative Perspective." *Industrial Relations Journal* 23(3):244–263.

Bhowmik, Sharit K. 2009. "India: Labor Sociology Searching for a Direction." *Work and Occupations* 36:126–144.

Blackburn, Daniel, et al. 2011. "Focus on Global Framework Agreements." *International Union Rights* 18(2). Accessed May 29, 2012. http://www.ictur.org/pdf/IUR182.pdf.

Bloom, Joshua. 2010. "Ally to Win: Black Community Leaders and SEIU's L. A. Security Unionization Campaign." In *Working for Justice: The L.A. Model of Organizing and Advocacy*, Ruth Milkman, Joshua Bloom, and Victor Narro, eds., 167–190. Ithaca, NY: ILR Press.

Bond, Patrick and Ashwin Desai. 2008. "Foreign Policy Bottom Up." [Report of the University of KwaZulu-Natal Centre for Civil Society]. Accessed January 30, 2013. http://ccs.ukzn.ac.za/files/Bond%20Desai%20Foreign%20Policy%20Bottom%20Up%20July%202008.pdf.

Bond, Patrick. 2009. "In Power in Pretoria?" *New Left Review*. Accessed January 30, 2013. http://newleftreview.org/II/58/patrick-bond-in-power-in-pretoria.

Boswell, Terry, and Dimitris Stevis. 1997. "Globalization and International Labor Organizing." *Work & Occupations* 24:288–308.

Bowers, Gina. 2008. "Security Officers Ratify Historic Union Contract in Los Angeles. SEIU: United Service Workers West."Accessed May 7, 2012. http://draft.seiu-usww.org/SECURITY_OFFICERS_RATIFY_HISTORIC_UNION_CONTRACT_IN_LOS_ANGELES.aspx.

Bowker, John. 2012. "Update 1-Security Giant G4S Says Will Avoid Soccer World Cup." Reuters. Accessed October 4, 2012. http://www.reuters.com/article/2009/05/20/g4s-idUSLK4638820090520.

Bramble, Tom. 2003. "Social Movement Unionism since the Fall of Apartheid: The Case of NUMSA on the East Rand." In *Rethinking the Labour Movement in the 'New South Africa,'* Tom Bramble and Franco Barchiesi, eds., 187–204. Aldershot, UK: Ashgate.

Brecher, Jeremy, and Tim Costello. 1990. *Building Bridges: The Emerging Grassroots Coalition between Labor and Community*. New York: Monthly Review Press.

Brecher, Jeremy, Tim Costello, and Brendan Smith. 2000. *Globalization from Below*. 10th ed. Cambridge, MA: South End Press.

Brecher, Jeremy, Tim Costello, and Brendan Smith. 2006. "International Labor Solidarity: The New Frontier." *New Labor Forum* 15:9–18.

Breman, Jan. 1976. "A Dualistic Labour System? A Critique of the 'Informal Sector' Concept: I: The Informal Sector." *Economic and Political Weekly* 11:1870–1876.

Bronfenbrenner, Kate, Sheldon Friedman, Richard W. Hurd, Rudolph A. Oswald, and Ronald L.Seeber. 1998. *Organizing to Win*. Ithaca, NY: Cornell University Press.

Bronfenbrenner, Kate, and Robert Hickey. 2003. "Winning Is Possible: Successful Union Organizing in the United States—Clear Lessons, Too Few Examples." *Multinational Monitor*. Accessed June 6, 2012. http://www.multinationalmonitor.org/mm2003/062003/bronfenbrenner.html.

Bronfenbrenner, Kate, and Robert Hickey. 2004. "Changing to Organize: A National Assessment of Union Strategies." In *Rebuilding Labor: Organizing and Organizers in the New Union Movement*, ed. Ruth Milkman and Kim Voss, 17–61. Ithaca, NY: ILR Press.

Bronfenbrenner, Kate, and Tom Juravich. 1999. *Ravenswood: The Steelworkers' Victory and the Revival of American Labor*. Ithaca, NY: ILR Press.

Bronfenbrenner, Kate, and Tom Juravich. 2001. "The Evolution of Strategic and Coordinated Bargaining Campaigns in the 1990s: The Steelworkers' Experience." In *Rekindling the Movement: Labor's Quest for Relevance in the Twenty-First Century*, ed.

Lowell Turner, Harry C. Katz, and Richard W. Hurd. Ithaca, NY: ILR Press: 211–237.

Bronfenbrenner, Kate, ed. 2007. *Global Unions: Challenging Transnational Capital Through Cross-Border Campaigns*. Ithaca, New York: ILR Press.

Buhle, Paul. 1999. *Taking Care of Business: Samuel Gompers, George Meany, Lane Kirkland, and the Tragedy of American Labor.* New York: Monthly Review Press.

Buketov, Kiril, Paul Garver, Hyewon Chong, and Beatrice Sosa Martinez. 2007. "Global Labor Organizing in Theory and Practice." *Labor Studies Journal* 32: 237–256.

Burawoy, Michael. 1985. *The Politics of Production: Factory Regimes under Capitalism and Socialism*. London: Routledge.

Burawoy, Michael. 2010. "From Polanyi to Pollyanna: The False Optimism of Global Labor Studies." *Global Labour Journal* 1:301–313.

Burawoy, Michael, et al. 2000. *Global Ethnography: Forces, Connections, and Imaginations in a Postmodern World*. 1st ed. Berkeley: University of California Press.

Burawoy, Michael, Alice Burton, Ann Arnett Ferguson, and Kathryn J. Fox. 1991. *Ethnography Unbound: Power and Resistance in the Modern Metropolis*. Berkeley: University of California Press.

Busch, Gary K. 1983. *The Political Role of International Trade Unions*. New York: Palgrave Macmillan.

Candland, Christopher. 1999. "Labour, Industry and the State in India and Pakistan." In *Labour Worldwide in the Era of Globalization: Alternative Union Models in the New World Order, International Political Economy Series*, ed. Ronaldo Munck and Peter Waterman. New York: Palgrave Macmillan, 175–196.

Cardoso, Fernando Henrique and Enzo Faletto. 1979. *Dependency and Development in Latin America*. Berkeley: University of California Press.

Carew, Anthony, Michel Dreyfus, Geert Van Goethem, Rebecca Gumbrell-McCormick, and Marcel Van der Linden, eds. 2000. "The International Confederation of Free Trade Unions." *International and Comparative Social History*. Bern, Switzerland: Peter Lang.

Carter, Bob and Rae Cooper. 2002. "The Organizing Model and the Management of Change: a Comparative Study of Unions in Australia and Britain," *Relations Industrielles* 57(4): 712–742.

Carter, Bob. 1997. "Politics and Process in the Making of MSF." *Capital & Class* 45:35–71.

Castells, Manuel. 2000. *The Rise of the Network Society (The Information Age: Economy, Society and Culture, Volume 1)*. 2nd ed. Malden, MA: Wiley-Blackwell.

Castree, Noel. 2009. "Geographic Scale and Grass-Roots Internationalism: The Liverpool Dock Dispute, 1995–1998." *Economic Geography* 76:272–292.

Castree, Noel, Neil Coe, Kevin Ward, and Mike Samers. 2004. *Spaces of Work: Global Capitalism and Geographies of Labour*. First edition. New York: SAGE Publications Ltd.

Catchpowle, Lesley, and Christine Cooper. 2003. "Neoliberal Corporatism: Origins and Implications for South Africa." In *Rethinking the Labour Movement in the "New" South Africa*, Tom Bramble and Franco Barchiesi, eds. 13–24. London: Ashgate.

Champagne, Jessica. 2007. "Unions Act Globally." Inside Indonesia. Accessed January 30, 2013. http://www.insideindonesia.org/weekly-articles/unions-act-globally.

Charnovitz, Steve. 1987. "The Influence of International Labour Standards on the World Trading Regime. A Historical Overview." *International Labour Review* 126:565–584.

Chen, Martha, and Renana Jhabvala. 2001. "Supporting Workers in the Informal Economy: A Policy Framework." WIEGO. Accessed November 11, 2012. http://wiego.org /sites/wiego.org/files/publications/files/Chen-Jhabvala-Lund-Supporting-Workers -policypaper.pdf.

Chibber, Vivek. 2005. "From Class Compromise to Class Accommodation: Labour's Incorporation in the Indian Political Economy." *Social Movements and Poverty in India*, ed. Mary Katzenstein and Rakha Ray, 32–61. London: Rowman & Littlefield.

Chun, Jennifer Jihye. 2009. *Organizing at the Margins: The Symbolic Politics of Labor in South Korea and the United States*. Ithaca, NY: Cornell University Press.

Clawson, Dan. 2003. *The Next Upsurge: Labor and the New Social Movements*. Ithaca, NY. ILR Press.

Clawson, Dan. 2010. "'False Optimism: The Key to Historic Breakthroughs? A Response to Michael Burawoy's From Polanyi to Pollyanna: The False Optimism of Global Labour Studies' (GLJ 1.2)." *Global Labour Journal* 1:398–400.

Cleeland, Nancy. 2004. "Surprising Opposition to Effort to Organize Guards." *Los Angeles Times*. Accessed May 17, 2012. http://articles.latimes.com/2004/jun/04/business/fi -guards4.

Cloward, Richard A., and Frances Fox Piven. 2000. "Power Repertoires and Globalization." *Politics & Society* 28(3):413–430. Accessed May 2, 2012. doi:10.1177/0032329200 028003006.

Cockburn, Alexander and Jeffrey St. Clair. 2000. *5 Days That Shook the World: Seattle and Beyond*. New York: Verso.

Cohen, Sheila. 2009. "Opening Pandora's Box: The Paradox of Institutionalised Organising." In *The Future of Union Organising: Building for Tomorrow*, Gregor Gall, ed., 28–44. New York: Palgrave Macmillan.

Community Resources and Information Centre (CRIC). 1990. "Public Sector Strikes: An Overview." *South African Labour Bulletin* 14:8–17.

Compa, Lance. 2004. "Trade Unions, NGOs, and Corporate Codes of Conduct." *Articles and Chapters* (February 1). http://digitalcommons.ilr.cornell.edu/articles/379.

COSATU. 2003. "Report to the Central Committee: Organizational Renewal to Deepen Service to Our Members!" COSATU. Accessed February 10, 2012. http:// www.cosatu.org.za/show.php?ID=2289.

COSATU. 2009. "Working Class Internationalism in the Era of Deepening Global Crisis: The Global Workers Struggle against Poverty and Inequalities Is a Struggle against Capitalism." Copy in possession of Jamie K. McCallum.

COSATU. 2010. "Renewal via Servicing Members." Accessed February 10, 2012. http:// www.cosatu.org.za/show.php?include=docs/reports/2003/ccreporte.htm&ID=2289.

Cowie, Jefferson R. 2001. *Capital Moves: RCA's 70-Year Quest for Cheap Labor*. New York: The New Press.

Crosby, Michael H. 2005. *Power at Work: Rebuilding the Australian Union Movement.* Annandale, Australia: Federation Press.

Croucher, Richard, and Elizabeth Cotton. 2009. *Global Unions, Global Business.* London: Middlesex University Press.

Dateline NBC. 2007. "Sweatshops Kathy Lee Scandal." Accessed October 6, 2012. http://www.youtube.com/watch?v=zCszZ5lwAgA&feature=youtube_gdata _player.

Davis, Mike. 1982. "The AFL-CIO's Second Century." *New Left Review: Anatomy of the Slump* (136, November-December):43–54.

Davis, Warren. 2009. "Philadelphia Museum Guards Finally Win Their Own Union." Accessed June 2, 2012. http://labornotes.org/2009/10/philadelphia-museum-guards -finally-win-their-own-union.

Deetz, S. A. 1992. *Democracy in an Age of Corporate Colonization: Developments in Communication and the Politics of Everyday Life.* Albany: State University of New York Press.

Delbridge, Rick, Edmund Heery, John Salmon, Melanie Simms, and Dave Simpson. "Organising Unionism Comes to the UK," *Employee Relations* 22(1): 38–57.

Democracy Now! 2008. "Puerto Rican Labor Struggle: Teachers Vote Against Joining SEIU." Democracy Now! [Video clip]. Accessed January 29, 2013. http://www.de mocracynow.org/2008/10/27/puerto_rican_labor_struggle_teachers_vote.

Desai, Ashwin. 2002. *We Are the Poors: Community Struggles in Post-Apartheid South Africa.* New York: Monthly Review Press.

Dubofsky, Melvyn. 1969. *We Shall Be All: A History of the Industrial Workers of the World.* New York: Quadrangle/The New York Times Book Company.

Early, S. 2008. "Puerto Rico's Teachers Beat SEIU Raid." *Labor Notes.* Accessed October 4. http://labornotes.org/node/1964.

Early, Steve. 2011. *The Civil Wars in U.S. Labor: Birth of a New Workers' Movement or Death Throes of the Old?* Chicago: Haymarket Books.

The Economist. 1982. "Europe's Unions are no Match for America's Multinationals." October 13. (7259):73.

Eder, Mine. 2002. "The Constraints on Labour Internationalism: Contradictions and Prospects." In *Global Unions? Theory and Strategies of Organized Labour in the Global Political Economy. RIPE Series in Global Political Economy*, ed. J. Harrod and R. O'Brien. London: Routledge, 167–184.

Erickson, Christopher L., Catherine L. Fisk, Ruth Milkman, Daniel J.B. Mitchell, and Kent Wong. 2003. "Justice for Janitors in Los Angeles: Lessons from Three Rounds of Negotiations." *Journal of British Industrial Relations* 40(3). Accessed May 7, 2012. http://www.ruthmilkman.info/rm/Articles_files/bjir%20jfj .pdf.

Esbenshade, Jill. 2004. "Codes of Conduct: Challenges and Opportunities for Workers' Rights." *Social Justice* 31(3):40–59.

Esbenshade, Jill. 2001. "The Social Accountability Contract: Private Monitoring From Los Angeles to the Global Apparel Industry." *Labor Studies Journal: Special Issue on Unions in the Global Economy* 26(1):98–120.

Eurofound. 2010. "European Works Councils." Accessed October 6, 2012. http://www .eurofound.europa.eu/areas/industrialrelations/dictionary/definitions/european workscouncils.htm.

Evans, Peter. 2000. "Fighting Marginalization with Transnational Networks: Counter-Hegemonic Globalization." *Contemporary Sociology* 29:230–241.

Evans, Peter. 2008. "Is an Alternative Globalization Possible?" *Politics & Society* 36:271–305.

Evans, Peter. 2010. "Is It Labor's Turn to Globalize? Twenty-First Century Opportunities and Strategic Responses." *Global Labour Journal* 1:352–379.

Fairbrother, Peter. 2010. *Unions and Globalization.* 1st ed. London: Routledge.

Fairbrother, Peter, and Nikolaus Hammer. 2005. "Global Unions Past Efforts and Future Prospects." *RI/IR* 60:405–431.

Fairbrother, Peter, and Charlotte Yates. 2003. *Trade Unions in Renewal: A Comparative Study.* 1st ed. London: Routledge.

Fantasia, Rick and Kim Voss. 2004. *Hard Work: Remaking the American Labor Movement.* Berkeley: University of California Press.

Fantasia, Rick. 1988. *Cultures of Solidarity: Consciousness, Action, and Contemporary American Workers.* Berkeley: University of California Press.

Featherstone, Liza, and United Students against Sweatshops. 2002. *Students Against Sweatshops: The Making of a Movement.* New York: Verso.

Fichter, Michael. 1982. "Support and Dissent, German and American Labor's Transnational Ties" In Detlef Junker, *The United States and Germany in the Era of the Cold War, 1945–1990, A Handbook,* Volume 1, 566–572. Cambridge: Cambridge University Press.

Fichter, Michael, and Ian Greer. 2004. "Analysing Social Partnership: A Tool for Renewal?" In *Varieties of Unionism: Strategies for Labor Movement Renewal in the Global North,* ed. Carola Frege and John Kelly, 71–92. Oxford: Oxford University Press.

Fichter, M. and M. Helfen. 2011. "Going Local with Global Policies: Implementing International Framework Agreements in Brazil and the United States." In *Shaping Global Industrial Relations. The Impact of International Framework Agreements.* Konstantinos Papadakis, ed. New York: Palgrave Macmillan. Co-published with International Labour Office.

Fichter, Michael, Jorg Sydow, Markus Helfen, L. Arruda, O. Agtas, Indira Gartenberg, Jamie McCallum, K. Sayim, and Dimitris Stevis. 2012. *Globalizing Labour Relations: A Critical Geopolitical Perspective.* Berlin: Friedrich-Ebert-Stiftung.

Fichter, Michael, Markus Helfen and Jörg Sydow. 2011. "Employment Relations in Global Production Networks: Initiating Transfer of Practices via Union Involvement." *Human Relations* 64(4):599–622.

Fiorito, Jack T., and Gregor Gall. 2011 "The Backward March of Labour Halted? Or, What Is to Be Done with 'Union Organising'? The Cases of Britain and the USA." *Capital & Class* 35(2): 233–251.

Fletcher Jr., Bill, and Fernando Gapasin. 2009. *Solidarity Divided: The Crisis in Organized Labor and a New Path Toward Social Justice.* Berkeley: University of California Press.

Fletcher Jr., Bill, and Richard Hurd. 1998. "Beyond the Organizing Model: The Transformation Process in Local Unions."In *Organizing to Win, Research on New Union Strategies,* ed. Kate Bronfenbrenner, Sheldon Friedman, Richard W. Hurd, Rudolph A. Oswald, and Ronald L. Seeber, 37–53. Ithaca, NY: Cornell University Press.

Fortune. 2007. "101 Dumbest Moments in Business 2007." Accessed August 20, 2012. http://money.cnn.com/galleries/2007/fortune/0712/gallery.101_dumbest.fortune/69.html.

Frankel, Francine R. 2005. *India's Political Economy 1947–2004: The Gradual Revolution*. 2nd ed. New York: Oxford University Press.

Freeman, Richard B., and Joel Rogers. 2002. "Open Source Unionism: Beyond Exclusive Collective Bargaining." *WorkingUSA: The Journal of Labor and Society* 5(4):8–40. Accessed May 19, 2012. http://scholar.harvard.edu/freeman/rfreeman/publications/open-source-unionism-beyond-exclusive-collective-bargaining.

Frege, Carola M., and John Kelly. 2004. *Varieties of Unionism: Strategies for Union Revitalization in a Globalizing Economy*. New York: Oxford University Press.

French, John D. 2002. "Towards Effective Transnational Labor Solidarity between NAFTA North and NAFTA South." *Labor History* 43:451–459.

Frundt, Henry J. 2001."Cross-Border Organizing Models in Maquila Industries." In *U.S. Unions in a Globalized Environment*, Bruce Nissen, ed., 45–75. Armonk, NY: M.E. Sharpe.

Frundt, Henry J. 2004. "Unions Wrestle with Corporate Codes of Conduct." *WorkingUSA* 7(4):36–69.

G4S. 2007a. *Annual Report and Accounts 2007.*Accessed September 26, 2012. http://www.g4s.com/~/media/Files/Annual%20Reports/g4s_annualreport_2007.ashx.

G4S. 2007b. *Report on Group 4 Securicor, Written in Response to UNI's Allegations about the Conduct of G4S in Relation to the OECD's Guidelines for Multinational Enterprises*. Copy in possession of Jamie K. McCallum.

G4S. 2008a. "G4S and UNI Sign Global Agreement." Accessed May 18, 2012. http://www.g4s.com/en/Media%20Centre/News/2008/12/16/G4S%20and%20UNI%20sign%20global%20agreement/.

G4S. 2008b. "G4S Wackenhut and SEIU Reach Agreement." Accessed September 26, 2012. http://www.g4s.com/en/Media%20Centre/News/2008/12/16/G4S%20Wackenhut%20and%20SEIU%20Reach%20Agreement/.

G4S. 2009. "Global United Front." Accessed October 4, 2012. http://www.g4s.com/~/media/Files/International%20magazine/2009%20Issue%201/g4s_international-g4s17-unitedfront_10-11.ashx.

Gall, Gregor. 2009. *The Future of Union Organizing: Building for Tomorrow*. New York: Palgrave Macmillan.

Gallin, Dan. 1997. "Funeral Speech of Charles Levinson." *Global Labour Institute*. Accessed April 21, 2012. http://www.globallabour.info/en/2006/10/funeral_speech_for_charles_lev.html.

Gallin, Dan. 2001. "Propositions on Trade Unions and Informal Employment in Times of Globalization." In *Place, Space, and the New Labour Internationalisms*, P. Waterman and J. Wills, eds. 227–245. Oxford: Blackwell.

Gallin, Dan. 2002. "Labour as a Global Social Force: Past Divisions and New Tasks." In *Global Unions? Theory and Strategies of Organized Labour in the Global Political Economy*, ed. J. Harrod and R. O'Brien, 235–251. London: Routledge.

Gallin, Dan. 2008. "The American Debate; Looking for the Quick Fix: Reviewing Andy Stern." Global Labour Institute. Accessed April 17, 2012. http://www.globallabour.info/en/2008/04/looking_for_the_quick_fix_revi.html.

Gallin, Dan. 2012. "Summer Days on Utøya." In *Confronting Finance: Mobilizing the 99% for Economic and Social Progress*, Nicolas Pons-Vignon and Phumzile Ncube, eds., 15–19. Geneva: International Labour Office.

Gamiz Jr., Manuel. 2008. "Private Security Industry Grows as Pay Rate Stays Flat." *The Morning Call*. Accessed June 17. http://www.mcall.com/business/outlook/all-security-030908,0,7324098.story.

Garver, Paul, Kirill Buketov, Hyewon Chong, and Beatriz Sosa Martinez. 2007. "Global Labor Organizing in Theory and Practice." *Labor Studies Journal* 32 (3) (September 1): 237–256. doi:10.1177/0160449X07299712.

Geertz, Clifford. 1977. *The Interpretation of Cultures*. New York: Basic Books.

George, Alexander L., and Andrew Bennett. 2005. *Case Studies and Theory Development in the Social Sciences*. Cambridge, MA: The MIT Press.

Goitom, Hanibal. 2012. "South Africa: Proposal to Tighten Rules of Private Security Industry." Library of Congress. *Global Legal Monitor*. Accessed August 15, 2012. http://www.loc.gov/lawweb/servlet/lloc_news?disp3_l205403267_text.

Goldman, Michael. 2011. "Speculative Urbanism and the Making of the Next World City." *International Journal of Urban and Regional Research* 35(3):555–581. doi:10.1111/j.1468-2427.2010.01001.x.

Gordon, James, and Poonam Gupta. 2003. "Understanding India's Services Revolution."Paper prepared for the IMF-NCAER Conference, *A Tale of Two Giants: India's and China's Experience with Reform*, November 14–16, New Delhi.http://www.perjacobsson.org/external/mp/apd/seminars/2003/newdelhi/gordon. pdf.

Gordon, Kathryn, and Maiko Miyake. 2000. "Deciphering Codes of Corporate Conduct: A Review of Their Contents." OECD Working Papers on International Investment. Number 1999/2. Accessed March 5, 2012. http://www.oecd.org/dataoecd/23/19/ 2508552.pdf. http://www.asria.org/ref/library/csrguidelines/lib/OECD%20Deciphering%20Codes%20of%20Corp%20Conduct.pdf.

Gordon, Michael E., and Lowell Turner. 2000. *Transnational Cooperation among Labor Unions*. Ithaca, NY: Cornell University Press.

Gorz, Andre. 1967. *Strategy for Labor: A Radical Proposal*. Boston: Beacon Press.

Government of India (GOI). 2008. "Report on Conditions of Work and Promotion of Livelihoods in the Unorganized Sector." New Delhi: Academic Foundation.

Graeber, David. 2002. "The New Anarchists." *New Left Review* (13, January-February). http://newleftreview.org/II/13/david-graeber-the-new-anarchists.

Greenfield, Gerard. 1998. "The ICFTU and the Politics of Compromise." In *Rising from the Ashes? Labor in the Age of "Global" Capitalism*, Ellen Meiksins Wood, Peter Meiksins, and Michael Yates, eds., 180–189. New York: Monthly Review Press.

Greenwood, Ian, Christy Hoffman, Jenni Myles, and Tom Powdrill. 2009. "Progress Report on the G4S-UNI Ethical Partnership Agreements." Webinar. Principles for Responsible Investment. Copy in possession of Jamie K. McCallum.

Grieco, Joseph M., and G. John Ikenberry. 2002. *State Power and World Markets: The International Political Economy*. First edition. New York: W. W. Norton & Company.

Gumedze, Sabelo. "To Embrace or not to Embrace: Addressing the Private Security Industry Phenomenon in Africa." In *Private Security in Africa: Manifestations, Chal-*

lenges, and Regulations, Sabelo Gumedze, ed. ISS Monograph Series. Accessed January 30, 2013. http://www.iss.co.za/uploads/MONO139FULLPDF.PDF.

Hall, Mimi. 2003. "Private Security Guards Are Homeland's Weak Link." *USA Today.* January 23. Accessed October 4, 2012. http://usatoday30.usatoday.com/news/nation /2003-01-22-security-cover_x.htm.

Hammer, Nikolaus. 2005. "Global Framework Agreements: Global Industrial Relations between Rights and Bargaining." *Transfer: European Review of Labour and Research* 11:511–530.

Hammer, Nikolaus. 2008. "Global Framework Agreements in the Context of Global Production." In *Cross-Border Social Dialogue and Agreements: An Emerging Industrial Relations Framework?,* ed. Konstantinos Papadakis and Dominique Bé, 89–111. Geneva: ILO.

Hampson, Ian. 2004. "International Unionism: Recovering History, Reshaping Theory, Recasting Practice?" *Labour History* 87:253–264.

Hanley, Glennis and Peter Holland. December 2002. "'Organising Works' Is it Meeting the Challenge of Declining Trade Union Membership?" Monash University Faculty of Business and Economics, Working Paper Series, Working Paper 48/02.

Hardt, Michael, and Antonio Negri. 2001. *Empire.* Reprint. Cambridge, MA: Harvard University Press.

Harriss-White, Barbara. and Nandini Gooptu. 2001. "Mapping India's World of Unorganized Labour." *Socialist Register.* 89–118.

Harrod, Jeffrey, and Robert O'Brien. 2002. *Global Unions?: Theory and Strategies of Organized Labour in the Global Political Economy.* 1st ed. New York: Routledge.

Harvey, David. 1991. *The Condition of Postmodernity: An Enquiry into the Origins of Cultural Change.* Reprint. Oxford: Wiley-Blackwell.

Harvey, David. 2005. *The New Imperialism.* New York: Oxford University Press.

Harvey, David. 2007. *A Brief History of Neoliberalism.* 1st ed. New York: Oxford University Press.

Haworth, Nigel and Stephen Hughes. 1997. "Trade and International Labour Standards: Issues and Debates Over a Social Clause." *Journal of Industrial Relations* 39 (2) (June 1): 179–195.

Hayek, Friedrich. A. 2007. *The Road to Serfdom: Text and Documents—The Definitive Edition.* Edited by Bruce Caldwell. Chicago: University of Chicago Press.

Heery, Edmund. 2002. "Partnership Versus Organising: Alternative Futures for British Trade Unionism," *Industrial Relations Journal* 33(1):20–35.

Heery, E., R. Delbridge, J. Salmon, M. Simms, D. Simpson, and P. Stewart. 1998. "Trade Union Organising in Britain." [Document 2/1.] Trade Union Research Unit, Cardiff University.

Helfand, Duke. 2006. "Deal Reached to Let Hundreds of Guards Unionize." *Los Angeles Times.* Accessed June 7, 2012. http://articles.latimes.com/2006/apr/12/local/me -labor12.

Heller, Patrick. 2000. *The Labor of Development: Workers and the Transformation of Capitalism in Kerala, India.* Ithaca, NY: Cornell University Press.

Hensman, Rohini. 2001. "World Trade and Workers' Rights: In Search of an Internationalist Position." In *Place, Space and the New Labour Internationalisms,* ed. Peter Waterman and Jane Wills, 123–146. Oxford: Blackwell.

Hensman, Rohini. 2010. "Labour and Globalization: Union Responses in India." *Global Labour Journal* 1:112–131.

Herod, Andrew. 1998. *Organizing the Landscape: Geographical Perspectives on Labor Unionism.* 1st ed. Minneapolis: University of Minnesota Press.

Herod, Andrew. 2001. *Labor Geographies: Workers and the Landscapes of Capitalism.* 1st ed. New York: The Guilford Press.

Herod, Andrew. 2002 "Labor Internationalism and the Contradictions of Globalization: Or, Why the Local Is Sometimes Still Important in a Global Economy." In *Place, Space and the New Labour Internationalisms,* ed. Peter Waterman and Jane Wills, 103–122. Oxford: Blackwell.

Herod, Andrew. 2009. *Geographies of Globalization: A Critical Introduction.* 1st ed. Hoboken, NJ: Wiley-Blackwell.

Hill, Elizabeth. 2009. "The Indian Industrial Relations System: Struggling to Address the Dynamics of a Globalizing Economy." *Journal of Industrial Relations* 51:395–410.

Hobbs, S. R. 2008. "SEIU, Wackenhut Reach Neutrality Agreement." *Daily Labor Report*, A7.

Hoffman, Christy. 2008 [Letter to Jenni Myles, October 14]. Copy in possession of Jamie K. McCallum.

Hoffman, Christy. 2008. "Global Campaigns: A Case Study with G4S." *Journal of the International Centre for Trade Union Rights* 15(3):4–5.

Holdt, Karl Von. 2003. *Transition from Below: Forging Trade Unionism Workplace Change in South Africa.* Pinetown: University of Kwazulu Natal Press.

Horn, Laura. 2011. *Regulating Corporate Governance in the European Union.* New York: Palgrave Macmillan.

Howard, Alan. 2007. "The Future of Global Unions: Is Solidarity Still Forever?" *Dissent* 54(4):62–70. doi:10.1353/dss.2007.0104.

Hurd, R. W. 2004. "The Rise and Fall of the Organizing Model in the U.S." Cornell University ILR School. Accessed May 11, 2012. http://digitalcommons.ilr.cornell.edu/articles/301/.

Hurd, Richard, Ruth Milkman, and Lowell Turner. 2003. "Reviving the American Labour Movement: Institutions and Mobilization." *European Journal of Industrial Relations* 9:99–117.

Huxtable, David. 2008. *The Failing Strategy of International Trade Unionism: The Need for a Global Labour Organization.* Saarbrücken: VDM Verlag.

Hyde, Jessie. 2009. "Wackenhut Stands Up to Miami-Dade." *Miami New Times News.* Accessed May 8, 2012. http://www.miaminewtimes.com/2009-05-07/news/wackenhut-stands-up-to-miami-dade/.

ICFTU. 2005. "Labour Standards and Trade—What Is the Social Clause?" Accessed November 12, 2012. http://www.icftu.org/www/english/els/escllst.html.

International Labour Organization (ILO). 1999. *South Africa: Studies on the Social Dimensions of Globalization.* Geneva: ILO Press.

International Transport Workers' Federation. 2006. "ITF on SATAWU." *Organising Globally* . Accessed May 16, 2012. http://www.itfglobal.org/congress/news-online.cfm/newsdetail/904.

IOE. 2007. "International Organization of Employers." *International Organisation of Employers.* Accessed March 12, 2012. http://www.ioe-emp.org/.

ITF. 2006. "Congress Daily News Archive SATAWU: Our Host Union." *The 41st Congress of the ITF.* Accessed May 1, 2012. http://www.itfglobal.org/congress/news-on line.cfm/newsdetail/904.

ITF. 2008. "ITF: South African Dockers Act against Zimbabwe Arms Shipment." *Organising Globally.* Accessed May 1, 2012. http://www.itfglobal.org/press-area/index. cfm/pressdetail/1915.

Jameson, Fredric, Masao Miyoshi, Stanley Fish, and Enrique Dussel. 1998. *The Cultures of Globalization.* Durham, NC: Duke University Press Books.

Jenkins, Rhys. 2001. "Corporate Codes of Conduct: Self-Regulation in a Global Economy." United Nations Research Institute for Social Development; Technology, Business and Society Programme Paper Number 2.

Jennings, Philip, Bernadette Ségol, and UNI Global Union. 2008. "Responsible UnionToolbox: UNI's Global Union's Guide to International Codes of Practice."UNI Global Union. Accessed May 13, 2012. http://www.uniglobalunion.org/Apps/UNI Pub.nsf/vwLkpById/A7AA327842A5A549C125754C004E6E60/$FILE/RB %20TOOLBOX-E%20.PDF.

Jessop, Bob. 1994. "Post-Fordism and the State." In *Post-Fordism: A Reader*, A. Amin, ed., 251–279. Oxford: Blackwell.

Jonas, Andrew. 1999. "Investigating the Local-Global Paradox." In *Organizing the Landscape: Geographical Perspectives on Labor Unionism*, ed. Andrew Herod, 115–127. Minneapolis: University of Minnesota Press.

Joyce, Amy. 2005. "AFL-CIO to Cut 167 Jobs, Spend More to Organize."*Washington Post.* Accessed October 4, 2012. http://www.washingtonpost.com/wp-dyn/content /article/2005/05/03/AR2005050301597.html.

Juravich, Tom. 2007. "Beating Global Capital: A Framework and Method for Union Strategic Corporate Research and Campaigns." In *Global Unions: Challenging Transnational Capital through Cross-Border* Campaigns, Kate Bronfenbrenner, ed. 16–39. Ithaca, NY: ILR Press.

Kaplan, Erin Aubrey. 2006. "The Black-Brown Divide." *Los Angeles Times.* Accessed June 20, 2012. http://articles.latimes.com/2006/may/24/opinion/oe-kaplan24.

Kay, Tamara. 2005. "Labor Transnationalism and Global Governance: The Impact of NAFTA on Transnational Labor Relationships in North America." *American Journal of Sociology* 111:715–756.

Kay, Tamara. 2011. *NAFTA and the Politics of Labor.* New York: Cambridge University Press.

Keck, Margaret E., and Kathryn Sikkink. 1998. *Activists beyond Borders: Advocacy Networks in International Politics.* Ithaca, NY: Cornell University Press.

Kilimnik, Ken. "Landmark European Labor Law Nears Passage." *The Multinational Monitor* 4(5) 1983.

Klein, Naomi. 1999. *No Logo: Taking Aim at the Brand Bullies.* First Edition. New York: Picador.

Klein, Naomi. 2007. *The Shock Doctrine: The Rise of Disaster Capitalism.* New York: Metropolitan Books/Henry Holt.

Kloosterboer, D. 2007. "Innovative Trade Union Strategies." FederatieNederlandse-Vakbeweging. Accessed October 4, 2012. http://www.newunionism.net/library /organizing/FNV%20-%20Innovative%20Trade%20Union%20Strategies%20 -%202007.pdf.

Koch-Baumgarten, Sigrid. 1998. "Trade Union Regime Formation under the Conditions of Globalization in the Transport Sector: Attempts at Transnational Trade Union Regulation of Flag-of-Convenience Shipping." *International Review of Social History* 43:369–402.

Koelble, Thomas A. 1999. *The Global Economy and Democracy in South Africa*. Piscataway, NJ: Rutgers University Press.

Kohr, Martin. 2000. "Globalization and the South: Some Critical Issues." *United Nations Conference on Trade and Development. Discussion Papers. No. 147*. Accessed April 3. 2012. http://www.unctad.org/Templates/Page.asp?intItemID=2101&lang=1.

Kolben, Kevin. 2006. "The New Politics of Linkage: India's Opposition to the Workers' Rights Clause." *Indiana Journal of Global Legal Studies* 13:225–259.

Kolko, Gabriel. 1994. *Century of War: Politics, Conflict and Society since 1914*. New York: The New Press.

Kraak, Andre. 1996. "Transforming South Africa's Economy: From Racial-Fordism to Neo-Fordism?" *Economic and Industrial Democracy* 17(1):39–74.

Kristoff, Nicholas. 2012. "A Failed Experiment." *The New York Times*. Accessed January 10, 2013. http://www.nytimes.com/2012/11/22/opinion/kristof-a-failed-experiment.html?_r=0

Kuruvilla, S., S. Das, H. Kwon, and S. Kwon. 2002. "Trade Union Growth and Decline in Asia." *British Journal of Industrial Relations* 40:431–461.

Kuruvilla, Sarosh, and Christopher Erickson. April 1, 2002. "Change and Transformation in Asian Industrial Relations." Faculty Publications - Collective Bargaining, Labor Law, and Labor History. Accessed January 30, 2013. http://digitalcommons.ilr .cornell.edu/cbpubs/36.

La Botz, Dan. 1991. "A Troublemaker's Handbook. How to Fight Back Where You Work–And Win!" Detroit: Labor Notes.

Lambert, Rob, and Eddie Webster. 2001. "Southern Unionism and the New Labour Internationalism." *Antipode* 33(3):337–362. doi:10.1111/1467-8330.00188.

Lambert, Rob. 2002. "Labour Movement Renewal in the Era of Globalization: Union Responses in the South." In *Global Unions? Theory and Strategies of Organized Labour in the Global Political Economy. RIPE Series in Global Political Economy*, Jeffrey Harrod and Robert O'Brien, eds., 185–203. New York: Routledge.

Landau, Micah. 2008. "Puerto Rico Teachers' Union Trounces SEIU." North American Congress on Latin America. Accessed Feb 5, 2012. http://nacla.org/node/5257.

Lee, Eric. 1996. *The Labour Movement and the Internet: The New Internationalism*. London: Pluto Press.

Lefebvre, Henri. 1968. *The Explosion: Marxism and the French Upheaval*. New ed. New York: Monthly Review Press.

Lehulere, Oupa. 2003. "The Road to the Right: COSATU Economic Policy in the Post-Apartheid Period." In *Rethinking the Labour Movement in the "New" South Africa*, Tom Bramble and Franco Barchiesi, eds., 25–42. Burlington, VT: Ashgate.

Leigh, Andrew. March 7, 2005. "The Decline of an Institution." *Australian Financial Review.* Accessed January 30, 2013. http://people.anu.edu.au/andrew.leigh/pdf/Deunionisation.pdf.

Lerner, Stephen. 1991. "Let's Get Moving: Labor's Survival Depends on Organizing Industry-Wide for Justice and Power." *Labor Research Review* 1(18). Accessed April 7, 2012. http://digitalcommons.ilr.cornell.edu/cgi/viewcontent.cgi?article=1174&context=lrr.

Lerner, Stephen. 1996. "Stephen Lerner Replies." *Boston Review.* Accessed September 26, 2012. http://www.bostonreview.net/BR21.3/Lerner.html.

Lerner, Stephen. 2007. "Global Unions: A Solution to Labor's Worldwide Decline." *New Labor Forum* 16:23–37.

Lerner, Stephen. 2007. "Global Corporations, Global Unions." *Contexts* 6(3):16–22.

Levinson, Charles. 1972. *International Trade Unionism.* 1st ed. London: Allen & Unwin.

Lillie, Nathan. 2006. *A Global Union for Global Workers: Collective Bargaining and Regulatory Politics in Maritime Shipping.* New York: Routledge.

Logue, J. 1980. *Toward a Theory of Trade Union Internationalism.* Gothenburg: University of Gothenburg Press.

Lorwin, Lewis L. 1953. *The International Labor Movement.* New York: Harper and Brothers Publishing.

Luebke, Paul and Terry W. Mullins. 1982. "Symbolic Victory and Political Reality in the Southern Textile Industry: The Meaning of the J.P. Stevens Settlement for Southern Labor Relations." *Journal of Labor Research* 3(1):81–88.

Luff, Jennifer. 2007. "Justice for Janitors." In *Encyclopedia of U.S. Labor and Working-class History,* Eric Arnesen, ed., vol. 3, 729–731. New York: Routledge.

Magic City Media. 2008. "Protesting FPL Headquarters over Sleeping Wackenhut Guards." Video. Accessed June 1, 2012. http://www.youtube.com/watch?v=gCdb0dMhOgw.

Makgetla, Tumi. 2007. "Threats to Security: A Case Study of the 2006 Security Guard Strike." Unpublished article. Copy in possession of Jamie K. McCallum.

Malawi News. 2009. "G4S Wants Workers Unionist Fired." [Newspaper excerpt from national news section.] Copy in possession of Jamie K. McCallum.

Manheim, Jarol B. 2000. *The Death of a Thousand Cuts: Corporate Campaigns and the Attack on the Corporation.* New York: Routledge.

Mann, Tom. 1897. *The International Labour Movement.* London: Clarion.

Mantsios, Gregory, ed. 1998. *A New Labor Movement for the New Century.* First edition. New York: Routledge.

Marais, Hein. 2001. *South Africa: Limits To Change: The Political Economy of Transition.* Revised. London: Zed Books.

Marginson, Paul and Keith Sisson. 1996. "European Works Councils–Opening the Door to European Bargaining?" *Industrielle Beziehungen* 3(3):229–236.

Matthews, Joe, and Vincent Rogers. 2006. "Owners to Let Guards Unionize." *Los Angeles Times.* Accessed June 2, 2012. http://articles.latimes.com/2006/nov/16/business/fi-security16.

Mazur, Jay. 2000. "Labor's New Internationalism." *Foreign Affairs.* Accessed February 6, 2011. http://www.foreignaffairs.com/articles/55634/jay-mazur/labors-new-internationalism.

McCabe, James P. 1985. "Voluntary Recognition of a Mixed-Guard Union under Section 9(b)(3) of the National Labor Relations Act—Bargaining at Will: Truck Drivers Local 807 v. NLRB." *St. John's Law Review* 60(1). Accessed June 1, 2012. http://scholarship.law.stjohns.edu/lawreview/vol60/iss1/7.

McAlevey, Jane, and Bob Ostertag. 2012. *Raising Expectations (and Raising Hell): My Decade Fighting for the Labor Movement*. New York: Verso.

McCallum, J. K. 2011a. "Organizing the 'Unorganized': Varieties of Transnational Trade Union Collaboration and Social Dialogue in Two Indian Cities." *The Journal of Workplace Rights* 15(3/4): 399–419.

McCallum, J. K. 2011b. "Trade Union Renewal and Labor Transnationalism in South Africa: The Case of SATAWU."*Working USA: The Journal of Labor and Society* 14:161–176.

McCallum, J.K., and S. Toff. 2012. "Supporting Dissent versus Being Dissent." In *Confronting Finance: Mobilizing the 99% for Economic and Social Progress*, ed. Nicolas Pons-Vignon and Phumzile Ncube, 57–63. Geneva: International Labour Office.

McGuiness, Jeffrey C., John E. Abodeely, and Robert E. Williams. 1989. *Guard Unions and the Problem of Divided Loyalties*. Philadelphia: Industrial Research Unit, Wharton School, University of Pennsylvania.

McNamara, Kevin. 2010. *The MacBride Principles: Irish American Strikes Back*. Liverpool: Liverpool University Press.

Medland, Colin. November 2006. "Global Framework Agreements." Slide presentation given in Turin, Italy. Slides in possession of Jamie K. McCallum.

Mendonca, Lenny T. 2006. "Shaking up the Labor Movement: An Interview with the Head of the Service Employees International Union: Andy Stern Discusses His Ideas for Reversing the Long Decline of US Organized Labor. *McKinsey Quarterly* (1): 53–61.

Meyerson, Harold. 2003. "Organize or Die" The American Prospect. Accessed February 5, 2012. http://prospect.org/article/organize-or-die.

Meyerson, H. 2007. "Harold Meyerson—Labor's Global Push."*Washington Post*. Accessed October 4, 2012. http://www.washingtonpost.com/wp-dyn/content/article/2007/12/11/AR2007121101837.html.

Milkman, Ruth. 2010. "Introduction." In *Working for Justice: The L.A. Model of Organizing and Advocacy*, Ruth Milkman, Joshua Bloom, and Victor Narro, eds., 1–22. Ithaca, NY: ILR Press.

Milkman, Ruth, Joshua Bloom, and Victor Narro, eds. 2010. *Working for Justice: The L.A. Model of Organizing and Advocacy*. Ithaca, NY: ILR Press.

Milkman, R., and K. Wong. 2001. "Organizing Immigrant Workers: Case Studies from Southern California." In *Rekindling the Movement: Labor's Quest for Relevance in the 21st Century*, ed. L. Turner, H. Katz, and R. Hurd, 99–128. Ithaca, NY: Cornell University Press.

Milkman, Ruth. 2006. *L.A. Story: Immigrant Workers and the Future of the U.S. Labor Movement*. New York: Russell Sage Foundation.

Milkman, Ruth, and Kim Voss. 2004. *Rebuilding Labor: Organizing and Organizers in the New Union Movement*. Ithaca, NY: ILR Press.

Minnaar, Anthony. 2007. "Oversight and Monitoring of Non-State/Private Policing: The Private Security Practitioners in South Africa." In *Private Security in Africa: Manifestations, Challenges, and Regulations*, Sabelo Gumeze, ed., 127–150. ISS Monograph Series. Accessed January 30, 2013. http://www.iss.co.za/uploads /MONO139FULLPDF.PDF.

Moberg, David. 2005a. "The Lay of Labors New Land." *In These Times*. Accessed May 15, 2012. http://www.inthesetimes.com/article/2368/.

Moberg, David. 2005b. "Power to the Pictures." In These Times. Accessed October 2011. http://www.inthesetimes.com/article/2245/power_to_the_pictures/.

Moberg, David. 2010. "Translating Solidarity." *American Prospect*. Accessed May 11, 2012. http://prospect.org/article/translating-solidarity.

Moberg, David. 2012a. "The New Face of SEIU." *In These Times*. Accessed May 14, 2012. http://www.inthesetimes.com/article/5980/the_new_face_of_seiu/.

Moberg, David. 2012b. "Wrong Union for the Job." *In These Times*. Accessed July 7, 2012. http://www.inthesetimes.com/article/13471/wrong_union_for_the_job/.

Moody, Kim. 1997. *Workers in a Lean World: Unions in the International Economy*. New York: Verso.

Moody, Kim. 1998. "American Labor: A Movement Again?" In *Rising from the Ashes? Labor in the Age of "Global" Capitalism* ed. Ellen Meiksins Wood, Peter Meiksins, and Michael Yates, 57–72. New York: Monthly Review Press.

Moody, Kim. 2007. *U.S. Labor in Trouble and Transition: The Failure of Reform from Above, the Promise of Revival from Below*. New York: Verso.

Morgan, Ted. 1999. *A Covert Life: Jay Lovestone: Communist, Anti-Communist, and Spymaster*. New York: Random House.

Mtyingizana, Beata. 2007. "Group 4 Securicor Labour Practices in Mozambique." [Final report, May 2007, prepared for SEIU.] Copy in possession of Jamie K. McCallum.

Mufson, Steven. 2008. "Executive Resigns in Storm over Sleeping Guards." *Washington Post*. Accessed June 2, 2012. http://www.washingtonpost.com/wp-dyn/content/article /2008/01/09/AR2008010903368.html.

Muller, T., M. Rüb, and Hans-Wolfgang Platzer. 2005. "Towards Internationalisation of Labour Relations? Global Union Networks and Global Framework Agreements—Status Quo and Prospects." *International Labor Organization*. Accessed May 5, 2012. www.ilo.org/wcmsp5/groups/public/---ed . . . /wcms_122176.pdf.

Muller, Torsten, Hans-Wolfgang Platzer, and Stefan Rüb. 2008. "Global Framework Agreements—Opportunities and Limitations of a New Tool of Global Trade Union Policy." *International Labor Organization*. Accessed April 5, 2012. http://library.fes.de /pdf-files/iez/05814.pdf.

Multinational Monitor. 1986. "Concessions and Convictions: Striking Meat Packers Face Off Against the UFCD and Hormel." *The Multinational Monitor* 7(5). Accessed April 22, 2012. http://www.multinationalmonitor.org/hyper/issues/1986/0315/con cessions.html.

Munck, Ronaldo. 2002. *Globalization and Labour: The New "Great Transformation."* New York: Zed Books.

Munck, Ronaldo. 2009. "Afterword: Beyond the 'New' International Labour Studies." *Third World Quarterly* 30:617–625.

Munck, Ronaldo. 2010. *Globalisation and Migration: New Issues, New Politics*. Reprint. New York: Routledge.

Munck, Ronaldo, and Peter Waterman. 1999. *Labour Worldwide in the Era of Globalization: Alternative Union Models in the New World Order*. New York: Palgrave Macmillan.

Murray, Jill. 1998. "Corporate Codes of Conduct and Labor Standards." *Corporate Codes of Conduct* (March 5). http://digitalcommons.ilr.cornell.edu/codes/7.

Myles, J. 2007. "Letter to Daniel Graymore." Copy in possession of Jamie K. McCallum.

Myles, Jenni. 2009. " 'We're not in Kansas Anymore:' The Challenge for Global Labour Relations." In *International Labour and Social Policy Review*, International Organisation of Employers, 63-62. Geneva, Switzerland: International Organisation of Employers.

Myles, J., C. Hoffman, I. Greenwood, and T. Powdrill. 2009. "Progress Report on the G4S-UNI Ethical Partnership Agreement."[Webinar]. Copy in possession of Jamie K. McCallum.

Naipaul, V. S. 1991. *India: A Million Mutinies Now*, New York: Viking.

Niforou, Christina. 2012. "International Framework Agreements and Industrial Relations Governance: Global Rhetoric Versus Local Realities." *British Journal of Industrial Relations* 50(2):352–373. doi:10.1111/j.1467-8543.2011.00851.x.

Newland, Kathleen. 1999. "Workers of the World, Now What?"*Foreign Policy* 114:52–64.

Nissen, Bruce. 2002. *Unions in a Globalized Environment: Changing Borders, Organizational Boundaries, and Social Roles*. Armonk, NY: M.E. Sharpe.

Northrup, Herbert R., and Richard L. Rowan. 1979. *Multinational Collective Bargaining Attempts*. Philadelphia: Industrial Research Unit, Wharton School, University of Pennsylvania.

Northrup, Herbert R., and Charles H. Steen. 1999. "Union 'Corporate Campaigns' as Blackmail." *Harvard Journal of Law and Public Policy* 22(771). Accessed April 7, 2012. https://litigation-essentials.lexisnexis.com/webcd/app?action=DocumentDisplay&crawlid=1&srctype=smi&srcid=3B15&doctype=cite&docid=22+Harv.+J.L.+%26+Pub.+Pol%27y+771&key=9b842c92bdbcd687af0783883dee27e0.

Northrup, Herbert. 1994. "Union Corporate Campaigns and Inside Games as a Strike Form." *Employee Relations Law Journal* 19(4):507–549.

O'Brien, Robert, Anne Marie Goetz, Jan AartScholte, and Marc Williams. 2000. *Contesting Global Governance: Multilateral Economic Institutions and Global Social Movements*. New York: Cambridge University Press.

OECD. 2011. *OECD Guidelines for Multinational Enterprises: Recommendations for Responsible Business Conduct in a Global Context*. Paris: OECD. Accessed June 7. http://www.tuac.org/en/public/e-docs/00/00/09/74/document_doc.phtml.

Ohmae, Kenichi. 1996. *The End of the Nation State: The Rise of Regional Economies*. 1st ed. New York: Free Press Paperbacks.

Olle, Werner, Wolfgang Schoeller, and Robin Mann. 1977. "World Market Competition and Restrictions upon International Trade-Union Policies." *Capital & Class* 1(2) 56–75. doi:10.1177/030981687700200103.

Ong, Aihwa. 2006. *Neoliberalism as Exception: Mutations in Citizenship and Sovereignty*. Durham, NC: Duke University Press Books.

Orecklin, Michele. 2001. "Airlines: Why Argenbright Sets Off Alarms." *Time*. November 19. Accessed September 15, 2012. http://www.time.com/time/magazine/article/0,9171,1001252,00.html.

Oxenbridge, Sarah. 1999. "The Individualisation of Employment Relations in New Zealand: Trends and Outcomes." In *Individualisation and Union Exclusion in Employment Relations: An International Study*, Stephen Deery and Richard Mitchell, eds., 227–250. Sydney, Australia: Federation Press.

Papadakis, Konstantinos, ed. 2011. *Shaping Global Industrial Relations: The Impact of International Framework Agreements*. New York: Palgrave Macmillan. Co-published with International Labour Office.

Papadakis, Konstantinos, Dominique Bé, Brian Bercusson, Giuseppe Casale, and Isabel De Costa. 2008. *Cross-Border Social Dialogue and Agreements: An Emerging Global Industrial Relations Framework?* Geneva: International Labour Office.

Paul Jarley and Cheryl L. Maranto. July 1990. "Union Corporate Campaigns: An Assessment," *Industrial and Labor Relations Review* 43(5):505–524.

Pearson, R. and G. Seyfang. 2001. "New Hope or False Dawn? Voluntary Codes of Conduct, Labour Regulation and Social Policy in a Globalizing World." *Global Social Policy* 1(1):49–78.

Perry, Charles R. 1987. "Union Corporate Campaigns." Philadelphia: Industrial Research Unit, The Wharton School, University of Pennsylvania.

Perry, Charles. 1996. "Corporate Campaigns in Context." *Journal of Labor Research* 17(3):329–343.

Piven, Frances Fox. 2008. *Challenging Authority: How Ordinary People Change America*. Lanham, MD: Rowman & Littlefield.

Polanyi, Karl. 2001. *The Great Transformation*. 2nd ed. Boston, MA: Beacon Press.

Portes, Alejandro. 1997. "Globalization from Below: The Rise of Transnational Communities." Princeton University. Accessed May 2, 2012. http://maxweber.hunter.cuny.edu/pub/eres/SOC217_PIMENTEL/portes.pdf.

Portes, Alejandro, Luis E. Guarnizo, and Patricia Landolt. 1999. "The Study of Transnationalism: Pitfalls and Promise of an Emergent Research Field." *Ethnic & Racial Studies* 22:217–237.

Prashad, Vijay. 2003. *Keeping Up with the Dow Joneses: Stocks, Jails, Welfare*. Cambridge, MA: South End Press.

Ramsay, Harvie. 1997. "Solidarity at Last? International Trade Unionism Approaching the Millennium." *Economic and Industrial Democracy* 18(4, November 1):503–537. doi:10.1177/0143831X97184002.

Rattay, Vivian A. 1983. "Representational Rights of Security Guards under the National Labor Relations Act: The Need for Balancing Interests." *Fordham Urban Law Journal* 12(4):657–701.

Rehfeldt, Udo. 1997. "The Renault-Vilvorde Affair: "Euro-Strike" against the Closure of Its Belgian Plant." *Eurofound*. Accessed October 6, 2012. http://www.eurofound.europa.eu/eiro/1997/03/feature/fr9703122f.htm.

Repya, Robyn. 2002. "Security Officers Allege Discrimination at Firm." *Minnesota Daily*. Accessed April 16, 2012. http://www.mndaily.com/2002/02/18/security-officers-allege-discrimination-firm.

Riisgaard, L. 2005. "Global Framework Agreements: A New Model for Securing Worker Rights?" *Industrial Relations* 44:707–737.

Rodriguez-Garavito, C. A. 2005. "Global Governance and Labor Rights: Codes of Conduct and Anti-Sweatshop Struggles in Global Apparel Factories in Mexico and Guatemala." *Politics & Society* 33:203–233.

Rogers, Joel, and Wolfgang Streeck. 1995. *Works Councils: Consultation, Representation, and Cooperation in Industrial Relations*. Chicago: University of Chicago Press.

Roozendaal, Gerda van. 2002. *Trade Unions and Global Governance: The Debate on a Social Clause*. First edition. New York: Routledge.

Rosenau, James N., and Ernst-Otto Czempiel. 1992. *Governance without Government: Order and Change in World Politics*. New York: Cambridge University Press.

Rosenblum, P., and C. Drew. 2007. *The Human Rights of Private Security Firm G4S*. Unpublished manuscript, Human Rights Clinic, Columbia Law School, and SOAS, University of London.

Ross, Andrew, ed. 1997. *No Sweat: Fashion, Free Trade and the Rights of Garment Workers*. New York: Verso.

Rüb, Stefan. 2002. "World Works Councils and Other Forms of Global Employee Representation in Transnational Undertakings." *Arbeits Papier* 55. Accessed May 15, 2012. http://www.boeckler.de/pdf/p_arbp_055.pdf.

Rudolph, L. I., & Rudolph, S. H. 1987. *In Pursuit of Lakshmi: The Political Economy of the Indian State*. Chicago: University of Chicago Press.

Sabel, Charles, Dara O'Rourke, and Archon Fung. 2000. "Ratcheting Labor Standards: Regulation for Continuous Improvement in the Global Workplace," Washington, D.C.: The World Bank, Social Protection Discussion Paper No. 11.

Sassen, Saskia. 2001. *The Global City: New York, London, Tokyo*. 2nd ed. Princeton, NJ: Princeton University Press.

Savage, L. 1998. "Geographies of Organizing: Justice for Justice in Los Angeles." In *Organizing the Landscape: Geographical Perspectives on Labor Unionism*, Andrew Herod, ed., 225–252. Minneapolis: University of Minnesota Press.

Scherrer, Christoph. 1998. "Protecting Labor in the Global Economy: A Social Clause in Trade Agreements?" *New Political Science* 20(1):53–68.

Scherrer, C., and T. Greven. 2001. *Global Rules for Trade: Codes of Conduct, Social Labelling, Workers' Rights Clauses*. Munster: Westfalisches Dampfboot.

Scheuerman, William E. 2001. "False Humanitarianism?: US Advocacy of Transnational Labour Protections." *Review of International Political Economy* 8(3): 359–388.

Schirm, Stefan A. 2004. *New Rules for Global Markets: Public and Private Governance in the World Economy*. Hampshire, England: Palgrave Macmillan.

Schömann, Isabelle, André Sobzack, Voss Eckhard, and Peter Wilke. 2008. "Global Framework Agreements: New Paths to Workers' Participation in Multinationals' Governance?" *European Review of Labour and Research* 14:111–126.

Schömann, Isabelle, André Sobzack, Eckhard Voss, and Peter Wilke. 2008. "Codes of Conduct and International Framework Agreements: New Forms of Governance at Company Level." European Foundation for the Improvement of Living and Working Conditions. Accessed January 23, 2013. http://www.academia.edu/678230/Codes

_of_conduct_and_international_framework_agreements_New_forms_of_gover nance_at_company_level.

Security Letter Inc. 2007. "Wackenhut Sues SEIU in Federal Court as a 'Racketeering Enterprise.'"*Security Business*, 37(21). Part 3.7-8.

Seidman, Gay. 2008. "Transnational Labour Campaigns: Can the Logic of the Market Be Turned Against Itself?" *Development and Change* 39:991–1003.

Seidman, Gay W. 2003. "Monitoring Multinationals: Lessons from the Anti-Apartheid Era." *Politics and Society* 31:381–406.

Seidman, Gay W. 2009. *Beyond the Boycott: Labor Rights, Human Rights, and Transnational Activism*. New York: Russell Sage Foundation.

SEIU, AFL-CIO, CLC. ca.2011. "Contract Campaign Manual." Accessed February 5, 2013. http://ia600403.us.archive.org/27/items/gov.uscourts.vaed.264094/gov.uscourts .vaed.264094.1.8.pdf.

SEIU. 2007a. (November 2). *SEIU Statement on Wackenhut Law Suit*. News Release. Copy in possession of Jamie K. McCallum.

SEIU. 2007b. "Wackenhut/G4S Security Firm Faces Debarment from City Contracts." *PR Newswire*. Accessed June 29, 2012. http://www.contractormisconduct.org/ass/con tractors/88/cases/687/723/group-4-securicor-la-contractor-responsibility-probe_pr.pdf.

SEIU. 2008a. "Background on SEIU's Efforts to Secure an Agreement with Group 4 Falck/Wackenhut to Work Cooperatively with the Union and the Industry to Raise Security Standards in America." Copy in possession of Jamie K. McCallum.

SEIU. 2008b.(January 29). *G4S/Wackenhut Business at Risk: News Update*. Copy in possession of Jamie K. McCallum.

SEIU 1199. 2010. "Awesome Exchange among Australian Unionists and SEIU 119ers in MD." SEIU blog. Accessed April 6, 2012. http://www.seiu.org/2010/06/awesome -exchange-among-australian-unionists-and-seiu1199ers-in-md.php.

SEIU, CTW, CLC. "Improving Security." Washington, DC: Change to Win Federation and Canadian Labor Congress. Accessed April 6, 2012. http://www.seiu.org/a /standforsecurity/improving-security.php.

Selby, W. G. October 24, 2004. [Corporate Memorandum to National Account Posts, The Wackenhut Corporation.] Copy in possession of Jamie K. McCallum.

Sengupta, A.K, &P.K. Sett. 2000. "Indian Industrial Relations Association Digest." *Industrial Relations Journal* 21:144–153.

Sengupta, Mitu. 2009. "Economic Liberalization, Democratic Expansion and Organized Labour in India: Towards a New Politics of Revival?" *Just Labour: A Canadian Journal of Work and Society* 14: 13–32.

Sharma, Alakh. 2006. "Flexibility, Employment and Labour Market Reforms in India." *Economic and Political Weekly* 41(21): 2078–2085.

Silver, Beverly J. 2003. *Forces of Labor: Workers' Movements and Globalization since 1870*. New York: Cambridge University Press.

Sims, Beth. 1999. *Workers of the World Undermined: American Labor's Role in U.S. Foreign Policy*. Cambridge, MA: South End Press.

Smith, Martin. 2008. "Focus: A Critical Look at Global Strategic Campaigns." *International Union Rights* 15(3):8–9. http://www.scribd.com/doc/48505810/ICTUR-Union -Rights-Focus-on-Strategic-Orporate-Campaigns.

Snow, David A. and Robert D. Benford. 1988. "Ideology, Frame Resonance, and Participant Mobilization," *International Social Movement Research* 1: 197–217.

Southall, Roger. 1987. *Trade Unions and the New Industrialization of the Third World*. London: Zed Books.

Southall, Roger. 1995. *Imperialism or Solidarity?: International Labour and South African Trade Unions*. Cape Town: Uct Press.

Southall, Roger & Andries Bezuidenhout. 2004. "International Solidarity and Labour in South Africa." In *Labour and Globalisation: Results and Prospects*, R. Munck, ed. 128–148. Liverpool: Liverpool University Press.

Stanley, Deetz. 1992. *Democracy in an Age of Corporate Colonization*. Albany: State University of New York Press.

Stevis, Dimitris. 2009. "Global Framework Agreements: Globalizing or Escaping European Industrial Relations?" Presented at the Law and Society Conference, Denver, May 29–31.

Stevis, Dimitris, and Terry Boswell. 2007a. *Globalization & Labor: Democratizing Global Governance*. Lanham, MD: Rowman & Littlefield.

Stevis, Dimitris, and Terry Boswell. 2007b. "Global Framework Agreements: Opportunities and Challenges for Global Unionism." In *Global Unions: Challenging Transnational Capital through Cross-Border Campaigns*, ed. Kate Bronfenbrenner, 174–195. Ithaca, NY: ILR Press.

Stillman, D. 2010. *Stronger Together: The Story of SEIU*. Burlington, VT: Chelsea Green Publishing.

Streek, Wolfgang. 1998. "The Internationalization of Industrial Relations in Europe: Prospects and Problems." *Politics & Society* 26:429–460.

Strom, Kevin, Marcus Berzofsky, Bonnie Shook-Sa, Kelle Barrick, Crystal Daye, Nicole Horstmann, and Susan Kinsey. 2010. "Private Security Industry: A Review of the Definitions, Available Data Sources, and Paths Moving Forward." National Criminal Justice Reference Service. Accessed December 1, 2012. https://www.ncjrs.gov/App/Publications/abstract.aspx?ID=254874.

Sweeney, John J. 1998. "Afterword." In *A New Labor Movement for the New Century*, Gregory Mantsios, ed., 329–335. New York: Monthly Review Press.

Sweeney, John J. 2001. "Not a Backlash, but Birth Pangs of a New Internationalism." *New York Times*, (January 27) Accessed May 13, 2013. http://www.nytimes.com/2001/01/27/opinion/27iht-edsween.t.html.

Szulanski, Gabriel. 1996. "Exploring Internal Stickiness: Impediments to the Transfer of Best Practice Within the Firm." *Strategic Management Journal* 17(Special issue, Winter): 27–43.

Tait, Vanessa. 2005. *Poor Workers' Unions: Rebuilding Labor from Below*. Cambridge, MA: South End Press.

Tarrow, Sidney. 2005. *The New Transnational Activism*. New York: Cambridge University Press.

Tattersall, Amanda. 2007. "Labor-Community Coalitions, Global Union Alliances, and the Potential of SEIU's Global Partnerships." In *Global Unions: Challenging Transnational Capital through Cross-Border Campaigns*, Kate Bronfenbrenner, ed. 155–173. Ithaca, NY: ILR Press.

Tattersall, Amanda. 2010. *Power in Coalition: Strategies for Strong Unions and Social Change*. Ithaca, NY: Cornell University Press.

Taylor, Matthew. 2012. "How G4S is 'Securing Your World': Budgetary Pressure, Political Will and the Lack of a Debate over Public Service Privatisation Has Seen G4S Grow Exponentially." The Guardian. Accessed September 15, 2012. http://www.guardian.co.uk/uk/2012/jun/20/g4s-securing-your-world-policing.

Tilly, Charles. 1992. *Coercion, Capital and European States: AD 990–1992*. Rev. ed. Malden, MA: Wiley-Blackwell.

Tilly, Charles. 1995. "Globalization Threatens Labor's Rights," *International Labor and Working-Class History* (47, Spring):1–23. Retrieved April 12, 2012. http://www.jstor.org/stable/27672207.

Timmons, Heather. 2009. "Security Guards Become the Front Lines in India." *New York Times*. Accessed May 15, 2012. http://www.nytimes.com/2009/03/03/business/worldbusiness/03security.html?_r=1.

Tørres, Liv, and Stein Gunnes. 2003. "Global Framework Agreements: A New Tool for International Labour." Geneva: Global Labor Institute. Accessed January 31, 2013. http://www.globallabour.info/en/2007/11/global_framework_agreements_a.html.

Traub-Werner, Marion. 2002. "Sustaining the Student Antisweatshop Movement: Linking Workers' Struggles." In *The Global Activist's Manual: Local Ways to Change the World*, Mike Prokosch and Laura Raymond, eds., 191–198. New York: Thunder's Mouth Press/Nation Books.

Tsogas, George. 2000. *Labor Regulation in a Global Economy*. Armonk, NY: M.E. Sharpe.

Turner, Lowell. 2005. "From Transformation to Revitalization: A New Research Agenda for a Contested Global Economy." *Work and Occupations* 32:383–399.

Uba, Katrin. 2008. "Labor Union Resistance to Economic Liberalization in India: What Can National and State Level Patterns of Protests against Privatization Tell Us?" *Asian Survey* 48:860–884.

Uchitelle, Louis. 2010. "Globalization, Union-Style." *American Prospect* (November 5). Accessed January 30, 2013. http://prospect.org/article/globalization-union-style.

UK National Contact Point for the OECD. 2008. (December 12). *Guidelines for Multinational Enterprises*. Accessed September 26, 2012. http://www.oecd.org/corporate/guidelinesformultinationalenterprises/43750644.pdf.

UNI. 2007. *Press Release on G4S*. Copy in possession of Jamie K. McCallum.

UNI. 2008. (December 3). *Draft Timelines: Global G4S Campaign*. Copy in possession of Jamie K. McCallum.

UNI. 2009. *Progress Report February 2009*. Copy in possession of Jamie K. McCallum.

UNI. ca. 2008. *Project to Support Satawu's Organizing Initiatives in the Security Industry*. Copy in possession of Jamie K. McCallum.

UNI. ca. 2009 (March). *UNI Property Services Activity Report March 2008–March 2009*. Copy in possession of Jamie K. McCallum.

UNI Global Union. 2009. "The Inequality Behind India's Economic Boom: G4S Security Workers Fight For Their Rightful Place in a Growing Economy." [Report]. Copy in possession of Jamie K. McCallum.

UNI Property Services. 2007. "Who Protects the Guards? The Facts behind G4S in Southern Africa: Findings of a Global Fact-Finding Team." Report. Copy in possession of Jamie K. McCallum.

UNI Property Services Alliance for Justice at Group 4 Securicor. 2007. *Can G4S Do More for Africa? G4Solidarity.* Nyon, Switzerland: UNI Global Union.

U.S. Department of Labor, Bureau of Labor Statistics. 2006. "Occupational Employment and Wages, May 2006." Occupational Employment Statistics. Accessed December 10, 2012. http://bls.gov/oes/current/oes339032.htm.

U.S. Government Printing Office. 2008. "Examining Whether Combining Guards and Other Employees in Bargaining Units Would Weaken National Security." Accessed October 4, 2012. http://www.gpo.gov/fdsys/pkg/CHRG-109hhrg30079/html/CHRG-109hhrg30079.htm.

Van der Walt, Lucien. 2004. "Bakunin's Heirs in South Africa: Race and Revolutionary Syndicalism from the IWW to the International Socialist League, 1910–21." *Politikon: South African Journal of Political Studies* 31:67.

Van der Walt, Lucien. 2007. "The First Globalisation and Transnational Labour Activism in Southern Africa: White Labourism, the IWW, and the ICU, 1904–1934." *African Studies* 66:(2/3):223–251.

Van Driel, Maria. 2003 "Unions and Privatization in South Africa, 1990–2001." In *Rethinking the Labour Movement in the 'New South Africa,'* Tom Bramble and Franco Barchiesi, eds. 62–80. Aldershot, UK: Ashgate.

Venkataratnam, C.S. 1998. "Judicial Activism: Implications for Workers and Consumers." *Indian Industrial Relations Association Digest* 4:1–7.

Vertovec, Steven. 1999. "Conceiving and Researching Transnationalism." *Ethnic & Racial Studies* 22:447–462.

Vogel, David. 2006. *The Market for Virtue: The Potential and Limits of Corporate Social Responsibility.* New ed. Washington, DC: Brookings Institution.

Von Bergen, Jane M. 2006. "A Union Loses Bid to Protect Records." *The Philadelphia Inquirer*, December 7. Accessed April 19, 2012. http://www.highbeam.com/doc/1G1-155629394.html.

Voss, Kim, and Rachel Sherman. 2000. "Breaking the Iron Law of Oligarchy: Union Revitalization in the American Labor Movement." *American Journal of Sociology* 106:303–349.

Waddington, J., ed. 1999. *Globalization and Patterns of Labor Resistance.* New York: Mansell Publishing.

Waddington, Jeremy. 2010. *European Works Councils: A Transnational Industrial Relations Institution in the Making.* New York: Routledge.

Waldinger, R., C. Erickson, R. Milkman, D. Mitchell, A. Valenzuela, K. Wong, et al. 1998. "Helots No More: A Case Study of the Justice for Janitors Campaign in Los Angeles." In *Organizing to Win: New Research on Union Strategies*, ed. K. Bronfenbrenner, S. Friedman, R. W. Hurd, R. A. Oswald, and R. L. Seeber, 102–119. London: ILR Press.

Walker, Richard P. 1983. "The Vredeling Proposal: Cooperation versus Confrontation in European Labor Relations." *International Tax and Business Law.* 177 (1983). Accessed February 11, 2013: http://scholarship.law.berkeley.edu/bjil/vol1/iss1/6.

Wallerstein, Immanuel. 1979. *The Capitalist World-Economy*. New York: Cambridge University Press.

Waterman, Peter. 2001. *Globalization, Social Movements, and the New Internationalism*. Reprint. New York: Continuum.

Waterman, Peter. 2001. "Trade Union Internationalism in the Age of Seattle." In *Place, Space and the New Internationalisms*. Peter Waterman and Jane Wills, eds., 8–32. Oxford: Blackwell.

Waterman, Peter, and Jane Wills. 2002. *Place, Space and the New Labour Internationalisms*. Malden, MA: Wiley-Blackwell.

Webster, Edward. 2010. "From Critical Sociology to Combat Sport? A Response to Michael Burawoy's 'From Polanyi to Pollyanna: The False Optimism of Global Labour Studies' (GLJ 1.2)." *Global Labour Journal* 1:384–387.

Webster, Edward, and Glenn Adler. 1999. "Toward a Class Compromise in South Africa's 'Double Transition': Bargained Liberalization and the Consolidation of Democracy." *Politics and Society* 27:347–385.

Webster, Edward, and Sakhela Buhlungu. 2004. "Between Marginalisation & Revitalisation? The State of Trade Unionism in South Africa." *Review of African Political Economy* 31:229–245.

Webster, Edward, Rob Lambert, and Andries Beziudenhout. 2008. *Grounding Globalization: Labour in the Age of Insecurity*. Malden, MA:Wiley-Blackwell.

Wills, Jane. 1998. "Taking on the CosmoCorps? Experiments in Transnational Labor Organization." *Economic Geography* 74:111–130.

Wills, Jane. 2002. "Bargaining for the Space to Organize in the Global Economy: A Review of the Accor-IUF Trade Union Rights Agreement." *Review of International Political Economy* 9:675–700.

Windmuller, J. 1981. *The International Trade Union Movement*. First edition. New York: Springer.

Winslow, Cal. 2010. *Labor's Civil War in California: The NUHW Healthcare Workers' Rebellion*. Oakland: PM Press.

Wood, Geoffrey, and Mark Harcourt. 1998. "The Rise of South African Trade Unions." *Labor Studies Journal* 23(1):74–92.

Wood, Geoffrey, and C. Psoulis. 2001. "Mobilization, Internal Cohesion, and Organized Labour: The Case of COSATU." *Work & Occupations* 28:293–313.

Workers Rights Consortium. 2012. "The Designated Suppliers Program—Revised." Accessed January 13, 2013. http://www.workersrights.org/dsp/DSP%20Program%20Description,%202012.pdf.

Wright, Erik Olin. 2000. "Working-Class Power, Capitalist-Class Interests, and Class Compromise." *American Journal of Sociology* 105:957–1002.

Yadav, Y. 2004. "Economic Reforms in the Mirror of Public Opinion." *The Hindu*. Accessed June 13, 2012. http://www.hindu.com/2004/06/13/stories/2004061301681600.htm.

Yin, Dr. Robert K. 2008. *Case Study Research: Design and Methods*. 4th ed. Thousand Oaks, CA: Sage Publications.

Zolberg, Aristide R. 1986. "How Many Exceptionalisms?" In *Working-Class Formation: Nineteenth-Century Patterns in Western Europe and the United States*, Ira Katznelson and Aristide R. Zolberg, eds., 397–456. Princeton: Princeton University Press.

Index